MULTINATIONALS, ENVIRONMENT AND GLOBAL COMPETITION

RESEARCH IN GLOBAL STRATEGIC MANAGEMENT

Series Editor: Alan M. Rugman

RESEARCH IN GLOBAL STRATEGIC MANAGEMENT
VOLUME 9

MULTINATIONALS, ENVIRONMENT AND GLOBAL COMPETITION

EDITED BY

SARIANNA M. LUNDAN

University of Maastricht, The Netherlands

2004

ELSEVIER
JAI

Amsterdam – Boston – Heidelberg – London – New York – Oxford – Paris
San Diego – San Francisco – Singapore – Sydney – Tokyo

ELSEVIER Ltd
The Boulevard, Langford Lane
Kidlington, Oxford OX5 1GB, UK

First edition 2004

A catalogue record from the British Library has been applied for.

ISBN: 0-7623-0966-0
ISSN: 1064-4857 (Series)

⊗ The paper used in this publication meets the requirements of ANSI/NISO Z39.48-1992 (Permanence of Paper).
Printed in The Netherlands.

CONTENTS

LIST OF CONTRIBUTORS

Thomas L. Brewer	McDonough School of Business, Georgetown University, Washington, DC, USA
Kristel Buysse	Research Department, National Bank of Belgium, Brussels, Belgium
Petra Christmann	The Darden School, University of Virginia, Charlottesville, USA
Michael W. Hansen	Copenhagen Business School, Denmark
James J. Kennelly	Skidmore College, Saratoga Springs, New York, USA
Ans Kolk	Amsterdam Graduate Business School, University of Amsterdam, The Netherlands
David L. Levy	Department of Management, University of Massachusetts, Boston, USA
Eric E. Lewis	Itacha College, Ithaca, New York, USA
Sarianna M. Lundan	Faculty of Economics and Business Administration, University of Maastricht, The Netherlands
Glen Taylor	Sykes College of Business, University of Tampa, Florida, USA
Rob van Tulder	Rotterdam School of Management, Erasmus University, The Netherlands
Alain Verbeke	Haskayne School of Business, University of Calgary, Canada, and Templeton College, University of Oxford, UK

PREFACE

What if the Academy actually mattered, was the title of a Presidential address at the annual conference of the Academy of Management in the United States ten years ago. My purpose in putting together this volume is no less ambitious than trying to show that in a very real sense, research on strategic management and business economics matters, at least when it comes to the environment. The studies contained in this volume have been selected because all of them reflect empirical research of a high standard that aims to shed some light on the relationship between multinationals and environmental standards. The first chapter by Lundan presents the general theoretical framework within which all of the research reported in this volume can be placed. While each chapter addresses a specific topic, and can be read independent of the other chapters, the sequence of the chapters aims to highlight the most salient aspects of the relationship between multinationals and the environment in the global economy.

We begin with two chapters that deal with the fundamental relationships between multinationality and environmental and financial performance. The chapter by Kennelly and Lewis asks if there is a connection between the degree of multinationality of the firm and its environmental performance. In other words, are more multinational firms on the whole greener or less green than their more domestic counterparts, in this case American firms? The subsequent chapter by Buysse and Verbeke addresses another basic relationship, which is whether firms that are high performing in terms of their environmental performance also do better in terms of their financial performance. In other words, are some firms green because they have excess resources to invest in environmental protection, or do they have excess resources because they have invested in the environment?

We then move on to consider what happens when multinationals from environmentally demanding home countries go to developing countries – do they carry their green credentials with them? The chapter by Hansen looks at the greenness of Danish multinationals in developing countries, particularly in India and Poland. The following chapter by Kolk and van Tulder looks more broadly at the issue of how firms from developed home countries display their green credentials. Their chapter focuses on the environmental reporting of European, American and Japanese multinationals, and the differences between firms from more and less environmentally sensitive home countries. Both of these chapters address the extent to which the greenness of the home country is translated into green performance in multinationals.

While the two previous chapters could be described as depicting a home country push towards green practices, the following chapter by Lundan describes a case where both home country push in the form of regulation, as well as market pull from abroad brought about significant changes in the pulp and paper industry. Another example of external pull is provided in the subsequent chapter by Christmann and Taylor, who look at ISO 14000 certification and the characteristics of Chinese firms that are planning to apply for this certification. In this case, the pressure for upgrading practices is very much driven by the market preference for supplier firms that have obtained ISO 14000 certification.

The final two chapters deal with the issue of climate change, which is not only important in terms of the possible cost implications for multinationals operating in countries that are signatories to the Kyoto protocol, but also because multinationals are due to play a major role in the Kyoto protocol implementation mechanisms by way of technology transfer in exchange for pollution credits. The chapter by Kolk and Levy describes the changing political dynamics of the issue of climate change within the oil and automobile industries, which are clearly industries that are very likely to be fundamentally transformed by the issue of climate change. The book concludes with the chapter by Brewer, which first looks at the issue of climate change from the perspective of the rules governing the global economy, namely the rules of the World Trade Organization (WTO), and then considers the related issue of tariffs on trade in environmental products and services, and their position under the WTO rules.

While it is clear that no single volume can exhaust the issue of multinationals and the environment, this book represents a unique effort in bringing together empirical work that aims to understand how the issues of multinational strategy and environmental standards are intertwined in the global economy. Several of the findings discussed in this volume contradict the predictions based on the pollution haven hypothesis, which saw multinationals as evading responsibility and likely to transfer dirty production. This does not mean that the presence of multinationals is unequivocally good for the recipient countries, but it does suggest, that the presence of multinationals is not unequivocally bad either, and that under the right circumstances, some of the technological and financial resources of multinationals can indeed be employed to advance common objectives. If we do not pursue research that tries to uncover and explain the interconnections within the global economy, and instead are happy to assume that we know how multinationals react to regulation or market pressures, we risk diverting our attention from the dynamics that are genuinely changing the world we live in. In order to make intelligent public policy, we must understand how the relationship between governments, multinationals and non-governmental organizations (NGOs) is evolving, and for that, if not for any other reason, the results presented in this volume do matter.

Sarianna Lundan
Maastricht
May 2003

MULTINATIONALS, ENVIRONMENT AND GLOBAL COMPETITION: A CONCEPTUAL FRAMEWORK

Sarianna M. Lundan

ABSTRACT

This chapter presents a conceptual framework to understand the role of multinational enterprises in the process of environmental standard setting in the global economy. Inside the multinational, we discuss the impact of path-dependency and irreversibility on environmental investment, and the importance of the integrated network structure of the multinational in enabling the transfer of standards within the firm. Outside the firm, we discuss the impact of regulation and market forces, and particularly the role of NGOs, in triggering change in firm behavior both at home and abroad. We conclude by considering the impact of supranational institutions on the environmental behavior of multinationals.

INTRODUCTION

Ever since the birth of the modern environmental movement in the early 1970s, multinationals have been suspected of contributing to environmental degradation by engaging in production in so-called pollution havens where regulations and enforcement are lax. The rationale behind this suspicion is based on comparative costs, where it is assumed that the lower cost of production in the pollution haven

Multinationals, Environment and Global Competition
Research in Global Strategic Management, Volume 9, 1–22
Copyright © 2004 by Elsevier Ltd.
ISSN: 1064-4857/doi:10.1016/S1064-4857(03)09001-6

location will be sufficient to offset any costs of moving production abroad. In time, the consequence of this movement of production would be to increase specialization in the global economy with cleaner processes remaining in the developed countries, while pollution intensive processes would gradually shift abroad, typically to developing countries whose need for foreign investment would override their environmental concerns. As a consequence of the relocation of production, exports in pollution intensive industries from pollution haven locations to developed countries would also be expected to increase.

However, the available evidence on the aggregate patterns of foreign investment and trade do not betray much evidence of such increased specialization. Leonard and Duerksen (1980) and Leonard (1988) found that in the United States foreign direct investment (FDI) in pollution-intensive industries grew no more rapidly than in other manufacturing, that the share of United States FDI in pollution intensive industries to the developing countries was no higher than to the developed ones, and that the share of United States imports in pollution-intensive industries grew at the same rate as other imports. While outward foreign investment from developed countries into developing countries in the most polluting industries has increased in absolute terms, this is in the context of the dramatic overall increase in foreign investment over the past 30 years. In fact, the proportion of investment in the traditionally pollution intensive sectors has increased less than in many other sectors, and although countries like South Korea or Malaysia have more pollution intensive industry now than they did 20 years ago, this is in the overall context of a rapidly rising GDP per capita. Similarly, if one looks at the results of studies analyzing changes in the patterns of trade reviewed in Dean (1992) and Jaffe, Peterson and Portney (1995), for example, there is no evidence to indicate that increasing specialization would have taken place, and in fact the ratio of imports to exports of polluting products in the United States was the same in the 1990s as it was in the 1970s (Mani & Wheeler, 1998).

In this volume, the contributors explore the reasons why the pollution haven hypothesis turned out to be false by presenting empirical evidence across countries and across industries on the interplay between multinational operations and environmental standards. There is growing evidence over the past fifteen years to suggest that under certain circumstances, the tradeoff between environmental investments and profitability is not as clear-cut as once thought, and some research has suggested that firms could actually increase their profitability as a result of environmental investments. However, most of these studies have centered on the domestic operations of American firms, and have not considered the influence of foreign operations on domestic standards, or domestic standards on foreign operations. The studies in this volume move beyond the pollution haven problematic that centers solely on the shifting of production to foreign locations, and look at the range of impacts multinational corporations have on environmental standards in the global economy.

The aim of this chapter is to complement the existing studies on the relationship between multinationals and environmental standards by offering a comprehensive framework that looks at the full range of interactions between multinationals and different constituents in the global economy. We will build on the framework presented by Rugman and Verbeke (1998a), which concentrated on the interplay between regulatory pressures and multinational standards. Specifically, we update the Rugman and Verbeke (1998a) framework by explicitly incorporating two additional elements, namely the role of consumers and the influence of non-governmental organizations (NGOs), and the growing importance of industry self-regulation on the development of multinational environmental strategy.

The discussion will be developed in two parts. In the first part we begin by reviewing the growing literature on strategic management and the environment employing the resource-based view of the firm, in order to gain an understanding of environmental investment as a strategic issue within the firm. We will argue, that the path dependencies in the innovation process of the firm will result in the creation of persistent environmental leaders and laggards, which has important implications for public policy and environmental quality. Additionally, in order to reflect the current understanding on the structural evolution of multinationals, we give due consideration to the influence of the multinational network and the learning that takes place between subsidiaries and the corporate headquarters. We conclude this discussion by expanding the treatment of firm-level strategic factors in Rugman and Verbeke (1998a) regarding the influence of flexibility and timing on the development of successful corporate environmental initiatives. By looking at environmental investments from a real options perspective, which is intended to explicitly value flexibility and reversibility, we can gain a better understanding of environmental investments, and particularly the investments companies are making to advance self-regulation.

Having explored the drivers for environmental investment within the firm, in the second part we aim to gain a more realistic understanding of the elements outside of the firm that drive multinational environmental performance in the global economy. We employ the framework developed by Lundan (1996) which characterizes these forces as a matrix with domestic and foreign consumers on one side, and domestic and foreign regulation on the other. Of particular importance in this context is the role of NGOs in campaigning on behalf of consumers in multiple markets. In addition to the market and regulatory forces, we will consider the implications of two supranational institutions, the World Trade Organization (WTO) rules on trade and trade-related investment measures, and the possible consequences of the adoption of the Kyoto protocol. We will argue that the pressures exerted on multinational firms intensify the division between leading and lagging firms already inherent in their domestic performance. While there are considerable pressures on the leading multinationals to improve their performance, and thus realistic possibilities for a race to the top to develop (cf. Vogel, 1995), the opposite is true of the lagging (domestic) firms, who neither face the same pressures nor have the resources to change their behavior.

MULTINATIONAL STRATEGY AND ENVIRONMENTAL INVESTMENT

Path Dependence and Performance

The resource-based view of the firm (see, e.g. Barney, 1991; Conner, 1991; Peteraf, 1993), which has come to dominate much of the research in the field of strategy, postulates that differences in performance between firms are due to their different resource endowments. The answer to the question of what makes one firm outcompete another is said to lie in the possession of resources that are value creating, rare and difficult to imitate. The resource-based view complements the work in evolutionary economics on the importance of path dependence on the firm's future (technological) trajectory (Nelson & Winter, 1982). Path dependence suggests that differences in performance between firms arise from the cumulative process of learning that is shaped by the initial bundle of resources of the firms. Not surprisingly, nearly all the studies published so far on strategy and environmental issues have adopted the resource-based view.

At the process level, most environmental investments involve improving efficiency by minimizing waste and maximizing resource use, and it is logical to suppose that firms can possess different capabilities when it comes to redesigning their processes. The connection between environmental performance and resource efficiency also opens up the possibility that environmental investments are not a zero-sum game. While many of the studies on environmental strategy try to link environmental initiatives with improved environmental or financial performance, this is not strictly necessary for a win-win argument to hold. For any given level of environmental performance, whether demanded by regulators or consumers, one firm can achieve a lower long-term cost of compliance than another firm, thus acquiring a competitive advantage. In order for environmental investments to "pay" in the economic sense, it does not have to be the case that the resulting improvements fully recover the initial cost, but merely that the resulting improvements are greater than those achieved by competing firms.

In the literature thus far there have been three kinds of studies on environmental investments and performance. There are studies that look at environmental initiatives and subsequent environmental performance, those that look at environmental initiatives and subsequent financial performance relying on accounting measures, and those that look at indicators of environmental performance and the market performance of firms. In the first group, Sharma and Vredenburg (1998) identified environmentally related corporate capabilities such as a technological advantage in cleaner technology, as well as intangibles such as a corporate culture predisposed to accepting environmental responsibility, or a capability for generating a long-term vision of competitiveness and sustainability, that could be competitively valuable for the firm. Klassen and Whybark (1999) looked at a sample of 69 plants from the United States (U.S.) furniture industry, associating the plant's portfolio of investments in environmental technologies in manufacturing to its performance, both in terms of environmental performance as well as manufacturing performance. Their results provide support for a win-win scenario, in that process improvements in manufacturing that were instigated for pollution prevention also improved manufacturing performance, whereas investments in pollution control (end-of-pipe solutions) had a deleterious effect on performance.

In a study of 88 chemical companies in the United States, Christmann (2000) looked at the role of complementary assets in allowing firms to obtain a cost advantage from the implementation of best practices of environmental management. The results indicate that such benefits are not universal, and require process innovation and effective implementation to mediate between best practices and cost advantage. Kennelly and Lewis (in this volume) looked specifically at the link between multinationality and environmental performance in a sample of U.S. firms drawn from the S&P 500. Their results indicate that more multinational firms do perform better in environmental terms, although this may be due to their overall better performance vis-à-vis purely domestic firms.

The second group of studies aim to link environmental performance with accounting measures of financial performance. Levy's (1995) study on 80 multinational enterprises (MNEs) found no evidence of a relationship between environmental performance and subsequent financial performance, whereas Russo and Fouts (1997) found a positive relationship between environmental performance and profitability for a sample of 243 U.S. multinationals. A subset of this literature are studies where the long-term expected efficiency gains are coupled with the strategic value of being identified as a first mover in the market. Freedman and Jaggi (1993) and Nehrt (1996) have attempted to quantify the effects on the long-term financial performance of firms in the pulp and paper industry that have engaged in significant (pro-active) environmental investments, and both studies concluded with cautiously positive results. In one the few studies outside of the U.S., Buysse and Verbeke (in this volume) found that for a sample of Belgian multinationals, an environmental leadership strategy was associated with better financial performance, while a more moderate environmental profile did not result in any better performance than a reactive strategy. Additionally, improvements in the firm's environmental profile had a positive effect on domestic firms, but no effect on foreign subsidiaries in Belgium, although this may be an artifact of the financial accounting of subsidiary profits.

In the final group, there is a small body of evidence on how well the market-place rewards environmentally conscious firms. Using event study methodology, Klassen and Mc Laughlin (1996) studied the stock market reaction for companies on the NYSE and AMEX exchanges on a sample of 118 positive and 18 negative (non-contemporaneous) environmental events. The results indicated that positive shocks, such as environmental performance awards, and particularly first time announcements, could initiate a significant increase in the stock price, while an environmental crisis had the predicted dampening effect on stock price. In another event study, Gilley et al. (2000) looked at the effects of announcements of product-driven (more visible) and process-driven (less visible) environmental initiatives, but found no effect on subsequent stock returns.

In an interesting study on a sample of 89 firms from the S&P 500, Dowell, Hart and Yeung (2000) attempted to evaluate whether changes in environmental standards (upgrading or downgrading) were associated with corporate value creation. They attempted to show, that if past market performance could not predict current changes in environmental standards, but past changes in environmental standards explained current changes in market value, the underlying causality could be established beyond mere coincidence or correlation. In other words, they sought to go beyond showing that firms that in general are high performing, are also more likely to perform well on the environmental dimension, by showing that environmental performance itself is linked to increased market value. Interestingly, in their sample the majority of the firms had adopted a stringent internal standard, which was applied globally, rather than simply adjusting to each host country standard, or simply observing U.S. standards, and the firms with the highest Tobin's q values were also the firms that applied their own internal standard around the world. The authors were not, however, able to prove that past years' environmental standards would predict future values of Tobin's q, or that past changes in market valuations would lead firms to change their environmental standards. This may have been because only 17 out of the 89 firms actually changed their standards during the period under study, or it may be further proof that environmental performance is largely invisible to the stock market.

Together these results indicate, that under certain conditions it is indeed possible for firms to improve their performance as a consequence of environmental investments, and that for some firms such improvements may even result in a noticeable improvement in the overall performance of the firm. However, even in the absence of this win-win dynamic, path dependence suggests that the more capable firms will find it easier, and thus in the long term more beneficial, to make environmental investments. Correspondingly, lagging firms will find it less appealing to engage in similar investments since they cannot hope to match the efficiency of the leading firms, and they are thus unlikely to improve their overall performance. This implies that while there are strong drivers for well performing firms to make environmental investments, due to the dynamics of the investment process, there are very few such drivers for the lagging firms.

Timing and Flexibility
Even if a firm has the underlying capabilities and resources to engage in environmental investments, two major constraining factors are the timing and the degree of flexibility involved in the investment. The real options literature (see, e.g. Damodaran, 2000), Dixit and Pindyck (1995) and Kogut and Kulatilaka (2001) have developed to address some of the shortcomings of traditional investment literature, exemplified by the discounted cash flow model, where an investment is made today that pays back a stream of income at different points in the future, and these streams are discounted back to the present day to assess the net present value of the proposed investment. In a discounted cash flow model, investments are typically considered either implicitly or explicitly to be reversible, and made at a single point in time. By contrast, the real options literature aims to make explicit the sequential character of much of real life investment. In this case, the flexibility afforded by sequential investment is a way for firms to mitigate the effects of investment irreversibility, and thus to control risk. While the literature also offers the possibility of valuing the real options, there are significant problems in defining the underlying asset and estimating its volatility. Nonetheless, on a conceptual level, this literature can be very useful in assessing environmental investments.

Two scenarios deserve particular consideration in connection with the option value of environmental investments. One is the case of the timing of large one-time capital investments, where process improvements and redesign are expected to result in improved environmental performance. In this case, the lack of flexibility, and the inability of the firm to exercise sequential options places a great emphasis on the timing of the investment, and results in waves of investment in the industry. By contrast, the second case, relating to the firm's efforts at getting its environmental standard approved in the marketplace, is a classic real options scenario, where sequential investments give the firm the possibility of acquiring better information before proceeding further with the investment.

Large capital investments are severely conditioned by their degree of irreversibility, and such investments can only be carried out as part of the overall capital investment plan of the firm. For example, as Lundan (in this volume) shows in her chapter on the introduction of the chlorine free pulping process, the required investments could only be undertaken as part of the ongoing capacity increases in the pulp and paper industry. Although a market for used pulping equipment does exist, when the question is about a one billion dollar investment in a state-of-the-art facility, should anyone come to the market selling the equipment only a few years after it had been installed, there would be very few willing buyers. This is because investment in highly capital intensive industries is often characterized by follow-my-leader behavior, particularly in cases where the global market price for the final product fluctuates. In a period of sustained high prices, firms often have the means as well as the approval of their shareholders to engage in capacity expansion. However, since scale economies are extremely important, each large-scale investment increases overall production capacity considerably, leading into overcapacity and depressed prices in a few years' time. Consequently, at least within the first cycle of price increases and decreases, large-scale investments in capacity expansion are irreversible.

The importance of timing due to irreversibility of investment characterizes a great deal of the investment that is undertaken in the traditional pollution intensive industries (pulp and paper, chemicals, oil and mining) to improve environmental performance. While the environmental improvements do not make the investment process more volatile on their own, they are linked to an underlying cycle that has its own dynamics. In large capital investments, the sheer scale of the resource commitment makes every major investment decision a strategic one, because of the need to consider competitive developments up to 30 years into the future. Consequently, while the timing of large-scale capital investments can be affected by outside forces, as was seen in the case of the pulp and paper industry, this can only happen when a critical mass of large firms is ready to undertake such investment.

The second kind of environmental investment related to option value is the flexibility inherent in the sequence of investments firms make in order to legitimate the environmental standards related to the product they are bringing to the market. Most of these efforts would fall under the banner of self-regulation as discussed by Christmann and Taylor (2002), in that they are not required by any regulatory authority, but they might bring benefits to the firm in one or more of the markets within which they operate. Such schemes include sponsorship and participation in eco-labeling schemes, such as the Forest Stewardship Council (FSC), the European Union eco-label, or the Nordic swan. The myriad of such schemes also include industry codes of conduct, like the chemical industry's much publicized Responsible Care initiative, as well as industry-wide efforts to curb child labor, such as in the case of sporting goods manufacturers and textile manufacturers (for example see Kolk, Tulder & Welters, 1999) on the overall use of codes by multinationals and Kolk (2001) for a study of codes of conduct in the sporting goods industry.

One clear problem with self-regulation by codes of conduct is, that there is not always an incentive for firms within the same industry to agree on common principles that are substantive, since this would tie their hands with respect to the development of their own environmental strategy, and it would eliminate any possibility of reaping first mover advantages from innovations in cleaner process technology. Indeed, while the chemical industry's Responsible Care was one of the earliest codes initiated by firms, two recent studies by King and Lenox (2000) and Howard, Nash and Ehrenfeld (2000) found that members of Responsible Care included poor performers, and that members did not improve their environmental performance any faster than non-members. However, self-regulation schemes should not simply be dismissed as an exercise in "green washing," because many of the firms have made substantial resource commitments in the form of environmental investments. Rather, these schemes represent a way for firms to make their standards known and accepted in the marketplace, which is essential if they are to reap the full benefit of the investments they have made. (This is a variant of Teece's (1986) seminal analysis of appropriability conditions in technological investments.)

Taken together, voluntary schemes share a few common characteristics. Firstly there is a proliferation of competing standards, and the efforts of the firm are geared towards ensuring that their proprietary standards will be endorsed in the marketplace. While in some cases firms may have to be satisfied with being one of a half a dozen recognized labels within a given market segment, such as in the case of paper manufacturers, in other instances particular firms have been successful in virtually dominating the standards in their own industry. The second important characteristic is that not only are the standards contested as part of the process, but establishing standards is typically a long sequence of small steps intended to find out more about the market, as well as to increase the acceptance and familiarity of the firm's proprietary standards. These two characteristics make the firms' efforts at environmental self-regulation a real options strategy. By moving ahead in small steps, and by keeping open the possibility of participating in multiple schemes, and if necessary even endorsing a competitor's scheme, firms maintain maximum flexibility in terms of their environmental commitments.

Self-regulation of this kind is predicated on the idea that the markets should guide firms when they move beyond the parameters set by environmental regulation. The expectation is, that this will minimize the need for firms to engage in investments that offer no real benefit to the consumers, while also offering consumers the ability to express to industry the kind of environmental performance they expect, and in the end, this should deliver a cleaner environment at a lesser cost (cf. Hahn, 1993). As a consequence, an inherent feature of self-regulation is the relative unpredictability of market-based standards in contrast to the regulatory context, where at least if firms enjoy open communication with the regulatory authorities, regulation is quite predictable, and subject to negotiation in terms of timing (cf. Harrison, 1999). Since market-based regulation is unpredictable but popular, it necessitates an investment strategy that offers flexibility of the kind characterized by real options.

One problem with treating sequential investment as real options is that at least in theory, every incremental investment option that secures a part of a future investment that is potentially beneficial, has positive value. Consequently, it can be difficult to determine when to stop investing in the creation of new options. The bursting of the internet bubble was a graphic illustration of how bundles of real options, and options on options with nothing underlying them, could not be a viable business model in the long run. The more uncertainty there is in the market, the higher the option value becomes. However, an increase in market volatility also makes it more difficult to determine the true value of the real option, and consequently at some point the added value arising from the flexibility of being able to decide whether to invest today, or wait, will be diminished.

In the case of environmental investments, extensive efforts to play the market to see which standard is accepted, and to tailor one's products to suit that standard, are not likely to be long lived. Without the underlying investments in fundamental process redesign and efficiency improvements, the effects of this kind of green positioning are going to be limited, particularly if the voluntary schemes are subjected to scrutiny by an independent auditor. However, we believe that by recognizing that environmental investments have important constraints in terms of both timing and flexibility, a better understanding of multinational environmental behavior can be achieved.

Learning Networks

The final issue we wish to consider in looking at environmental investment in multinational firms is the influence of the network structure of the modern multinational. Learning through subsidiaries about different consumer tastes or changes in the regulatory climate are important parts of the knowledge that forms the basis for the competitiveness of an integrated multinational. In order to achieve a bi-directional flow of information within the firm, multinationals have become less hierarchical, resulting in the advent of new conceptual forms, such as Hedlund's (1986) Heterarchy and Bartlett and Ghoshal's (1989) Transnational.

In addition to the changing configuration of internal activities, the boundaries of the multinational firm have become more porous, incorporating many forms of co-operative relationships, such as joint ventures and strategic alliances, with the two often distinguished by the presence and lack of an equity investment share. Increasingly, what is traveling through the network in addition to intermediate goods and finished products is knowledge. The kind of knowledge that is likely to be both valuable and rare is tacit knowledge, i.e. knowledge and experience embodied in people and the connections between people (see, e.g. Cantwell, 1991; Spender, 1996). Since it is tied to skilled employees, a great deal of valuable knowledge tends to be location specific. The challenge for the multinational then becomes to absorb the locally generated knowledge held by the subsidiary, and to leverage it with the financial and other resources available within the firm. (There are several recent studies on knowledge management in multinationals, e.g. the Centres of Excellence project on a cross-national sample of European subsidiaries by Holm and Pedersen (2000) and the various contributions in Lundan (2002).)

The multinational network also extends beyond the boundaries of the firm, and the multinational has the ability to affect standards throughout the supply chain, thus extending its practices to distant members of the network. This is particularly important in the context of developing countries, where local firms supplying multinational networks are in a position to upgrade standards locally, such as in the adoption of ISO 14000 standards in China, as described by Christmann and Taylor (in this volume). The Rugman and D'Cruz (2000) five partners network provides a model of the extended network of the multinational. This model relies on the existence of a flagship firm, which provides the primary guidance for strategic decision making within the network. This flagship firm is an MNE which has through trade, FDI, licensing, or joint ventures acquired skills in executing global strategies. The asymmetry that exists between the role of the flagship firm and the other four partners, namely key customers and suppliers, competitors, and the non-business infrastructure, creates credible commitments (Williamson, 1983) between the five partners, as the MNE provides both skills and a narrow strategic purpose for the network. This model acknowledges learning from both suppliers and customers and the role of non-business institutions, such as universities, research institutions and trade associations, as a forum for a cooperative exchange of ideas, as well as an institutionalized locus of memory. Such network relationships play an important role in the pulp and paper industry, for example, where cooperative linkages between equipment manufacturers, research institutions, and trade associations are longstanding in Scandinavia, as discussed by Lundan (in this volume).

By virtue of collecting and assessing information on developments in various markets around the world, the multinational firm makes assessments about the range of options available, and the strategic implications of choosing a course of action. The network of connections forms the conduit through which standards are disseminated within the multinational. Since the integrated network is based on a two-way flow of information, the multinational can both collect information and disseminate best practice throughout its network of subsidiaries. The multinational firm is thus the perfect conduit for the dissemination of new standards, but whose standards are they adopting? In the second part of this chapter, we will concentrate on the external influences on multinational environmental behavior, particularly on the role of regulation and NGOs in guiding corporate practices.

EXTERNAL DRIVERS FOR ENVIRONMENTAL INVESTMENT IN THE GLOBAL ECONOMY

Regulation

What is the role of regulation in the global marketplace, and if firms are engaging in more self-regulation, does this do away with the role of national governments? The answer by all accounts is no, whether one looks at the kinds of standards adopted by multinationals from developed economies in developing countries, or one looks at how environmental reporting differs between countries, or indeed if one looks at the reactions among European firms as opposed to American firms on the issue of climate change. In all these cases national regulation matters.

While there are substantial differences in the relationship between firms and governments across countries, even in the United States, where the relationship has traditionally been adversarial, there has been a movement towards what the Environmental Protection Agency has labeled "negotiated regulation." Since the early 1990s, incentive-based systems of regulation, that focus on target setting rather than command-and-control, and incorporate market-based instruments of regulation, such as tradable permits, have become the norm rather than the exception (Hahn, 1993). Over time, both governments and firms have become more familiar with the possibilities for strategic interaction (or co-optation), and have evolved an ability to accommodate each other's timetables for implementation. The role of the modern regulator is to set targets, and the means to achieve the targets are selected by the firms, with few if any guidelines as to best available technology (BAT) (cf. Harrison, 1999). In practice, flexible regulatory measures can include reduced monitoring for firms with certified environmental management systems, such as EMAS or ISO 14001, and they can also involve negotiated timetables and individual compliance agreements for firms that pursue innovative pollution control strategies. Some evidence is already available on the effectiveness of flexible regulation, and at least data from the electric utilities indicates, that regulations that allow firms to develop new technologies according to their own schedule result in a competitive advantage for the firms (Majumdar & Marcus, 2001).

Hansen (in this volume) demonstrates how Danish multinationals, thanks to stringent Danish environmental policies and the linking of development assistance and environmental objectives, have generally maintained very high standards in their investments in developing countries. Similarly, firms from the small open economies of Europe, which also tend to be environmentally more conscious, have been the clear leaders in improving their environmental communication, first by issuing separate environmental reports, and then by moving towards third party verification of their environmental reports. This is in contrast to firms from France, for example, which have not operated under similar pressures for openness and transparency in corporate communication in their home market (Kolk & van Tulder, in this volume). One can also look at the contrast in how European firms early on accepted climate change as a challenge to their future viability, while American firms engaged in attempts to challenge the science and to negate the impact of climate change. This is but one of many issues, such as those involving hormone treated beef and genetically modified food, where Europeans have adopted very different political strategies as compared to their American counterparts. As Kolk and Levy (in this volume) show in their study of the leading oil multinationals, the strategic option of challenging the science of climate change was considered not just unviable, but an anathema by the Europeans. They also suggest that the Americans soured to renewable forms of energy already in the 1970s, when the Californian wind rush came to an abrupt end, and their particular learning path taught them to remain wary of all alternative forms of energy.

On this and several other major issues, national preferences and beliefs still matter, and national regulation continues to play a major role in influencing the investment decisions made by multinationals. Although there are isomorphic pressures in the global economy, and in many ways the leading firms have become more alike, as was seen for instance in the changes in the environmental reporting by French firms, most multinationals still have their headquarters located at home, which reinforces the importance of domestic regulation. It appears that charity does indeed begin at home, and while regulation in foreign markets can influence the standards adopted by multinational firms, domestic regulation is still a major driver of environmental strategy (see also Jaffe, Peterson & Portney, 1995) and Rugman and Verbeke (1998b) on the impact of domestic and foreign regulation.

Of course, what makes multinationals different from domestic firms is that they are exposed to different kinds of regulation in the various markets they serve, and they have to decide whether a uniform corporate set of standards is appropriate, or whether different standards will be maintained in different markets. We argued earlier, that on efficiency grounds alone, proactive (leading) firms are more likely to adopt uniform internal standards, and to trade up rather than down between different jurisdictions. While in some markets multinationals may not strive beyond minimum compliance, in other markets they may maintain standards that are higher than those required by regulation or prevalent among indigenous firms. It is also possible that multinationals would seek to influence governments to dissuade them from enacting further regulation, but there is no reason to suspect that this would be the only, or even prevalent, form of interaction between the firms and their hosts (see Gray, 2002 for examples of such "regulatory chill").

Markets and NGOs
While regulation has thus not become any less important, it has changed its character, as market-based regulation in various forms has taken hold in Europe as well as in the United States. In addition to the regulatory changes, the direct influence of markets on the environmental behavior of firms has also changed substantially. In large economies, such as the United States, domestic consumers often play an important role in shaping corporate activity (this is the original Porter & van der Linde, 1995 scenario). In smaller economies, domestic consumers have typically been of lesser importance, since large-scale production has necessitated substantial export sales. This is the case for Canada and the Scandinavian countries, for example.

In terms of changing consumer demands, the most important change has occurred in the rise of the importance of NGOs in shaping the marketplace. For example, Lundan (in this volume) shows how Greenpeace initiated the campaign to bring about chlorine free pulping, while Christmann and Taylor (2002) discuss the range of voluntary initiatives firms have adopted in order to meet specific demands arising in the marketplace. These are not isolated cases, but a part of a growing reality that under market-based regulation the firms are not led by atomistic markets of individual consumers, but by large environmental NGOs such a Greenpeace and Friends of the Earth.

The question here is how important are these two kinds of triggers relative to each other. To what extent will firms in pollution-intensive industries still be pushed by regulation into making environmental changes, and to what extent will they follow the market in making their investment decisions? NGOs' mode of operation is targeted campaigning on specific issues, and they are geared towards achieving a visible impact in a short amount of time. NGOs are not publicly accountable in the same way as national regulators, and their unpredictability makes them more difficult for the firms to accommodate. (This is somewhat akin to arguments concerning the effects of corruption on investment that characterize corruption as a random form of taxation (see, e.g. Campos, Lien & Pradhan, 1999; Habib & Zurawicki, 2002).)

On the whole, firms do not have an easy time in getting their environmental standards accepted in the marketplace, and this seems to be an issue of credibility. The credibility of environmental organizations in opinion polls is often considerably higher than that of industrial firms, and this has not eroded even in instances where environmental organizations have been caught spreading false information, as Greenpeace did in the case of the Brent Spar for example. Increased self-regulation by way of voluntary initiatives and third-party verification is a way for firms to counter the unpredictability of the marketplace, although so far it would appear that the firms have not been able to "sell" their proprietary standards to the NGOs with the same degree of success that they have enjoyed with national regulators.

Supranational Institutions
The final issue to be addressed in connection with external influences on corporate environmental behavior is the influence of the supranational institutions that mitigate disputes at the national level, and provide the superstructure of rules in the global economy. The picture that is emerging regarding the environmental actions of multinationals is one of increased political involvement at multiple levels of influence. At the supra-national level, the fundamental issue of sovereignty has been revisited in the drafting of multilateral agreements, like the North American Free Trade Agreement (NAFTA), and the now defunct Multilateral Agreement on Investment (MAI) under the auspices of the OECD, which would have given multinationals the right to sue governments if non-discrimination was not exercised in the markets in which they operate. As is illustrated by the climate change issue (see Levy, 1997) and Kolk and Levy (in this volume), for example, multinationals (and NGOs) are increasingly influencing national policy through their role in the standard setting process. The political role of the MNE has stretched, as it now encompasses elements which were previously solely the domain of national governments, as well as involvement in "grass-roots" issues in response to market demand.

The changing configuration of environmental decision making can be split into three levels (see also Lundan, 2001). At the top level, there are supranational issues such as climate change, and multilateral agreements, such as the Montreal protocol to curb the use of chlorofluorocarbons (CFCs), for instance. At the level below are the bodies specifically designed to establish rules and codes of conduct in the international domain. Thus WTO rules are operative at this level, as are codes of conduct for multinationals designed by the OECD, and the provisions of the proposed MAI agreement. Below this level are the national policy makers, who set the basis for industry standards in their geographical area, and below them are the firms. While a few decades ago, the entire chain of environmental policy would have consisted of the bottom two, or at the most, bottom three levels, today we find not only four levels of governance, but also two new entrants, the MNEs and environmental NGOs, who engage with all four levels of policy making. The expanding role of the multinationals has in turn given rise to anti-globalization protests, fueled by fears that the supranational institutions would allow multinationals to ride roughshod over environmental regulations (see Brewer & Young, 2000; Graham, 2000 for evidence countering this viewpoint).

The supranational bodies with the greatest impact on multinationals and environmental standards are the World Trade Organization (WTO) rules that govern trade and trade-related investment, the provisions of the environmental side agreement of the North American Free Trade Agreement (NAFTA), and European Union (EU) regulations. Some of the well-known decisions arising from the GATT/WTO dispute settlement process involved the tuna-dolphin dispute, which restricted the extraterritoriality of environmental measures, and the Thai cigarettes and Danish bottles cases, both of which required less-trade distorting measures to be adopted in implementing polices on public health and the environment (see, e.g. Esty, 1994 on these and other cases). The results of cases such as the tuna-dolphin dispute have been interpreted by environmental groups as signaling that the WTO lets trade concerns override environmental concerns. However, as emphasized by Brewer (in this volume), the provisions of the WTO provide ample room for countries to engage in legitimate measures to protect the environment, as long as this is done in the least trade-distorting manner. In fact, while the existing rules do not significantly curtail countries' ability to impose legitimate environmental rules, they still leave some room for the opportunistic tailoring of environmental rules to suit domestic producers. For example, in connection with NAFTA, Rugman, Kirton and Soloway (1999) have shown how American firms have tried to use environmental measures to close out Canadian firms in several industries.

All three supranational institutions (WTO, NAFTA and EU) provide fora within which conflicts arising from divergent environmental standards can be addressed. Since environmental policy, like any other form of policy, is subject to political capture in addition to being based on unique political, economic and natural conditions in each country, there are likely to be persistent differences between countries in the emphasis given to different areas of environmental policy. The existence of such differences has given rise to discussions regarding cross-border harmonization of environmental rules. While the rationale for adopting uniform regulations regarding trans-border pollution is compelling, the practical obstacles to reaching such agreements are considerable. As a consequence, the NAFTA environmental side agreement explicitly rejects the objective of harmonization in favor of a (market-led) process of gradual convergence, and in the European

Union, domestic and community measures complement each other under the principle of subsidiarity (Ziegler, 1996).

Outside of the trade rules and the limited range of investment rules governing the global economy, the Kyoto protocol agreement is potentially of tremendous significance for multinational firms, and it is therefore worthwhile reviewing its basic implications. In the 1997 Kyoto agreement on the reduction of greenhouse gases the EU, for example, has committed itself to a reduction of 8% of carbon dioxide emissions by 2008–2012, based on the emissions level of 1990. The cost of phasing out fossil fuels is going to be sizable, and it will require firms to adopt clean sources of energy as part of a holistic policy on environmental concerns. In the most heavily affected sectors, like the oil and gas markets, firms will have to gradually shift their business to new areas, and the firms in deregulated energy markets will have to decide how and when to integrate renewable energy sources into the mix they offer their customers. Developing competitively priced renewable sources of energy will be particularly important in Europe, since the EU has decided to bring about its own emissions trading scheme that is independent of the Kyoto agreement, in case the agreement fails to be ratified. In the beginning stages this means that the European Union will institute mandatory caps (with negotiated opt-outs) for greenhouse gas emissions from industrial sectors with the largest emissions, such as power generation, oil refineries and pulp and paper mills.

In addition to substantial investment in renewable forms of energy, the Kyoto treaty calls for significant improvements in energy efficiency in manufacturing, services and transportation. The fact that the United States pulled out of the agreement due to the concerns about the adverse effects on the American economy is an indication of the potential magnitude of the effect. On the other hand, if the treaty is ratified, even American multinationals operating outside of the United States will have to comply by its provisions. There are also possible direct implications of the Kyoto protocol for foreign investment, both in terms of a possible deterrent effect due to higher costs, and as an opportunity for multinationals to engage in environmental investments in less developed countries as part of an emissions trading scheme. Due to the chosen base year of 1990, which represented the last boom year under the old regime for the ten EU accession countries in Central and Eastern Europe, a shrinking economy produced fewer emissions, and consequently all the accession countries (with the exception of Slovenia) were on track in 1999 for meeting their Kyoto targets. Furthermore, some of the accession countries far exceed the required reductions in greenhouse gases, which opens up the possibility that these countries will become the sellers in a future market for tradable emissions permits.

The emission trading scheme is one of the compliance mechanisms included in the Kyoto protocol, along with joint implementation (JI) programs aimed at the economies in transition, and clean development mechanisms (CDM) aimed at the developing countries. For example, since the accession countries are counted among the Annex I countries along with the EU-15, firms from the European Union can engage in JI projects in the economies in transition to install cleaner technology in order to reduce the emission of greenhouse gases, and in return receive credit for the reduced emissions against their domestic quota. The ten accession countries who will join the EU in 2004 face a considerable challenge in meeting the EU environmental standards within the agreed timetable, and multinationals will have to play a major role in generating the required investment, with or without the Kyoto mechanisms in place (Lundan, 2003).

While the influence of the supranational institutions on the environmental in-vestment behavior of multinationals is mostly indirect, an illustration of the direct influence of world trade rules on environmental standards and the efforts to combat global warming can be seen in the issue of tariffs on environmental equipment. As Brewer shows (in this volume) such tariffs still persist under the WTO, and they have a negative impact on the firms that develop environmental technology by limiting their growth and further technological development. For developing countries that do not have the indigenous technological capability, and need to buy environmental technology to meet the obligations under the Kyoto protocol for example, these tariffs can pose a serious hindrance in moving towards cleaner production.

DISCUSSION AND CONCLUSIONS

In this chapter, we presented a framework that sought to explain multinational environmental behavior by looking at the determining factors inside and outside the firm in a parsimonious manner. Inside the multinational firm, we argued that path dependencies in environmental investment would lead to a clear distinction between global firms, who are the leaders in their respective industries, and the lagging firms who operate primarily in the local and regional markets. This is because the initial differences between firms arising from available cash flow (and other resources) that enable the firm to make proactive investments grow larger over time, and are reinforced by market mechanisms. Additionally, we argued that much of environmental investment is conditioned by significant irreversabilities, which places emphasis on the importance of timing in the case of large capital investments, and on flexibility in a series of smaller investments. In the capital-intensive investment case, flexibility is constrained by the necessary scale of the investment, so the timing of the investment becomes critical. By contrast, timing is less critical, while flexibility is essential, in the case where companies make investments in promoting their proprietary environmental standards. We also argued, that the structural changes that have taken place in multinational firms to enable them to benefit from an integrated network structure provide an effective conduit for the transfer of environmental standards within the firm and across borders. These new structures have allowed multinationals to cultivate "centers of excellence" within their subsidiary network, and they have the explicit purpose of enabling the firm to not just disseminate resources and management practices from the headquarters to the subsidiaries, but to also gather knowledge from the subsidiaries and to integrate it into the process of corporate decision making.

Regarding important factors outside of the multinational firm, we argued that firms can be pushed into changing their behavior by changes in regulation in any of the main markets where the company is present, or they can be urged to change their practices by the demands of the marketplace, which are often channeled through the campaigning activities of an NGO. By necessity, the relationship between firms and their regulators has changed towards a more cooperative stance, since governments are eager to pursue market-led regulation, where firms are encouraged to find the most efficient organizational and technological means to meet specific targets. This in turn means, that the effective rules under which firms operate in any given country is a complex mixture of domestic regulation, which is often influenced by regulation in other countries, the firms' internal standards, which can also be influenced by regulatory standards abroad, as well as the prevailing market standards, which are influenced by NGO activity, and which in turn can also be influenced by prevailing standards abroad.

In spite of these developments, there is no reason to think that regulation is less important today than it has been before, but that in markets that are open to trade and investment, the process of regulation is more complex than ever before. Where national regulatory rules are in conflict, WTO rules determine the allowability of environmental exceptions for traded goods and services at the supranational level, and additional rules are imposed by the NAFTA environmental side agreement, as well as by EU directives. There is, however, at the present time very little regulation pertaining to the activities of multinationals as foreign investors. Nonetheless, since multinationals are typically the affected parties in any dispute concerning alleged anti-competitive application of environmental (trade) rules, they occupy center stage in the supranational arena as well.

The pollution haven hypothesis overstated the importance of investment reloca-tion in determining environmental standards, and by so doing it may have resulted in an unduly bleak view of the role of multinationals in shaping environmental standards. By limiting the focus on the effects of relocation of pollution-intensive industries, the pollution haven hypothesis covered only a small part of the effects of multinational activity. Multinational behavior is important not only in terms of where the investment takes place, but in terms of what kinds of standards are applied, where the standards originate, and how do they get transferred within industries and across borders. In an effort to capture the complexity of these interactions, this book presents a number of studies comparing the behavior of multinationals from different home countries, looking at the impact of multinationals in different host countries, and looking at the differences in how firms from different home countries react to regulation and how they respond to market demands. The movement of pollution intensive investment across borders is not the primary issue, and instead, we should direct more effort to understanding the process whereby multinational firms participate in the process of standard setting in the global economy.

REFERENCES

Barney, J. (1991). Firm resources and sustained competitive advantage. *Journal of Management, 17*(1), 99–120.

Bartlett, C., & Ghoshal, S. (1989). *Managing across borders: The transnational solution*. Boston, MA: Harvard Business School Press.

Brewer, T. L., & Young, S. (2000). *The multilateral investment system and multinational enterprises*. Oxford: Oxford University Press.

Campos, E., Lien, D., & Pradhan, S. (1999). The impact of corruption on investment: Predictability matters. *World Development, 27*(6), 1059–1067.

Cantwell, J. A. (1991). The theory of technological competence and its application to international production. In: D. G. McFetridge (Ed.), *Foreign Investment, Technology and Economic Growth*. Calgary: University of Calgary Press.

Christmann, P. (2000). Effect of "best practices" of environmental management on cost advantage: The role of complementary assets. *Academy of Management Journal, 43*(4), 663–680.

Christmann, P., & Taylor, G. (2002). Globalization and the environment: Strategies for international voluntary environmental initiatives. *Academy of Management Executive, 16*(3), 121–135.

Conner, K. R. (1991). A historical comparison of resource-based theory and five schools of thought within industrial organization economics. *Journal of Management, 17*(1), 121–154.

Damodaran, A. (2000). The promise of real options. *Journal of Applied Corporate Finance, 13*(2), 29–44.

Dean, J. M. (1992). Trade and the environment: A survey of the literature. In: L. Patrick (Ed.), *International Trade and the Environment – World Bank Discussion Papers*. Washington, DC: World Bank.

Dixit, A. K., & Pindyck, R. S. (1995). The options approach to capital investment. *Harvard Business Review, 73*(May–June), 105–115.

Dowell, G., Hart, S., & Yeung, B. (2000). Do corporate global environmental standards create or destroy market value? *Management Science, 46*(8), 1059–1074.

Esty, D. (1994). *Greening the GATT: Trade, environment and the future*. Washington, DC: Institute for International Economics.

Freedman, M., & Jaggi, B. (1993). *Air and water pollution regulation: Accomplishments and economic consequences*. Westport, CT: Quorum Books.

Gilley, K. M., Worrell, D. L., Davidson, W. N., & El-Jelly, A. (2000). Corporate environmental initiatives and anticipated firm performance: The differential effects of process-driven versus product-driven greening initiatives. *Journal of Management*, *26*(6), 1199–1216.

Graham, E. M. (2000). *Fighting the wrong enemy: Antiglobal activists and multinational enterprises*. Washington, DC: Institute for International Economics.

Gray, K. R. (2002). Foreign direct investment and environmental impacts: Is the debate over? *Review of European Community and International Environmental Law*, *11*(3), 306–313.

Habib, M., & Zurawicki, L. (2002). Corruption and foreign direct investment. *Journal of International Business Studies*, *33*(2), 291–307.

Hahn, R. W. (1993). Getting more environmental protection for less money: A practitioner's guide. *Oxford Review of Economic Policy*, *9*(4), 112–123.

Harrison, K. (1999). Talking with the donkey: Co-operative approaches to environmental protection. *Journal of Industrial Ecology*, *2*(3), 51–72.

Hedlund, G. (1986). The hypermodern MNC – A Heterarchy? *Human Resource Management*, *25*(1), 9–35.

Holm, U., & Pedersen, T. (Eds) (2000). *The emergence and impact of MNC centers of excellence*. Basingstoke: Macmillan.

Howard, J., Nash, J., & Ehrenfeld, J. (2000). Standard or smokescreen? Implementation of a voluntary environmental code. *California Management Review*, *42*(2), 63–82.

Jaffe, A. B., Peterson, S., & Portney, P. R. (1995). Environmental regulation and the competitiveness of U.S. manufacturing: What does the evidence tell us? *Journal of Economic Literature*, *XXXXIII*(March), 132–163.

King, A., & Lenox, M. (2000). Industry self-regulation without sanctions: The chemical industry's responsible care program. *Academy of Management Journal*, *43*(4), 698–717.

Klassen, R. D., & McLaughlin, C. P. (1996). The impact of environmental management on firm performance. *Management Science*, *42*(8), 1199–1214.

Klassen, R. D., & Whybark, D. C. (1999). The impact of environmental technologies on manufacturing performance. *Academy of Management Journal*, *42*(6), 599–615.

Kogut, B., & Kulatilaka, N. (2001). Capabilities as real options. *Organization Science*, *12*(6), 744–758.

Kolk, A. (2001). Multinationality and corporate ethics: Codes of conduct in the sporting goods industry. *Journal of International Business Studies*, *32*(2), 267–284.

Kolk, A., Tulder, R. v., & Welters, C. (1999). International codes of conduct and corporate social responsibility: Can transnational corporations regulate themselves? *Transnational Corporations*, *8*(1), 143–180.

Leonard, H. J. (1988). *Pollution and the struggle for the world product: Multinational corporations, environment, and international comparative advantage*. Cambridge: Cambridge University Press.

Leonard, J. H., & Duerksen, C. J. (1980). Environmental regulations and the location of industry – An international perspective. *Columbia Journal of World Business* (Summer), 52–68.

Levy, D. L. (1995). The environmental practices and performance of transnational corporations. *Transnational Corporations*, *4*(1), 44–67.

Levy, D. L. (1997). Business and international environmental treaties: Ozone depletion and climate change. *California Management Review*, *39*(3), 54–71.

Lundan, S. M. (1996). *Internationalization and environmental standards in the pulp and paper industry*. Ph.D. Dissertation, The Graduate School – Newark, Rutgers University, NJ, USA.

Lundan, S. M. (2001). Environmental standards and multinational competitiveness: A public policy proposal. In: F. Khosrow (Ed.), *International Public Policy and Regionalism at the Turn of the Century*. Oxford: Pergamon.

Lundan, S. M. (Ed.) (2002). *Network knowledge in international business*. Cheltenham: Edward Elgar.

Lundan, S. M. (2003). The role of environmental issues in the competition for inward investment within Europe. In: P. Ghauri & L. Oxelheim (Eds), *European Union and the Race for Foreign Direct Investment in Europe*. Oxford: Pergamon.

Majumdar, S. K., & Marcus, A. A. (2001). Rules versus discretion: The productivity consequences of flexible regulation. *Academy of Management Journal, 44*(1), 170–179.

Mani, M., & Wheeler, D. (1998). In search of pollution havens? Dirty industry in the world economy, 1960 to 1995. *Journal of Environment & Development, 7*(3), 215–247.

Nehrt, C. (1996). Timing and intensity effects of environmental investments. *Strategic Management Journal, 17*, 535–547.

Nelson, R. R., & Winter, S. G. (1982). *An evolutionary theory of economic change*. Cambridge, MA: Harvard University Press.

Peteraf, M. A. (1993). The cornerstones of competitive advantage: A resource-based view. *Strategic Management Journal, 14*(3), 179–191.

Porter, M. E., & van der Linde, C. (1995). Toward a new conception of the environment-competitiveness relationship. *Journal of Economic Perspectives, 9*(4), 97–118.

Rugman, A. M., & D'Cruz, J. R. (2000). *Multinationals as flagship firms*. Oxford: Oxford University Press.

Rugman, A., Kirton, J., & Soloway, J. (1999). *Environmental regulations and corporate strategy: A NAFTA perspective*. Oxford: Oxford University Press.

Rugman, A. M., & Verbeke, A. (1998a). Corporate strategies and environmental regulations: An organizing framework. *Strategic Management Journal, 19*, 363–375.

Rugman, A. M., & Verbeke, A. (1998b). Corporate strategy and international environmental policy. *Journal of International Business Studies, 29*(4), 819–834.

Russo, M. V., & Fouts, P. A. (1997). A resource-based perspective on corporate environmental performance and profitability. *Academy of Management Journal, 40*(3), 534–559.

Sharma, S., & Vredenburg, H. (1998). Proactive corporate environmental strategy and the development of competitively valuable organizational capabilities. *Strategic Management Journal, 19*, 729–753.

Spender, J. C. (1996). Making knowledge the basis of a dynamic theory of the firm. *Strategic Management Journal, 17*(Special Issue), 45–62.

Teece, D. J. (1986). Profiting from technological innovation: Implications for integration, collaboration, licensing and public policy. *Research Policy, 15*, 285–305.

Vogel, D. (1995). *Trading up: Consumer and environmental regulation in a global economy*. Cambridge, MA: Harvard University Press.

Williamson, O. (1983). Credible commitments: Using hostages to support exchange. *The American Economic Review, 73*(4), 519–540.

Ziegler, A. R. (1996). *Trade and environmental law in the European community*. Oxford: Clarendon Press.

DEGREE OF INTERNATIONALIZATION AND ENVIRONMENTAL PERFORMANCE: EVIDENCE FROM U.S. MULTINATIONALS

James J. Kennelly and Eric E. Lewis

ABSTRACT

We examine the relationship between the degree of internationalization (DOI) of a sample of 148 U.S.-based MNEs and measures of their corporate environmental performance. Using cross-sectional data for 1993 and 1998, and longitudinal data for 1993–1999, we tested for associations between the two variables of interest. Cross-sectional data suggested a positive relationship between DOI and highly rated environmental performance. Longitudinal findings were similar with positive correlations that grew stronger the longer the "lag" between measurement of DOI and environmental performance. This research supports arguments that MNEs tend to be proactive leaders rather than laggards in fostering better corporate environmental performance.

INTRODUCTION

The most recent *World Investment Report* (UNCTAD, 2002) notes that there are now some 68,000 multinational firms on this planet, with 850,000 foreign affiliates and worldwide sales of $18.5 trillion. If one accepts that firm turnover is

Multinationals, Environment and Global Competition
Research in Global Strategic Management, Volume 9, 23–41
Copyright © 2004 by Elsevier Ltd.
All rights of reproduction in any form reserved
ISSN: 1064-4857/doi:10.1016/S1064-4857(03)09002-8

an indicator comparable to the GNP of a nation, then fifty-one of the world's one hundred largest economies are multinationals (Anderson & Cavanagh, 1996). Whether one accepts such comparisons or not, it is clearly difficult to contest the importance of these primary instruments of a rapidly globalizing world economy. Indeed, to many observers, multinational enterprises (MNEs), with their considerable financial, technological, and human resources, now appear to be the dominant social institutions of the age (Barnet, 1994; Barnet & Cavanagh, 1994; Barnet & Mueller, 1974; Hawken, 1993; Kanter, 1995; Korten, 1995, 1999; Vernon, 1992, 1998; Viederman, 1997).

Although an appreciation of the economic muscle of MNEs is widely shared, observers of the broader social and environmental effects of globalization (and MNEs as the "shock troops" of globalization) have arrived at no such consensus. Attitudes towards the social and environmental effects of MNEs tend to vary widely, usually characterized by extreme positions. What *is* certain is that MNEs continue to be lightning rods for the critics of globalization, as the continuing public protests at meetings of the WTO, IMF and World Bank demonstrate.

Concerns over the environmental performance of MNEs, in particular, have been pronounced, and are characterized by a wide array of views, excessive emotion, the ritual recitation of anecdotal evidence, and very little in the way of empirical investigation. Proponents of globalization tend to argue that MNEs, armed with the powerful array of capabilities and advantages that have permitted them to succeed economically in the global arena, tend to propagate *higher* environmental standards around the world, as they diffuse their own "best practice" policies and standards throughout their worldwide operations. In this view, MNEs provide the spur to "raise all boats" in the arena of environmental performance. Critics, on the other hand, accuse MNEs of leading a "race to the bottom" as they search for locations where they may reap cost advantages by exercising the very *lowest* environmental standards commensurate with maximizing their economic bottom line.

Not only are the theoretical underpinnings of either perspective hardly robust, there is also scant empirical evidence to buttress either claim. Nevertheless, the battle lines are clearly drawn. Critics see MNEs, quite literally, as destroying the planet. Supporters, at least those "true believers" in the promise of globalization, tend to see MNEs as perhaps the planet's last best hope. The authors of this chapter hope to provide at least some evidence that may shed light on this emotional, but understudied, relationship between MNEs and the natural environment.

In this chapter, we summarize and extend our early efforts to sort out, admittedly to a limited extent, this complex and deeply contentious issue by collecting and examining a set of empirical data for U.S.-based MNEs. Specifically, we ask a question that on the surface is quite straightforward: *Is* there a relationship between the degree of internationalization of a firm and its environmental performance, and if so, is that relationship a positive or a negative one?

THEORETICAL BACKGROUND

It is not difficult to find critics of the environmental performance of multinational corporations. They embody a radical critique that frames the debate in very stark terms: MNEs are seen as effective and useful instruments for the economic success of organizations, their agents, and their owners themselves, and detrimental or, at best, indifferent to the societies, and the natural environments, in which they are embedded. Although some of this criticism has come from within the Academy, where even some of the founders of the field of International Business articulated their concerns about the power, motives, and impacts of MNEs (see Hymer, 1976; Kindleberger, 1974; Vernon, 1971, 1977), this has been fairly muted. Political activists (and particularly environmental organizations) on the other hand, have been no less than vociferous in their critique of MNEs' environmental misdeeds. That MNEs are almost compelled to behave in a manner that is destructive of the natural environments in which they are embedded is accepted nearly as an article of faith. This is considered a natural consequence of the logic of the global economic system of which they are a part. MNEs are footloose, stateless, flexible and mobile, able to leverage their power by playing nation-states off against one another, not tethered by the control of any particular nation, and in constant search of marginal advantage. The short-term dictates of financial markets, driven by the incessant and shifting flows of international capital, compel firms to utilize every opportunity to realize short-term economic advantage. These critics (Barnet, 1994; Barnet & Cavanagh, 1994; Barnet & Mueller, 1974; Hawken, 1993; Korten, 1995, 1999) observe the lack of commitment MNEs have to any one country, and their predilection to arbitrage their opportunities (Kogut, 1985) to optimal advantage.

A natural consequence of such motivations, argue the critics, is inevitably the compromise of MNEs' corporate environmental performance. Driven by the demands of an ever more competitive global arena, MNEs have every incentive to compromise their environmental performance, especially in cases where local environmental regulations are lax and enforcement uneven (Gladwin, 1987; Greider, 1997). One of the earliest, and most common, accusations leveled against MNEs is that they search for "pollution havens," opportunities to move dirty industrial processes to those locations with weak environmental regulations, usually less developed nations that are desperate for foreign direct investment (Daly, 1994). This "pollution haven hypothesis," however, has not been supported by most academic research (Lundan, 2000; Rugman & Verbeke, 1998). Kolk (2000) identifies several reasons for this. First, environmental costs in many instances are sufficiently low, so the considerable cost of creating a separate national organizational apparatus to take advantage of savings is not economically sensible. Second, compromising environmental performance, even when quite legal, is not worth the risk to corporate reputation. Third, applying differential environmental standards throughout the world is not worth the cost and complexity of the coordination required to accomplish this. All of this has not prevented critics from continuing to cite such behavior as high among their list of MNE misdeeds. To extend their argument further, even MNE environmental performance in its home country may be affected, since it can always avail itself of multiple opportunities to exit the home country if environmental regulations, and their attendant costs, become too troublesome. Yet, although the critics of MNEs' environmental performance are passionate, they have offered little more than anecdotal support for their claims. Empirical studies that would shed further light on such assertions are not only limited, but also generally fail to support the pollution haven claims, or even the salience of environmental regulatory regimes for international investment (Grossman & Krueger, 1993; Jaffe et al., 1995).

An (arguably) more mainstream view of the environmental performance of MNEs offers a significant contrast, and indeed, there is a growing body of empirical work that suggests that MNEs may in fact be associated with more *positive* levels of corporate environmental performance. Clearly, there is no lack of theory detailing the competitive advantages that multinational enterprises are thought to realize by virtue of their internationalization of operations and capabilities (Buckley & Casson, 1976; Dunning, 1993; Rugman & D'Cruz, 1997). In addition to such transaction cost and internalization advantages are the attributes that critics of MNEs find so threatening to environmental performance, the ability to play "options," "arbitrage" opportunities, and hedge risk, through the flexibility that internationalization offers (Kobrin, 1982; Kogut, 1983, 1985, 1992; Porter, 1990). As noted by Bartlett and Ghoshal (1998), these global networks of MNEs also permit them to source information from throughout the worldwide organization, digest it, build upon it, and ultimately diffuse it as *knowledge* throughout the organization. The form of knowledge most germane to this discussion is *environmental* knowledge, as demonstrated by the standards, practices, policies, processes, and ultimately environmental performance demonstrated by MNEs.

In this view, MNEs are still driven to achieve optimal performance through making best use of their worldwide opportunities and flexible options, just as their critics argue. But in this case, *superior* corporate environmental performance is seen as a type of operational efficiency that can be honed and developed through international activities, and one that is fully consistent with the overall economic objectives of the firm. To the extent that good environmental performance contributes to such economic efficiency, MNEs will have sufficient motivation to invest in such activities beyond the dictates of the regulations and law. Some scholars have already advanced the argument that such environmental capabilities may reflect distinct competitive advantages that contribute to overall production efficiency (Elkington, 1994; Hart, 1997; Kanter, 1995; Porter & van der Linde, 1995; Shrivastava, 1996). This "win-win" scenario, of course, is hardly unattractive in that it argues that better environmental performance is fully consistent with the (economic) bottom line (see Kolk, 2000, for a list of publications that advance this line of thinking). Following this logic, MNEs, as they attempt to maximize profits, will in fact tend to develop stricter environmental standards internal to the company, and will disseminate them throughout the worldwide organization as best organizational practice. Many, in fact, have formally committed to enforcing identical environmental practices and standards throughout their far-flung operations. In other cases, MNEs have committed to maintaining the same level of environmental performance, if not the identical environmental standards (arguing that there must be room to customize environmental practices to specific local conditions). Indeed, the more internationalized a firm is, the greater is the opportunity for both the development of environmental knowledge, and the dispersion of superior environmental standards, processes and practices. Additionally, and beyond their direct contribution to economic performance, better environmental performance may also provide intangible benefits, such as contributions to reputational capital, which itself may further organizational priorities and contribute to financial success (Dowell, Hart & Yeung, 1998; Hart & Ahuja, 1996). Some have suggested that MNEs, in particular, are highly visible and, conceivably, attractive targets for more than passing scrutiny of their environmental management and performance (Kolk, 2000).

Early research in this area has been promising. In their study of S&P 500 manufacturing firms, Hart and Ahuja (1996) found that capital spending on pollution prevention projects was associated with better financial performance (with clear lags between investment and performance). Nehrt (1996), studying paper and pulp manufacturers in eight countries, also found a positive relationship between capital spending on pollution control activities and financial performance (profit growth). Klassen and McLaughlin (1996) found that better financial returns were associated with evidence of strong and proactive environmental management activities, while Russo and Fouts (1997) found a strong positive relationship between independent environmental performance ratings and enhanced profitability for a large (238) sample of *Fortune* 500 firms. More recently, Dowell, Hart and Yeung (1998) found that MNEs that chose to adopt one stringent environmental standard worldwide for all worldwide operations realized higher market values than those that engaged in a lower level of environmental performance. It would appear that most empirical evidence at this point supports the proposition that good environmental performance is quite consistent with what most people understand as "good business."

Theory suggests that firms internationalize in order to develop, and reap advantage from, mobility advantages, flexibility, learning opportunities, and global scale and scope economies. The greater the level of internationalization of the firm, the more opportunities to develop, and utilize, such capabilities. If one accepts the argument (supported by the above-noted empirical studies) that positive, or proactive, environmental capabilities are merely one more such manifestation of these capabilities, then using them to produce superior environmental performance would not be entirely far-fetched. The logical extension is that MNEs, motivated by economic advantage, and prone to use those firm-specific advantages they have built by virtue of being MNEs, will tend to evince better environmental performance the more "multinational" or "international" they are.

The question of whether theory supports one view of MNEs' environmental performance, or another, is difficult; neither is particularly compelling, nor necessarily even "theory." We thus treat the question of the relationship between degree of firm internationalization, and environmental performance, as primarily an empirical question. There has been at least some empirical work in this area. For example, Kolk and van Tulder (2000), studied the degree of internationalization for one hundred of the largest transnational corporations, and found a positive relationship with "proactive" environmental reporting. Although environmental reporting is not the same as environmental performance, the fact that these MNEs often provide sufficient data in these reports to have their actual environmental performance monitored to some extent suggests that environmental reporting may be a reasonable proxy for environmental performance (Kolk & van Tulder, 2000).

THE STUDY

In this chapter, we present an update and extension of research originally reported in Kennelly and Lewis (2002), which examined the relationship between the degree of internationalization (DOI) of a sample of U.S.-based MNEs drawn from the S & P 500 and measures of their corporate environmental performance. Although there has been some research into the relationships between MNEs and environmental performance, there has been little that examines the degree or extent of firm internationalization, and its association with environmental performance. This study seeks to make a contribution by addressing this gap. In addition to reporting details of the original cross-sectional study (Kennelly & Lewis, 2002), we have added several years of data to conduct longitudinal tests (through 1999), and additional statistical treatments. Our research question is relatively straightforward: Is there any statistically significant correlation between the degree of internationalization (DOI) and the level of MNEs' environmental performance?

Sample

The focal firms in the study were 148 U.S.-based MNEs, taken from the S&P 500. The initial 500 firms were first reduced by the elimination of all non-manufacturing industries: only firms with a primary 2-digit SIC code between 20 and 49 were retained in the sample. This appeared logical given the potential environmental impacts of firms in these industrial sectors, their similarities to what have been termed "core" or "flagship" firms in the global economy (Kolk & van Tulder, 2000; Rugman & D'Cruz, 1997), and from a practical perspective, the greater likelihood of the availability of environmental performance data. The sample was further reduced as a function of data availability (for example, either measures of corporate environmental performance, or relevant measures of internationalization, were not available for every year from 1993 to 1999). Due to changes in the corporate reporting requirements regarding international segments, foreign asset data was in many cases unavailable for years after 1996. Fortunately it was possible to obtain reliable data for both the measure of environmental performance (discussed below) and the Foreign Sales to Total Sales (FSTS) ratio for 80 of the firms that were included in the initial study. This proved to be sufficient to allow for the extension of a portion of the initial study and also for a new test of the relationship between DOI and environmental performance.

Measures

Degree of Internationalization (DOI)

The most common measure of the extent of internationalization of firms used by researchers has clearly been the percentage of foreign sales to total sales revenue (see Ramaswamy, 1992). Unidimensional measures such as this have, however, been roundly criticized in the literature (Ramaswamy, 1992; Ramaswamy, Kroeck & Renforth, 1996; Sullivan, 1994, 1996).

Among those critical of unidimensional measures, Ramaswamy (1992) developed a multidimensional conceptualization of the internationalization construct, consisting of three independent factors: *Scope* (a count of 1–3 indicating the discrete number of functional activities pursued abroad: sales, production, R&D),

depth (the ratio of foreign assets to total assets, and foreign sales to total sales), and *dispersion* (a discrete count of the number of foreign countries in which an MNE has research labs, manufacturing facilities, sales offices and sales subsidiaries, respectively). In contrast, however, Sullivan (1994) argued for use of a single factor, a DOI (degree of internationalization) of MNEs comprised of five variables: foreign sales/total sales, overseas subsidiaries/total subsidiaries, foreign assets/total assets, psychic dispersion of international operations (dispersion of subsidiaries around the 10 psychic cultural zones as identified in Ronen and Shenkar (1985), and top management's international experience (as a percentage of total top management experience)).

This chapter reports both cross-sectional data from 1993 and 1998, and results of a longitudinal study of data for the period 1993–1999. Following Sanders and Carpenter (1998), this study utilized a variation of Sullivan's (1994) measure (for the cross-sectional analysis only) by developing a DOI measure that incorporates each firm's percentage of foreign sales, percentage of foreign assets, the ratio of foreign subsidiaries to total firm subsidiaries, and the number of regions in which a firm is active (Sullivan's "psychic dispersion of international operations"). More specifically, the data was sourced as follows:

Foreign sales percentage (FSTS). Data on the ratio of foreign sales to total firm sales (FSTS) was collected from firm annual report disclosures accessed through *Standard & Poor's Compact Disclosure/Worldscope* for 1991–1999.

Foreign assets percentage (FATA). Data on the ratio of foreign assets to total firm assets FATA) was also accessed through *Compact Disclosure/Worldscope* for 1991–1999.

Percentage of overseas subsidiaries (OSTS). Overseas subsidiaries as a percentage of total subsidiaries (OSTS) were sourced from the *Directory of Corporate Affiliations*.

Psychic dispersion of international operations (PDIO). The number of "psychic zones" in which the firm has subsidiaries. This measure was developed by Ronen and Shenkar (1985), who clustered countries into 10 cultural zones based on Hofstede and others. This data was gathered by counting the number of zones in which each firm had either sales, production, distribution or research & development operations, as indicated in the *Directory of Corporate Affiliations*.

Though recognizing that multidimensional measures of degree of internationalization (DOI) are preferable to the more common unidimensional measures, (Ramaswamy, 1992; Ramaswamy, Kroeck & Renforth, 1996; Sullivan, 1994, 1996) we chose to employ the percentage of foreign sales (FSTS) as our DOI measure for the *longitudinal* testing. This relates to the difficulties in obtaining reliable measures of other variables, and follows the results of Kennelly and Lewis (2002) that showed the strongest relationships between this DOI measure and the available measures of environmental performance.

Environmental Performance Measurement of firm-level environmental performance is problematic. Although more and more firms are preparing voluntary environmental reports for their various stakeholders, there is as yet little consensus on environmental rating (and reporting) criteria (Kolk, 1999). While organizations engage this issue and seek to develop widely applicable criteria, among them the Coalition for Environmentally Sustainable Economies, the United Nations Environmental Program, and the World Business Council for Sustainable Development, U.S.-based firms may report environmental data as they choose or, in many cases, not at all. In the United States, certain unidimensional data such as toxics release inventory (TRI) data detailing emissions and effluent containing a variety of listed ingredients is reported (at facility level) by law, and made available through the EPA. However even such data, in themselves, do not constitute "ratings." In assessing corporate environmental performance, a multidimensional rating is eminently preferable. For this study, measures of the level of corporate environmental performance were determined through use of environmental ratings supplied by Kinder, Lydenberg & Domini (KLD), a social research and investment firm that specializes in evaluating the social and environmental performance of publicly owned corporations. Although admittedly an imperfect measure (there is considerable scope for subjectivity in such triangulated ratings), KLD ratings have advantages over unidimensional measures (for example, emissions data, environmental lawsuits and fines, or extent of environmental reporting) and there is precedent for their use in business and society research (Graves & Waddock, 1994; Johnson & Greening, 1994; Ruf, Muralidhar & Paul, 1993). KLD identifies "strengths" and "concerns," related to various categories of environmental performance for a wide selection of publicly traded corporations. We have equally weighted the ratings for the various categories of environmental performance and converted this data into a 10-point ordinal scale, with a rating of ten reflecting the very highest level of environmental performance, and a level of zero reflecting the lowest.

Control variables. In the cross-sectional study, control variables such as sales, 5-year average return on sales (to measure organizational slack), research and development intensity, and industry concentration ratio were utilized to account for variability unrelated to the independent variable of DOI.

Methodology. In testing the research question, we performed both cross-sectional and longitudinal tests on the data. Using the more sophisticated measures of DOI we had developed for the 1993 and 1998 data, we tested the relationship between DOI and environmental performance through regression analysis. Longitudinal results (for the years 1993–1999) were developed from observations of correlation patterns between DOI and our KLD measures of environmental performance.

RESULTS

Stepwise OLS regressions were run on the cross-sectional data for both 1993 and 1998 (correlation matrices are shown in Tables 1 and 2). From the list of control variables (above) only the sales (a general measure of firm size) in log form showed a statistically significant relationship with the KLD measure of environmental performance. Also of note was the finding that this measure of firm size was

Table 1. Correlations for 1993.

	KLD	FATA	FSTS	RDI	DOIComp	LogSales	PDI
KLD	1	0.149^*	0.183^*	0.050	0.099	-0.261^{**}	-0.066
FATA		1	0.793^{**}	0.162^*	0.798^{**}	0.219^{**}	0.513^{**}
FSTS			1	0.347^{**}	0.849^{**}	0.207^{**}	0.549^{**}
RDI				1	0.430^{**}	-0.037	0.321^{**}
DOIComp					1	0.304^{**}	0.855^{**}
LogSales						1	0.428^{**}
PDI							1

*Correlation is significant at the 0.05 level.
**Correlation is significant at the 0.01 level.

Table 2. Correlations for 1998.

	KLD	FATA	FSTS	LogSales	DOIComp	PDI	OSTS
KLD	1	0.162	0.095	-0.113	0.106	-0.023	0.049
FATA		1	0.626^{**}	0.083	0.784^{**}	0.367^{**}	0.468^{**}
FSTS			1	0.224^{**}	0.845^{**}	0.524^{**}	0.512^{**}
LogSales				1	0.243^*	0.431^{**}	0.189^*
DOIComp					1	0.838^{**}	0.769^{**}
PDI						1	0.769^{**}
OSTS							1

*Correlation is significant at the 0.05 level.
**Correlation is significant at the 0.01 level.

Table 3. Regression Model Results for 1993 and 1998.

	Coefficient	Std. Error	Significance
Model 1 – 1993			
Constant	1.283	0.433	0.003
FSTS	1.031	0.291	0.001
LogSales	−0.238	0.053	0.000
Model 2 – 1993			
Constant	1.313	0.448	0.004
DOIComp	0.213	0.080	0.000
LogSales	−0.240	0.057	0.009
Model 3 – 1998			
Constant	0.000	Not significant	
FATA	0.879	0.493	0.078
LogSales	−0.045	0.017	0.009

Note: All but 1998 FATA are significant at the 99% level – 1998 FATA at 90%.

negatively correlated with environmental performance in both 1993 and 1998, and with a level of confidence greater than 99% for 1993. Table 3 shows the regression results for 1993 and 1998 , where the ratio of foreign sales to total sales (FSTS) and foreign assets to total assets were respectively employed as the DOI measures.

These results suggest that firms with a higher degree of internationalization will also tend to evince a higher (more positive) level of corporate environmental performance. Similar results were realized with the 1993 data using a multiple measure of DOI based on that suggested by Sullivan (1994). Table 3 also includes these results, which were again significant at the 99% level of confidence.

While the 1998 results pointed tepidly in the same direction as the 1993 results, only a single measure of DOI, foreign assets as a percentage of total assets (FATA), was found to be related to environmental performance with statistical significance at the 90% level. The firm size variable, logsales, retained both its statistical significance (at greater than 99%) and its directional impact on the environmental performance measure. The implications of this result are both interesting and, perhaps, counterintuitive. As one might suspect, there is a positive and statistically significant relationship between the size of a firm in the study group and its level of internationalization, as measured by the multidimensional measure of DOI and each of its unidimensional components. This rather intuitive result was observed in the overall correlation matrices for both the 1993 and 1998 data sets in the original study. However, while these measures of size and international breadth are positively correlated, the composite measure of environmental performance relates to them separately in a contrary fashion. That is to say that while the gross measure of size, given by the logsales variable, is negatively associated with environmental performance with a high level of statistical significance, all measures of DOI were positively associated with the composite measure of environmental performance in both 1993 and 1998, save the Psychic Dispersion measure in 1998 which exhibited no significant negative correlation coefficient. These results describe the statistical impression that, while overall firm size has a negative impact on environmental performance, increasing levels of DOI are associated with improving environmental performance.

These cross-sectional results formed the basis for the preliminary findings of our initial study (Kennelly & Lewis, 2002). These findings were further supported by reference to the overall correlation between the KLD environmental performance measure and the two measures of DOI to which it was most strongly related, foreign sales as a percentage of total sales (FSTS) and foreign assets as a percentage of total assets (FATA). The overall correlations and the accompanying analysis are abbreviated here (see Kennelly & Lewis, 2002), but deserving of mention, as their indications provided the only longitudinal results of the initial study. It was generally observed, and also supported by a time series regression, that the positive correlations between the FSTS and FATA DOI measures and the KLD measure were increasing through time from 1991 to 1996. It was also observed that these correlations were stronger between the levels of DOI observed for firms two to three years prior to observance of their KLD measures. This was the nearest to a suggestion of causality that the study data yielded. That is, since earlier DOI correlates with later environmental performance, some causal effect may at least be posited. A summary of these correlation phenomena is presented in Table 4. While the implications are supported statistically, a less formal examination of the Table 4 correlations indicates that the general level of association between the FSTS DOI measure and the KLD performance measure is increasing in recent years

Table 4. Lagged Correlations Between FSTS and KLD.

1991	1992	1993	1994	1995	1996
0.13362	0.133031	0.145353	0.169697	0.1809922	0.2257850
$n = 91$	94	53	38	24	08
	0.172351	0.085124	0.187598	0.2078612	0.2326568
	56	57	54	83	38
		0.125875	0.143445	0.2255561	0.2363355
		99	08	03	5
			0.174211	0.1853397	0.2552071
			89	53	5

(reading right to left). It is also generally apparent that there is a tendency toward stronger associations as the lag between observation of DOI and environmental performance is increased from zero to three years (reading top to bottom).

One difficulty presented by the form of the study data leaves the original OLS regression results with less force. The environmental performance measure, KLD, is an ordinal measure, providing a discrete variable in the data set, while the several and composite measures of DOI are continuous variables. This presents a problem if the KLD measure is to be used as the dependent variable in an OLS regression. Employing the KLD measure as the independent variable in a simple two-variable model can overcome a portion of this issue, though a potential argument for causality is lost. Future analysis of this multivariate model, using the KLD measure as the independent variable, may achieve the best non-regression result through the use of a Multiple Analysis of Variance (MANOVA). The results from the current study represent a one-way analysis of variance (ANOVA) to provide insight into the relationship between one measure of DOI, FSTS, and the KLD environmental performance measure through all years from 1993 through 1999.

As previously described, the KLD measure is provided in two pieces, a "strength" rating that ranges from 1 to 5, and a "concerns" rating that also ranges from 1 to 5. For the purposes of this study the strengths and concerns ratings were combined into a single measure with a range of zero to ten, with ten being the best possible performance and zero being the worst. As a practical matter no scores greater than seven were achieved through this combination, and few scores of zero or one were observed. This left the group of firms under study with practical performance levels ranging from two to seven.

The single measure of DOI that could be reliably obtained for all years from 1993 to 1999 was FSTS. This allowed for a one-way ANOVA that was designed to measure between firms who fell at the reported extremes of environmental performance according to KLD at any time during the period of study. The method was to match any composite KLD score of two or seven in any year with the FSTS measure for the same firm in the same year, thereby yielding all possible combinations of extreme environmental performance and contemporaneous DOI. The ANOVA then looked for differences in levels of DOI (FSTS) between the established KLD performance groups. Table 5 shows the results of this analysis.

It should be noted that this result shows a difference (significant with greater than 99% confidence) in DOI between the firms performing at the extremes of the KLD measure, and with the firms performing at the low extreme on the environmental measure exhibiting a lower degree of internationalization. This again supports the hypothesis that firms with higher levels of internationalization may be associated with more positive levels of environmental performance.

Table 5.   ANOVA of FSTS for KLD Levels 2 and 7 for Years 1993–1999.

Summary

Groups	Count	Sum	Average	Variance
KLD composite 7	15	693.72	46.248	283.1133
KLD composite 2	36	1212.57	33.6825	155.7023

ANOVA

Source of Variation	SS	df	MS	F	p-Value	F crit
Between groups	1,671.795	1	1,671.795	8.702489	0.004861	2.810822
Within groups	9,413.166	49	192.1054			
Total	11,084.96	50				

As the instances of performance ratings of seven were relatively few, and a far greater number of level six performances were observed, we applied the same ANOVA to the category two and six KLD performance firms, with the results reported in Table 6.

These results are consistent with those from Table 7 (with greater than 95% confidence). While the nature of this test precludes the implication of causality on the relationship, the results do indicate a measurable, strong and positive relationship between higher DOI and superior environmental performance. The authors also have preliminary indications that the results of logistic regressions using the full data set will provide similar support for this hypothesis. Of course these findings

Table 6.   ANOVA of FSTS for KLD Levels 2 and 6 for Years 1993–1999.

Summary

Groups	Count	Sum	Average	Variance
KLD composite 6	63	2,614.42	41.4987	298.9536
KLD composite 2	36	1,212.57	33.6825	155.7023

ANOVA

Source of Variation	SS	df	MS	F	p-Value	F crit
Between groups	1,399.595	1	1,399.595	5.660307	0.019311	2.757972
Within groups	23,984.7	97	247.265			
Total	25,384.3	98				

held well short of providing a definitive word on the matters of interest, that is, the relationship (if any) between DOI and the environmental performance of MNEs.

DISCUSSION AND LIMITATIONS

This study represents a limited exploratory analysis of the relationship between a firm's degree of internationalization and certain measures of its environmental performance. Although the results should be approached with due caution, and the limitations of this study are not inconsiderable, we believe they provide some relevant insights that may inform the ongoing debate over the environmental impacts of the largest multinational corporations.

The evidence presented here, while not the final word on the matter, does suggest that there may be a statistically significant *positive* relationship between the extent of a firm's internationalization (that is, how *multinational* it is) and a particular multidimensional measure of its corporate environmental performance. At least, it is to the best of our knowledge the first attempt to empirically test this relationship between degree of internationalization and environmental performance. Minimally, we hope that its findings, while not conclusive, at least suggest that future research in this area may be fruitful.

Any attempt to suggest that DOI leads to better environmental performance, however, is clearly exceeding the boundaries of what this study's results may legitimately permit us to claim. Our research suggests the presence of a significant relationship, but does not test for causality. It is better, perhaps, to focus upon what the study results do *not* support. Specifically, there is no evidence to support the thesis of critics that less acceptable levels of corporate environmental performance are attendant upon higher degrees of internationalization of corporations. Quite simply, for the environmental critics of MNEs, there is no "smoking gun." However, there may be many explanations for this.

First, it could be that MNEs, by virtue of being more internationalized, *are* in fact better environmental performers. The results here only hint at this. Second, it could be that the degree of internationalization, and the level of environmental performance, have no relationship whatsoever. Our research suggests that this is not the case, at least insofar as our measures of DOI and environmental performance adequately measure the relevant variables. Third, it could be that the operationalizations of the variables that we have employed are simply not up to the task of encompassing the considerable complexity of the phenomena they attempt to measure. This is a legitimate area of concern. Better specification of DOI, and surely better specification of measures of corporate environmental performance, is clearly needed.

Willis Harmon was famously quoted as saying (see Hawken, 1992, p. 100) that multinational corporations have "special" responsibilities, since "the dominant institution in any society needs to take responsibility for the whole. Every decision that is made, every action taken has to be viewed in light of, in the context of, that kind of responsibility." Given the global impact of environmental issues, the performance of MNEs in this area will be a critical feature of life in this century. The results of this empirical study do answer a real need. The more that discussions of the environmental performance of MNEs can be turned from arguments over political ideology to conversations focused upon empirical evidence, the sooner they will be grounded in solid science and grounded theory. This study, as one of the few to test for a relationship between degree of internationalization and environmental performance, supplies at least a modicum of such evidence. The results are relevant, interesting, and hopefully provocative. The evidence weakens the case of critics of MNEs, depriving them of the "smoking gun" of poor corporate environmental performance. Conversely, the findings offer support to those who see the largest MNEs as playing more positive and constructive roles in the spread of environmentally sustainable practices. Future researchers will have ample opportunity to proceed well beyond these first small steps.

Limitations

The results must be approached cautiously, and with sufficient circumspection. In themselves, they prove nothing. Measurement issues are not irrelevant, insofar as debates about the appropriate measurements of DOI have yet to settle out, and measurement of corporate environmental performance itself is only in its infancy. The sample itself is composed exclusively of very large, U.S.-based manufacturing firms, and consequently the results may not be readily generalizable to smaller, non-manufacturing, or non-U.S.-based MNEs. The double cross-sectional analyses performed in the study add richness, but are less helpful than a full longitudinal design. It is also quite possible that the environmental performance of U.S.-based MNEs outside of the U.S. may be far less visible than their performance at home. Assessing the environmental performance of U.S.-based MNEs may well be based largely on information provided on their operations in the U.S., while information on their environmental performance in their many foreign host countries is far more difficult to access. To the extent that MNEs perform differently abroad than at home, this may represent a significant limitation, and one that can only be addressed with the maturity of environmental reporting on a global basis.

In summary, this study represents a small first step in empirical research on the relationship between the growing multinational presence of business enterprises and their environmental performance. The significant positive relationship found between these two variables represents an interesting and potentially useful finding from which future research may derive some benefit.

REFERENCES

Anderson, S., & Cavanagh, J. (1996). *The top 200: The rise of global corporate power*. Washington: Institute for Policy Studies.

Barnet, R. J. (1994). Lords of the global economy. *The Nation*, December 19th, 754–757.

Barnet, R. J., & Cavanagh, J. (1994). *Global dreams: Imperial corporations and the new world order*. New York: Simon & Schuster.

Barnet, R. J., & Mueller, R. E. (1974). *Global reach*. New York: Simon & Schuster.

Bartlett, C. A., & Ghoshal, S. (1998). *Managing across borders: The transnational solution*. Boston: Harvard Business School Press.

Buckley, P. J., & Casson, M. (1976). *The future of the multinational enterprise*. London: Macmillan.

Daly, H. E. (1994). Fostering environmentally sustainable development: Four parting suggestions for the world bank. *Ecological Economics*, *10*, 183–187.

Dowell, G., Hart, S., & Yeung, B. (1998). Corporate global environmental standards: Altruism or value-added? *Academy of Management Best Paper Proceedings*.

Dunning, J. H. (1993). *Multinational enterprises and the global economy*. Reading, MA: Addison-Wesley.

Elkington, J. (1994). Towards the sustainable corporation: Win-Win-Win business strategies for sustainable development. *California Management Review*, *36*(2), 90–100.

Gladwin, T. N. (1987). Environment, development, and multinational enterprise. In: C. Pearson (Ed.), *Multinational Corporations, Environment and the Third World-Business Matters*. Durham: Duke University Press.

Graves, S. B., & Waddock, S. A. (1994). Institutional ownership and corporate social performance. *Academy of Management Journal*, *37*(4), 1034–1046.

Greider, W. (1997). *One world, ready or not*. New York: Simon and Shuster.

Grossman, G. M., & Krueger, A. B. (1993). Environmental impacts of a North American Free Trade Agreement. In: P. Garber (Ed.), *The U.S.-Mexico Free Trade Agreement* (pp. 13–56). Cambridge: MIT Press.

Hart, S. (1997). Beyond greening: Strategies for a sustainable world. *Harvard Business Review* (January–February), 67–76.

Hart, S., & Ahuja, G. (1996). Does it pay to be green? An empirical examination of the relationship between emission reduction and firm performance. *Business Strategy and the Environment*, *5*, 30–37.

Hawken, P. (1992). The ecology of commerce. *Inc.* April, 93–100.

Hawken, P. (1993). *The ecology of commerce*. New York: HarperCollins.

Hymer, S. H. (1976). *The international operations of national firms: A study in direct foreign investment* (Doctoral dissertation, MIT, 1960). Cambridge, MA: MIT Press.

Jaffe, A. B., Peterson, S. R., Portney, P. R., & Stavins, R. N. (1995). Environmental regulation and the competitiveness of U.S. manufacturing: What does the evidence tell us? *Journal of Economic Literature*, *33*, 132–163.

Johnson, R. A., & Greening, D. W. (1994). Relationships between corporate social performance, financial performance, and firm governance. *Academy of Management Best Paper Proceedings*, 314–318.

Kanter, R. M. (1995). *World class: Thriving locally in a global economy*. New York: Simon & Schuster.

Kennelly, J. J., & Lewis, E. E. (2002). Degree of internationalization and corporate environmental performance: Is there a link? *International Journal of Management, 19*(3), 478–489.

Kindleberger, C. P. (1974). Size of firm and size of nation. In: C. P. Kindleberger (Ed.), *Multinational Excursions* (pp. 14–34). Cambridge, MA: MIT Press.

Klassen, R. D., & McLaughlin, C. P. (1996). The impact of environmental management on firm performance. *Management Science, 42*(8), 1199–1214.

Kobrin, S. J. (1982). *Managing political risk assessment: Strategic response to environmental change*. Berkeley, CA: University of California Press.

Kogut, B. (1983). Foreign direct investment as a sequential process. In: C. P. Kindleberger & D. Audretsch (Eds), *The Multinational Corporation in the 1980s* (pp. 38–56). Cambridge, MA: MIT Press.

Kogut, B. (1985). Designing global strategies: Profiting from operational flexibility. *Sloan Management Review* (Fall), 27–38.

Kogut, B. (1992). The evolutionary theory of the corporation: Within and across country options. Conference on Perspectives on International Business Theory, Research, and Institutional Arrangements, May 21st–23rd, University of South Carolina.

Kolk, A. (1999). Evaluating corporate environmental reporting. *Business Strategy and the Environment, 8*, 225–237.

Kolk, A. (2000). *Economics of environmental management*. Harlow, England: Pearson Education Ltd.

Kolk, A., & van Tulder, R. (2000). Internationalization and environmental reporting: A greener face for multinationals? Paper presented at the Annual Meeting of the Academy of International Business, 17th–20th November 2000, Phoenix, Arizona.

Korten, D. C. (1995). *When corporations rule the world*. San Francisco: Berrett-Koehler Publishers.

Korten, D. C. (1999). *The post-corporate world: Life after capitalism*. San Francisco: Berrett-Koehler Publishers.

Lundan, S. M. (2000). Environmental standards and multinational competitiveness: A public policy proposal. In: K. Fatemi (Ed.), *International Public Policy and Regionalism at the Turn of the Century*. Oxford: Pergamon.

Nehrt, C. (1996). Timing and intensity effects of environmental investment. *Strategic Management Journal, 17*, 535–547.

Porter, M. E. (1990). *The competitive advantage of nations*. New York: Free Press.

Porter, M. E., & van der Linde, C. (1995). Green and competitive: Ending the stalemate. *Harvard Business Review, 73*, 120–134.

Ramaswamy, K. (1992). Multinationality and performance: A synthesis and redirection. *Advances in International Comparative Management, 7*, 241–267.

Ramaswamy, K., Kroeck, K. G., & Renforth, W. (1996). Measuring the degree of internationalization of a firm: A comment. *Journal of International Business Studies, 27*(1), 167–177.

Ronen, S., & Shenkar, O. (1985). Clustering countries on attitudinal dimensions: A review and synthesis. *Academy of Management Review, 10*(3), 435–454.

Ruf, B., Muralidhar, K., & Paul, K. (1993). Eight dimensions of corporate social performance: Determination of relative importance using the analytic hierarchy process. *Academy of Management Best Paper Proceedings*, 326–330.

Rugman, A. M., & D'Cruz, J. (1997). The theory of the flagship firm. *European Management Journal, 15*(4), 403–411.

Rugman, A. M., & Verbeke, A. (1998). Corporate strategies and environmental regulations: An organizing framework. *Strategic Management Journal, 19*, 363–375.

Russo, M. V., & Fouts, P. A. (1997). A resource-based perspective on corporate environmental performance and profitability. *Academy of Management Journal, 40*(3), 534–559.

Sanders, W., & Carpenter, M. A. (1998). Internationalization and firm governance: The roles of CEO compensation, top team composition, and board structure. *Academy of Management Journal, 41*, 158–178.

Shrivastava, P. (1996). *Greening business: Profiting the corporation and the environment.* Cincinnati, OH: Thomson Executive Press.

Sullivan, D. (1994). Measuring the degree of internationalization of a firm. *Journal of International Business Studies* (2nd Quarter), 325–342.

Sullivan, D. (1996). Measuring the degree of internationalization of a firm: A reply. *Journal of International Business Studies, 27*(1), 179–192.

United Nations Conference on Trade and Development (UNCTAD) (2002). World Investment Report. Geneva: UNCTAD.

Vernon, R. (1971). *Sovereignty at bay: The multinational spread of U.S. enterprises.* New York: Basic Books.

Vernon, R. (1977). *Storm over the multinationals: The real issues.* Cambridge, MA: Harvard University Press.

Vernon, R. (1992). Transnational corporations: Where are they coming from, where are they headed? *Transnational Corporations, 1*(2), 7–35.

Vernon, R. (1998). *In the hurricane's eye: The troubled prospects of multinational enterprises.* Cambridge, MA: Harvard University Press.

Viederman, S. (1997). Remarks at United Nations Correspondents Association Press Briefing (June 23rd).

ENVIRONMENTAL STRATEGY CHOICE AND FINANCIAL PROFITABILITY: DIFFERENCES BETWEEN MULTINATIONALS AND DOMESTIC FIRMS IN BELGIUM

Kristel Buysse and Alain Verbeke

ABSTRACT

This chapter aims to determine the financial performance impacts of environmental strategies. The chapter builds upon a sample of firms operating in Belgium and includes both domestic firms and affiliates of foreign multinational enterprises. It appears that an environmental leadership approach is associated with an increase in financial performance, much in line with the mainstream literature on this subject. The surprising result is that a clear linkage can be established between environmental strategy and financial performance for Belgium-based companies, but not for affiliates of foreign multinational enterprises. In contrast, the industry growth rate does not appear to affect the linkages between environmental leadership and financial performance.

Multinationals, Environment and Global Competition
Research in Global Strategic Management, Volume 9, 43–63
© 2004 Published by Elsevier Ltd.
ISSN: 1064-4857/doi:10.1016/S1064-4857(03)09003-X

INTRODUCTION

Industrial corporations increasingly need to respond to rapidly changing, complex and stringent environmental regulations. A growing number of firms is attempting to integrate environmental management into corporate strategy; such firms have identified the adoption of advanced environmental practices as critical to strategy formation. The broad variety of corporate responses to environmental regulation has been described extensively in the environmental management literature (Rugman & Verbeke, 2001; Schmidehiny, 1992; Schot & Fischer, 1993).

The financial impacts associated with different managerial approaches to environmental issues have been the subject of some debate, see Dowell et al. (2000) for a recent, albeit selective overview of the literature. Recent empirical work analyzing the relationship between environmental and financial performance has produced mixed results. The majority of econometric studies have found a positive relationship between environmental performance and profitability. Here, environmental performance can be measured by a variety of parameters. These include the development of unique organizational capabilities (Sharma & Vredenburg, 1998), environmental ratings (Russo & Fouts, 1997), the reduction in toxic releases (Hart & Ahuja, 1996), the integration of the natural environment into strategic planning (Judge & Douglas, 1998), and finally the timing and intensity of investments in environmental technologies (Nehrt, 1996). Similarly, research based on event study methodology has concluded that proactive environmental management leads to superior stock market performance, whereas news of high levels of toxic emissions results in significant negative abnormal returns (Hamilton, 1995; Klassen & McLaughlin, 1996). In addition, Khanna and Damon (1999) have shown that voluntary participation in the United States Environmental Protection Agency's 33/50 program has had a significant impact on profitability in the short run. In contrast, Levy (1995) did not find any significant link between measures of environmental performance and profitability.

This chapter revisits the linkages between more proactive environmental management and higher profitability. In addition, it attempts to establish whether such a linkage is strengthened by industry growth (Russo & Fouts, 1997). Unlike most empirical studies that have surveyed firms operating in large countries (especially the United States), this chapter will analyze the linkage between environmental performance and profitability in the context of firms competing in a small open economy, namely Belgium. The chapter should be viewed as a complement and an extension of the recent empirical work reported in Buysse and Verbeke (2003).

The chapter is organized as follows. In the next section, the possible strategic choices regarding environmental management practices are identified. These should allow the classification of firms according to their level of environmental proactiveness. The third section suggests a specific relationship between environmental strategy proactiveness and financial performance, drawing on the insights offered by the resource-based view of the firm. The fourth section discusses the data and the research methodology. The fifth section presents our main empirical findings. The last section concludes.

ENVIRONMENTAL MANAGEMENT: A CONCEPTUAL FRAMEWORK

As already explained by Buysse and Verbeke (2003), and repeated here, various typologies of firms have been proposed, based on their environmental management practices, see Hunt and Auster (1990), Roome (1992) and Azzone and Bertelé (1994). These classifications build upon the models developed by Carroll (1979) and Wartick and Cochrane (1985) on corporate social responsibility. Both models identified four "generic," firm level approaches to corporate social responsibility: reactive, defensive, accommodative and proactive. These strategies reflect an increasingly important focus on societal issues, both in terms of strategy formulation and implementation (Clarkson, 1995).

Firms with a reactive or defensive approach to environmental management mainly respond to legislation (Roome, 1992), but environmental issues have no strategic importance (Azzone & Bertelé, 1994). Such firms do not engage in efforts to establish formal environmental action plans, and due to this lack of internal communication, both managers and employees are left uninformed and uninvolved (Hunt & Auster, 1990). In contrast, firms with an accommodative approach to environmental management focus more on anticipating regulatory changes rather than restricting themselves to compliance, and attach some strategic importance to environmental issues. They tend to hire environmental management professionals, who may participate in strategic planning, but have little involvement with other functional activities inside the firm. In addition, these firms typically develop a formal environmental plan, specifying the environmental management responsibilities and the actions needed to improve environmental performance. Such a plan can be viewed as the outcome of several rounds of communication with various groups within and outside the firm (Henriques & Sadorsky, 1999). Finally, firms with a proactive approach view environmental management as a key component of their corporate strategy. Managers and employees within various functional areas are all heavily involved in reducing the firm's environmental impact. These efforts are communicated through internal and external environmental reports.

Building on the resource-based theory of the firm, Hart (1995) also developed a typology, based on the firm's linkages with the natural environment. The resource-based view of the firm suggests that corporate strategy will only lead to a sustainable competitive advantage if it is supported by competencies that cannot easily be duplicated by competitors (Barney, 1991). Such competencies reflect a unique combination of resources. Thus, resources are the basic unit of analysis and include physical and financial assets as well as e.g. employees' skills and organizational processes. Hart distinguished among four types of behavior:

(1) the *end-of-pipe* approach.
(2) *pollution prevention or total quality management* (TQM).
(3) *product stewardship*.
(4) *sustainable development*.

Investments in *end-of-pipe* technologies reflect a reactive posture to environmental issues in which limited physical and financial resources are committed to solving environmental problems. *Pollution prevention* implies that firms continually adjust their production process in order to reduce pollution levels below legal requirements. To the extent that prevention at the source allows firms to achieve regulatory compliance at a lower cost and to reduce liabilities, this environmental management strategy may be viewed as a cost leadership approach. This strategy requires employee involvement and continuous efforts to reduce emissions, rather than reliance on expensive pollution abatement (Roome, 1992). In addition, a pollution prevention strategy may become more transparent over time to outsiders, through the voluntary publication of annual environmental reports, detailing emissions, spills, accidents, fines as well as accomplishments in pollution prevention. *Product stewardship* can be viewed as a form of product differentiation, whereby products are designed so as to minimize the negative environmental burden during their entire life cycle. A minimal requirement for the successful implementation of this strategy is that some form of life cycle analysis (LCA) be implemented. LCA is used to assess the environmental burden created by a product from "cradle to grave," including material selection, production, distribution, packaging, consumption and disposal (Welford & Gouldson, 1993). This implies close working relationships among the various functional tasks such as product design, marketing, production, purchasing, storage and transportation, as well as extensive employee involvement. Finally, *sustainable development* aims to minimize the environmental burden of firm growth through the development of clean technologies. It requires a long-range vision shared among all relevant stakeholders and strong moral leadership, which according to Hart (1995) is a rare resource.

Table 1 summarizes the various typologies of environmental management approaches and describes the main characteristics of each approach. Building on these typologies, especially the one suggested by Hart (1995), and Buysse and

Table 1. Classification of Firms' Environmental Management Strategies.

Hunt and Auster (1990)	Roome (1992)	Azzone and Bertelé (1994)	Hart (1995)	Characteristics
Beginner	Non-compliance	Stable strategy		Environmental issues not addressed and no integration with strategic management No commitment of senior management No environmental reporting or other techniques No functional coverage No employee training or involvement
Fire fighter	Compliance	Reactive strategy	End-of-pipe approach	Environmental issues addressed when necessary, but little integration with strategic management Little commitment of senior management No environmental reporting, no LCA, limited planning Limited functional coverage Little employee training or involvement
Concerned citizen	Compliance plus	Anticipatory strategy	Total quality management	Minimization of emissions and waste and some integration with strategic management Some commitment of senior management Some internal but no external reporting, some planning but no LCA Moderate functional coverage Some employee training and involvement
Pragmatist	Commercial and environmental excellence	Proactive strategy	Product stewardship	Minimization of environmental burden of products and firm growth and deep integration with strategic management Strong commitment of senior management Internal and external reporting, planning and LCA Broad functional coverage Extensive employee training and involvement
Proactivist	Leading edge	Creative strategy	Sustainable development	Employee training and extensive involvement Moral leadership

Verbeke (2003) developed the first empirically grounded resource-based typology of micro-level environmental practices that permits to distinguish among three categories of environmental strategy, namely reactive, pollution prevention and environmental leadership strategies. Their analysis suggests that each strategy category is associated with a particular level of investments in five distinct resource domains, namely:

(1) investments in conventional green competencies related to green product technologies and manufacturing technologies.
(2) investments in employee skills, as measured by resource allocation to environmental training and employee participation.
(3) investments in organizational competencies, as measured by the involvement of functional areas such as R&D and product design, finance and accounting, purchasing, production, storage and transportation, sales and marketing, and human resources in environmental management.
(4) investments in formal (routine-based) management systems and procedures, at the input, process and output sides. At the input side, the development of a written environmental plan was used as a relevant parameter. More at the process side, the implementation of some form of LCA is important. At the output side, the publication of internal and external environmental reports and the importance attached to environmental performance as a parameter to evaluate top managers seem critical.
(5) efforts to reconfigure the strategic planning process, by explicitly considering environmental issues and allowing the individual(s) responsible for environmental management to participate in corporate strategic planning.

ENVIRONMENTAL MANAGEMENT AND PROFITABILITY

Firm-level expenditures for pollution abatement have risen rapidly over the past decades for firms in polluting industries, partly as a result of increasingly stringent environmental standards and the introduction of environmental taxes. However, the costs of satisfying environmental regulations also appear to be affected by the choice of corporate response to such regulations. Reactive firms, deploying "end-of-pipe" solutions to environmental problems have found this strategy to become an increasingly expensive and less effective response to ever-changing environmental regulation, since "end-of-pipe" equipment needs to be replaced, modified or supplemented with additional investments with each regulatory change (Barry & Rondinelli, 1998). In contrast, firms that focus on preventing pollution before it occurs, have found it easier to manage the costs of environmental regulation because pollution prevention offers the potential to reduce emissions well below the levels required by law. This makes firms less sensitive to regulatory changes (Hart & Ahuja, 1996). Firms with an environmental leadership strategy enjoy the same advantages, but in addition may be able to leverage their reputation for environmental proactiveness to influence public policies in ways that confer competitive advantage (Russo & Fouts, 1997). In fact, these firms are most likely to cooperate with regulators and international organizations in the context of developing international environmental standards and concluding voluntary agreements (Sharma & Vredenburg, 1998).

There are other reasons why corporations can expect their profitability to improve as their environmental management strategies become more proactive. First, pollution can be viewed as a sign of inefficiency within the manufacturing process, and waste is an unrecoverable cost (Shrivastava & Hart, 1992). By preventing pollution "at the source," a company can save on the costs of installing and operating end-of-pipe pollution control devices (Hart & Ahuja, 1996). In addition, less waste means better utilization of inputs, resulting in lower raw material costs and waste disposal costs (Schmidehiny, 1992).

Second, a more proactive environmental strategy may contribute to the creation of distinctive "eco-friendly" products, thereby creating a competitive advantage for firms (Shrivastava, 1995a, b). This assumes that at least some consumers will be prepared to pay a premium for products with lower environmental costs over their life cycle.

Third, by being more proactive, the risk of serious environmental accidents is reduced (Shrivastava, 1995a). Consequently, firms can avoid the costs of negative reactions to such incidents by key stakeholders, including customers, employees, shareholders and government agencies.

Fourth, a proactive environmental strategy may also improve the firm's image and enhance these key stakeholders' commitment to the firm and its products (Dechant & Altman, 1994; Hart, 1995).

Finally, an advanced environmental strategy offers the potential of reducing long-term risks in terms of micro-level impacts of resource depletion, fluctuations in energy costs, product liability, and waste management (Shrivastava, 1995a).

The above elements suggest a positive relationship between the extent to which an environmental strategy can be considered proactive, and the firm's economic performance. However, they do not provide a conceptual framework to explain how exactly environmental strategies affect the bottom line at the micro-level. To overcome this problem, environmental management researchers have recently turned to the resource-based view of the firm to refine their analyses of how environmental strategies influence the firm's financial performance

(Hart, 1995; Judge & Douglas, 1998; Russo & Fouts, 1997; Sharma & Vredenburg, 1998).

The resource-based view of the firm argues that the firm-specific combination of resources into organizational capabilities determines the firm's economic performance (Barney, 1991). Organizational capabilities include the coordinating mechanisms that enable the efficient use of the firm's resources (physical assets, human capital, technical know-how, etc...). Such capabilities are grounded in social complexity, deeply embedded in the organization (Hart, 1995; Teece, 1987), and rely on tacit learning occurring over a period of time (Dierickx & Cool, 1989). Such capabilities often result from the integration of various functional capabilities (Grant, 1995). They lack an identifiable "owner" in the organization and are not traded in factor markets (Barney, 1991; Hart, 1995). Thus, organizational capabilities are difficult to identify, thereby raising barriers to imitation.

A reactive environmental strategy, based on the introduction of "end-of-pipe" equipment leaves the production process virtually unchanged. In addition, such investments do not require the firm to develop proprietary expertise or skills in managing new environmental technologies. Thus, the implementation of this strategy is straightforward, and leaves the firm in essentially the same resource and capability situation as before any environmental action was undertaken.

A pollution prevention strategy builds upon the "quality principle." This principle implies that preventing pollution is better than correcting it after the fact. By integrating pollution prevention into total quality management and continuous improvement programs through the use of employee involvement and "green" teams, significant reductions in emissions become possible. Thus, prevention is a more comprehensive and more socially complex strategy, as it necessitates significant employee involvement, cross-disciplinary coordination and integration, and a forward thinking managerial style (Shrivastava, 1995b). Indeed, general management, R&D, purchasing, production, and marketing all must be involved and committed for an environmental action plan to be implemented successfully (Ashford, 1993). In addition, the continuous improvements approach is based on internal routines that enable the firm to deploy even the environmental technologies purchased from third parties in ways that are less transparent to competitors. To conclude, a pollution prevention strategy affects the resources and organizational capabilities of a firm in ways that are not easily identifiable, thereby creating barriers to imitation and thus potentially contributes positively towards the firm's economic performance.

An environmental leadership strategy can be expected to affect a firm's image and corporate culture. This corporate culture, in turn, influences human resources management approaches and shapes job design, recruitment, selection and training (Starik & Rands, 1995). Firms adopting sophisticated human resources management strategies linked to a proactive environmental management agenda are likely to capture productivity improvements (Koch & McGrath, 1995). A firm's image or reputation for environmental leadership will increase sales among the customers that are sensitive to such issues. Both the corporate culture and the firm's reputation are intangible, valuable and inimitable resources that may contribute significantly towards profitability.

Thus, the resource-based analysis of the relationship between environmental strategy choice and economic performance leads to our first hypothesis:

Hypothesis 1. A more proactive environmental management strategy will be associated with enhanced profitability.

In addition, it can be argued that firms are more likely to reap benefits from a proactive environmental strategy when they operate in high-growth industries rather than low-growth industries. There are three reasons for this. First, a more proactive environmental strategy requires a firm to redesign or replace its existing processes, and to adopt new, clean technologies that are relatively untested. This entails significant financial investments and substantial risks. From a financial perspective, the expected payoff of any investment risk is higher in high-growth industries.

Second, a more proactive environmental strategy is characterized by the development of organizational capabilities such as the extensive involvement of employees and managers on all levels, and close cooperation among functional divisions. Such capabilities are more easily developed in firms that use an organic management style than in firms with a hierarchical, relatively inflexible and bureaucratic structure. The latter structure is more common in low-growth industries populated by mature firms selling standardized industrial products, whereas the former is more likely to be found in younger firms concentrated in high-growth industries.

Third, older firms in mature (low-growth) industries are often stuck with a reputation of high pollution intensity. Once such a reputation is established, it is difficult to change. Moreover, it has been suggested that a firm with a poor reputation, active in an older, basic manufacturing industry, may affect consumer perceptions of the entire industry (Jennings & Zandbergen, 1995). Such negative spillovers are likely to reduce the expected returns to proactive environmental management in low-growth industries (older manufacturing industries, often characterized with severe pollution problems).

The above elements suggest that the industry growth rate amplifies the linkage between environmental performance and profitability, as expressed in the following hypothesis:

Hypothesis 2. A higher industry growth rate will lead to a stronger positive impact of a proactive environmental strategy on firm profitability.

SAMPLE, MEASURES AND METHODS

Sample: The sample of firms included in this study is identical to the sample reported in Buysse and Verbeke (2003). The data was gathered through a survey conducted in Belgium and completed in 1999. A firm was selected to participate in the survey when it contributed significantly to either water pollution or solid and hazardous waste production or both, as measured by the environmental taxes paid.[1] This approach resulted in a sample of 450 companies, which accounted for 80% of water pollution and 80% of solid waste production in 1998. The sample included mainly manufacturing firms, with companies from the chemical, food, and textile sectors particularly well represented (see Table 2 for a sector breakdown). This sample composition reflects the pattern of industrial specialization in Belgium, but is somewhat different from what would be expected in studies conducted in the United States, Canada or the Scandinavian countries, where natural resource-based industries would likely be more important. Other characteristics of the sample are

Table 2.   Industry and Sector Breakdown.

Industry	Number of Respondents
Food and beverages	45
Textiles	16
Wood and wooden products	3
Paper and pulp	6
Publishing	2
Chemicals, pharmaceuticals, cosmetics	19
Rubber and synthetics	7
Non-ferrous industry	7
Metals	10
Steel products	3
Industrial tools	4
Electrical-technical equipment, computers	6
Automobiles and car parts	3
Furniture	7
Recuperation of waste	2
Construction	2
Wholesale services and retailing	8
Transportation	2
Other services (cleaning, utilities, etc.)	5

its bias towards the largest manufacturing firms in Belgium and the substantial presence of subsidiaries of multinational enterprises (MNEs) (about half of the sample), which is a common feature of many small, open economies.

The relevant public agencies in Belgium provided the coordinates of companies contributing significantly to water pollution or solid waste production. These companies were then contacted in order to identify which manager[2] was responsible for environmental issues and to solicit their cooperation in the survey, which was subsequently sent to them. For firms with multiple production facilities, firm-level data rather than facility-level data were used for various reasons. First, for most of these firms, only consolidated annual statements are publicly available. Second, the environmental manager is hired at the level of the firm, implying that a single person is responsible for all facilities. The research team provided the opportunity to all participating managers to obtain extensive guidance when completing the questionnaire. A total of 197 usable responses was received by the authors. The first part of the study, reported in Buysse and Verbeke (2003), used all 197 responses in the quantitative analyses performed.

For the second part of the study, reported in this chapter, financial statistics were obtained from the balance sheets collected by the National Bank of Belgium for the years 1998, 1999 and 2000. A total of 40 firms had to be eliminated from the initial sample because they lacked an adequate set of financial data for the 3-year period, and this for a variety of reasons. First, a number of smaller firms (19 in total) were dropped from the sample, because they publish their annual statements following an abridged scheme, which includes no information on sales. Second, a few utilities whose activities were still subject to extensive government regulations, and therefore have little real autonomy at the strategic level (an electricity utility and the national railway company) were also excluded. Third, a small number of firms had grown or shrunk by more than 50% in the years considered due to major downsizing, restructuring, mergers or acquisitions. These observations were omitted because they would have substantially reduced the predictive power of the models. Fourth, firms with irregularities in the publication date of their annual statements were also removed. Fifth, some firms realized an extremely high or low return on assets; such outliers were also omitted from the sample. Sixth, each firm was matched with an industrial sector using the classification developed by the leading Belgian financial magazine, *Trends*, which also publishes some industry-level data. However, two firms had missing data on industry concentration, and had to be removed as well. The final sample consisted of 157 firms or 471 observations.

Measurement of environmental management profiles: as explained in Buysse and Verbeke (2003), investments in five distinct resource domains were used to classify respondents according to their posture towards environmental issues.

A methodological approach identical to the one suggested in Buysse and Verbeke (2003) was adopted, but now for only 157 firms. Here, cluster analysis again led to the identification of three fundamentally different types of resource-based company strategies: reactive, pollution prevention and environmental leadership. The present chapter tests whether the choice of one of these environmental strategies is associated with a better financial performance.

Dependent variable and control variables: the dependent variable chosen is the firm's return on assets (ROA) before taxes and financial costs in the years 1998, 1999 and 2000, a commonly accepted measure of firm performance. The choice of control variables is based on a meta-analysis of performance studies (Capon, Farley & Hoenig, 1990), which resulted in a list of eight control variables most prevalent in such studies. These were industry concentration, firm growth rate, firm size, capital intensity, research and development intensity, advertising intensity, market share, and risk tolerance. Research and development intensity and market share were dropped due to a lack of data. Belgian financial statements do not report separate data on advertising costs; these are included in the category "costs of purchasing services and goods other than raw and auxiliary materials." Using this as a proxy for advertising costs reduced the predictive power of the models, raising some doubts about the validity of the construct as a proxy for advertising costs. Industry growth was added in order to test the second hypothesis.

The remaining control variables, adopted in this study, were defined as follows: industry concentration was defined as the four-firm concentration ratio for each industry, using the industrial classification of the Belgian business magazine *Trends*. Industry level data was taken from the annual Trends Top 10,000 publications for 1998, 1999 and 2000. Industry growth was defined as the average annual increase in industry sales in the last four years (1995–1998, 1996–1999 and 1997–2000 respectively). The firm's growth rate was measured by the firm's annual percentage change in sales during the years considered (i.e. respectively 1998, 1999, 2000). The natural logarithm of the sales volume was used as a proxy for firm size in each year. Capital intensity was defined as the ratio of total assets to sales. Finally, risk tolerance was defined as the ratio of equity to assets. All variables except the environmental profile exhibited fluctuations between 1998 and 2000.

Two dummy variables were added to indicate whether an observation was taken from 1998 (year 1999 = 0 and year 2000 = 0), from 1999 (year 1999 = 1) or from 2000 (year 2000 = 1). This is a common approach in regressions that use pooled data.

Method: Ordinary least squares regression techniques were used to assess the impact of environmental leadership versus reactive environmental management styles on firm performance, after accounting for the influence of the other control variables. In order to test Hypothesis 2, two interaction terms were formed by multiplying industry growth rates with each of the two dummy variables, which reflected the different environmental management strategies.

RESULTS

A number of descriptive statistics are shown in Table 3. Correlations between the independent variables are generally low, except for the correlation between industry concentration and firm size. Furthermore, the correlations between ROA on the one hand, and risk tolerance, firm size, firm growth, and the proactive environmental strategy dummy variables are significant, thus providing initial support for the first hypothesis. Here, the trend should be noted that larger firms tend to be more environmentally proactive and smaller firms more reactive.

A further investigation of the descriptive statistics for the different types of firms (Belgian firms, Belgian and foreign MNEs and foreign MNEs only) demonstrates that MNEs, and in particular foreign MNEs enjoy a higher average return on assets and stronger growth at the firm level than Belgian companies. In addition, it appears that MNEs are more capital-intensive and more inclined towards the implementation of an environmental leadership strategy, see Table 4.

Table 5 shows the regression results. Model 1 included the control variables only. The coefficients associated with risk tolerance, firm size and firm growth are positive and significant. However, the coefficients associated with industry concentration, industry growth rate and capital intensity appeared not to be significant.

Model 2 allowed us to test Hypothesis 1 by including two dummy variables that reflect the different corporate approaches to environmental management. The resulting increase in R^2, the total explained variance, is important. Moreover, implementing an environmental leadership strategy contributes positively and significantly to corporate performance: it increases the ROA by 2.25% on average. Contrary to expectations, implementing a reactive environmental strategy at first sight also improves corporate performance, albeit only slightly: the ROA rises by 0.45% on average. However, the performance difference with firms that implement pollution prevention strategies is not statistically significant.

Past research has shown that firms manufacturing differentiated consumer products, typically associated with high advertising intensity, or firms with a strong capability to innovate, as measured by R&D intensity, are more likely to implement environmental leadership strategies. In addition, past studies have shown that both R&D intensity and advertising intensity contribute positively to firm performance. However, these control variables could not be included in the analysis due to a lack of data. As a result, it is possible that these effects are partially expressed through the dummy variables for environmental strategy. This

Table 3. Descriptive Statistics ($n = 471$).

	Mean	Std. Dev.	1	2	3	4	5	6	7	8	9
1. Return on assets	7.47	8.04	1.00								
2. Industry concentration	0.38	0.19	0.05	1.00							
3. Industry growth rate	3.35	4.99	0.02	0.00	1.00						
4. Firm size	11.15	1.51	0.16	0.38	0.02	1.00					
5. Risk tolerance	35.47	19.4	0.15	0.10	0.02	-0.11	1.00				
6. Capital intensity	0.89	0.62	0.01	0.08	-0.02	0.13	0.10	1.00			
7. Firm growth rate	4.42	15.87	0.12	0.00	0.13	0.14	-0.10	0.01	1.00		
8. Reactive environmental strategy	0.37	0.48	-0.06	-0.13	0.05	-0.23	-0.15	-0.04	0.04	1.00	
9. Environmental leadership strategy	0.20	0.40	0.17	0.07	0.06	0.27	0.06	0.03	0.04	-0.38	1.00

Table 4. Descriptive Statistics for Belgian Firms and MNEs (Standard Deviations Between Brackets).

	Belgian Firms ($n = 255$)	All MNEs ($n = 258$)	Foreign MNEs ($n = 216$)
1. Return on assets	6.06 (6.685)	8.705 (8.804)	9.14 (8.972)
2. Industry concentration	0.35 (0.187)	0.41 (0.199)	0.41 (0.196)
3. Industry growth rate	3.06 (5.46)	3.37 (4.53)	3.47 (4.528)
4. Firm size	10.8 (1.344)	11.6 (1.567)	11.56 (1.578)
5. Risk tolerance	0.35 (0.183)	0.376 (0.201)	0.376 (0.196)
6. Capital intensity	0.72 (0.389)	1.018 (0.745)	0.973 (0.725)
7. Firm growth rate	3.14 (14.88)	5.8 (16.84)	6.52 (17.12)
8. Reactive environmental strategy	0.418 (0.494)	0.331 (0.471)	0.331 (0.471)
9. Environmental leadership strategy	0.129 (0.336)	0.25 (0.434)	0.27 (0.447)

Table 5. Regression Results (t-Statistics in Parentheses, $n = 471$).

	Model 1	Model 2	Model 3
Industry concentration	−0.011 (0.551)	−0.010 (0.63)	−0.009 (0.449)
Industry growth rate	−0.082 (1.098)	−0.089 (1.168)	−0.044 (0.422)
Firm size	0.667*** (5.995)	0.599*** (5.208)	0.585*** (5.010)
Risk tolerance	0.071*** (4.003)	0.071*** (4.019)	0.071*** (4.033)
Capital intensity	−0.005 (0.885)	−0.005 (0.857)	−0.005 (0.932)
Firm growth rate	0.062 (2.749)	0.060*** (2.673)	0.060*** (2.671)
Reactive environmental strategy		0.448 (0.571)	0.907 (0.965)
Environmental leadership strategy		2.247** (2.267)	2.001 (1.552)
Industry growth rate × Reactive environmental strategy			−0.135 (0.865)
Industry growth rate × Environmental leadership strategy			0.055 (0.246)
Year 1999	−2.428*** (2.757)	−2.391*** (2.714)	−2.381*** (2.696)
Year 2000	−2.361*** (2.600)	−2.313** (2.552)	−2.306** (2.520)
R^2	0.086	0.096	0.098

**Significant at 5%.
***Significant at 1%.

possible linkage, if it were present, would imply that environmental leadership could be viewed as one expression of a broader, firm-level focus on quality (or the establishment of sustainable isolating mechanisms), encompassing a variety of upstream (R&D) and downstream (advertising) activities simultaneously.

Finally, Model 3 tested Hypothesis 2 by adding two interaction terms between each of the dummies and the industry growth rate. The explanatory power of the model improved only marginally. Contrary to predictions, the coefficient associated with the interaction term between industry growth and an environmental leadership strategy is negative and insignificant, as is the coefficient associated with the interaction term between industry growth and reactive environmental strategy. When evaluated at the average industry growth rate of 3.35%, the incremental impact on the ROA of implementing an environmental leadership strategy (instead of a pollution prevention strategy) is given by $2 - (0.055 \times 3.35) = 1.82\%$. This result suggests that although environmental leadership strategies are associated with better financial performance in general, firms in stagnating or slowly growing industries benefit more from an environmental leadership position than firms in rapidly growing industries. One explanation could be that consumers of products of mature, low-growth industries attach a higher value to the environmental characteristics of the products purchased than is the case in younger, high-growth industries. Another explanation could be that firms in low-growth industries are, by necessity, focused more on the financial performance implications of an environmental leadership program (in terms of internal cost efficiencies and gaining maximum industrial leverage) as compared to firms in high-growth industries. Similarly, again evaluated at the average industry growth rate of 3.35%, the incremental impact of implementing a reactive environmental strategy (rather than a pollution prevention one) is given by $0.907 - (0.135 \times 3.35) = 0.45\%$. Such a result could suggest that firms in faster growing industries may be slightly punished for pursuing a reactive environmental strategy, but it is not statistically significant.

As pointed out earlier, environmental leadership is more likely to be the strategy of choice for MNEs, whereby MNEs also experience stronger financial performance as measured by their return on assets. This could create the false impression of a positive linkage between environmental leadership and profitability, in cases whereby it is in fact the multinational character of the firm that explains superior profitability. It is therefore appropriate to assess whether an environmental leadership strategy has different financial performance implications for a purely domestic firm vis-à-vis an MNE (whether Belgian or foreign).

The environmental strategy choice appears to have a substantial impact on the financial performance of domestic firms: the implementation of an environmental leadership strategy rather than a pollution prevention strategy significantly

Table 6. Regression Results for MNEs and Belgian Firms (Model 2).

	Belgian Firms ($n = 255$)	All MNEs ($n = 258$)	Foreign MNEs ($n = 216$)
Industry concentration	−0.035 (1.536)	−0.011 (0.381)	0.018 (0.558)
Industry growth rate	0.042 (0.53)	−0.278** (2.183)	−0.357** (2.444)
Firm size	1.182*** (63.614)	0.325 (0.413)	0.147 (0.319)
Risk tolerance	0.056** (2.487)	0.096*** (3.608)	0.089*** (2.874)
Capital intensity	−0.010 (1.223)	−0.566 (0.790)	−0.006 (0.762)
Firm growth rate	0.090*** (2.994)	0.044 (1.411)	0.036 (0.997)
Reactive environmental strategy	0.264 (0.291)	−0.188 (0.143)	0.469 (0.320)
Environmental leadership strategy	3.263** (2.534)	2.351* (1.751)	2.008 (1.338)
Year 1999	0.287 (0.278)	−4.694*** (3.571)	−5.471*** (3.701)
Year 2000	−0.362 (0.351)	−4.211*** (3.083)	−5.363*** (3.416)
R^2	0.136	0.128	0.131

*Significant at 10%.
**Significant at 5%.
***Significant at 1%.

increases the ROA, namely by 3.26% on average, whereas the implementation of a reactive strategy reduces the ROA only marginally by 0.26% on average (see Table 6). For the MNEs, the implementation of an environmental leadership strategy rather than a pollution prevention strategy also increases domestic financial performance by 2.26% on average. However, when excluding Belgian MNEs from the sub-sample of MNEs, the incremental impact of implementing an environmental leadership strategy on financial performance becomes statistically insignificant. This finding suggests that it is mainly the Belgian MNEs that benefit from an environmental leadership strategy in the domestic market.

This result may be explained in two ways. First, it may indicate that even MNEs with superior environmental practices, shared among subsidiaries, face a substantial liability of environmental foreignness, when operating in host countries. In other words, the assumed non-location bound firm-specific advantages in the environmental sphere, derived from the MNE-network, may in reality not contribute to competitive advantage in all host countries. This occurs when host country characteristics make it difficult for the MNE to translate a corporate-level environmental leadership approach into subsidiary financial performance, for example because of idiosyncratic, host country environmental regulations, requiring high costs of national responsiveness and the fact that stakeholders assumed to "reward" a strong environmental performance do not "recognize" this performance, i.e. use a host country-specific set of criteria to judge this performance. Second, these results may indicate that subsidiary financial performance data may be affected by foreign MNE financial engineering practices, especially transfer pricing, adopted for funds positioning and tax reduction purposes. The results thus imply that any study whereby MNEs are included, should be very careful in drawing conclusions on the linkages between environmental and financial performance, as the broader MNE network "arbitration strategies" may completely eliminate any visible linkage between the two performance types at the level of individual subsidiaries.

CONCLUSIONS

This study has focused on the possible linkages between environmental management choices and financial performance, distinguishing between domestic firms and MNEs. It has provided some support for the suggestion that win-win situations do occur, whereby improvements in environmental practices and in financial performance can be achieved simultaneously. Firms with an environmental leadership strategy do tend to have a superior financial performance, as measured by their return on assets. However, firms with a reactive environmental strategy do not appear to be less profitable than firms with a pollution prevention strategy. This result suggests that environmental strategy choice only becomes a source of competitive advantage in cases of "deep involvement" in this area, and it also demonstrates the fallacy of the "one minute greening"-approaches often suggested in the popular management literature. These results are thus consistent with Rugman and Verbeke (1998) and Buysse and Verbeke (2003).

The study led to the important observation that only domestic firms (including Belgian MNEs) benefit visibly from shifting towards an environmentally more proactive strategy. The average financial performance improves as a Belgian firm moves from a reactive strategy towards a pollution prevention strategy, and from a pollution prevention strategy towards environmental leadership. In contrast, the choice of an environmental strategy has no visible financial implications for foreign MNE subsidiaries in Belgium. Two alternative explanations for this result were provided. First, the liability of environmental foreignness facing MNE subsidiaries. Second, the foreign MNEs' financial engineering practices, which may have eliminated any visible link between environmental strategy and financial performance.

In addition, this study found no evidence that industry growth amplifies the relationship between environmental strategy choices and profitability, as environmental leaders in fast growing industries exhibit a slightly weaker linkage between both parameters than similar firms in slow growing industries.

One limitation characterizing this type of research is the problem of reverse causality. This study has assumed that a more proactive environmental strategy choice will enhance profitability, but it cannot demonstrate the causal linkage between both parameters. For example, it cannot be excluded that firms with a superior financial performance in the past have used the resulting internal slack resources to invest in advanced environmental management practices, without such resource allocations having a negative impact on present financial performance. It is also possible that "virtuous cycles" exist between financial performance and environmental resource allocation, which can only be verified by longitudinal studies. However, a study by Henriques and Sadorsky (1995) found that prior financial performance was not predictive of subsequent environmental planning, one aspect of environmental management that was also included in this study.

A final limitation of this study is the use of self-reported data. The most senior executive responsible for environmental issues was contacted in each firm, but it is difficult to establish whether this person's views are truly representative of the entire organization. In addition, there is always a tendency for the respondent to present the firm's environmental efforts in a more favorable light than they deserve. To the extent that all respondents exhibit a similar bias, this may not affect the relative classification of firms very much. However, there appears to be a need for the development of indicators on environmental performance that rely on more objective data. Unfortunately, no agency in Belgium presently collects the data required as inputs for such an indicator, nor is there a legal requirement to make pollution data publicly available. External environmental reports are still published on a voluntary basis and differ very strongly in content among firms.

NOTES

1. In Belgium, the regions are responsible for environmental regulation and taxation. Taxes are currently levied on solid waste and water pollution. The water pollution load is calculated using a complex formula, which takes into account the different forms of water pollution. All three regions (Flanders, Wallonia and Brussels) have been applying the same formula since 1994. For large industrial consumers of water, the calculation of the pollution load is based on actual measurements of wastewater quality, conducted by the relevant public agencies.

2. Large firms are required by law to create a position for an environmental manager, whose responsibility it is to ensure that a company complies with all environmental regulations (including reporting requirements).

REFERENCES

Ashford, N. A. (1993). Understanding technological responses of industrial firms to environmental problems: Implications for government policy. In: K. Fischer & J. Schot (Eds), *Environmental Strategies for Industry*. Washington, DC: Island Press.

Azzone, G., & Bertelé, U. (1994). Exploiting green strategies for competitive advantage. *Long Range Planning, 27*(6), 69–81.

Barney, J. B. (1991). Firm resources and sustained competitive advantage. *Journal of Management, 17*, 99–120.

Barry, M. A., & Rondinelli, D. A. (1998). Proactive corporate environmental management: A new industrial revolution. *Academy of Management Executive, 12*, 38–50.

Buysse, K., & Verbeke, A. (2003). Proactive environmental strategies: A stakeholder management perspective. *Strategic Management Journal, 24*(5), 453–470.

Capon, N., Farley, J. U., & Hoenig, S. (1990). Determinants of financial performance: A meta-analysis. *Management Science, 36*, 1143–1159.

Carroll, A. B. (1979). A three-dimensional conceptual model of corporate social performance. *Academy of Management Review, 4*, 497–505.

Clarkson, M. B. E. (1995). A stakeholder framework for analyzing and evaluating corporate social performance. *Academy of Management Review, 20*(1), 92–117.

Dechant, K., & Altman, B. (1994). Environmental leadership: From compliance to competitive advantage. *Academy of Management Executive, 8*, 7–20.

Dierickx, I., & Cool, K. (1989). Asset stock accumulation and sustainability of competitive advantage. *Management Science, 35*, 1504–1511.

Dowell, G., Hart, S., & Yeung, B. (2000). Do corporate global environmental standards create or destroy market value? *Management Science, 46*(8), 1059–1074.

Grant, R. M. (1995). *Contemporary strategic analysis.* Oxford: Blackwell.

Hamilton, J. (1995). Pollution as news: Media and stock market reaction to toxic release inventory data. *Journal of Environmental Economics and Management, 28*, 98–113.

Hart, S. L. (1995). Natural resource-based view of the firm. *Academy of Management Review, 20*, 986–1014.

Hart, S. L., & Ahuja, G. (1996). Does it pay to be green? An empirical examination of the relationship between pollution prevention and firm performance. *Business Strategy and the Environment, 5*, 30–37.

Henriques, I., & Sadorsky, P. (1995). The determinants of firms that formulate environmental plans. In: J. E. Post (Ed.) and D. Collins & M. Starik (Vol. Eds), *Research in corporate social performance and policy: Sustaining the natural environment – Empirical studies on the interface between nature and organizations, supplement 1* (pp. 67–97). Greenwich, CT: JAI Press.

Henriques, I., & Sadorsky, P. (1999). The relationship between environmental commitment and managerial perceptions of stakeholder importance. *Academy of Management Journal, 42*(1), 87–99.

Hunt, C. B., & Auster, E. R. (1990). Proactive environmental management: Avoiding the toxic trap. *Sloan Management Review* (Winter), 7–18.

Jennings, P. D., & Zandbergen, P. A. (1995). Ecologically sustainable organizations: An institutional approach. *Academy of Management Review, 20*, 1015–1052.

Judge, W. Q., & Douglas, T. J. (1998). Performance implications of incorporating environmental issues into the strategic planning process: An empirical assessment. *Journal of Management Studies, 35*, 241–262.

Khanna, M., & Damon, L. (1999). EPA's voluntary 33/50 program: Impact on toxic releases and economic performance of firms. *Journal of Environmental Economics and Management, 37*, 1–25.

Klassen, R., & McLaughlin, C. (1996). The impact of environmental management on firm performance. *Management Science, 42*, 1199–1214.

Koch, M. I., & McGrath, M. R. (1995). Improving labor productivity: Human resource management policies do matter. *Strategic Management Journal, 17*, 335–354.

Levy, D. L. (1995). The environmental practices and performance of transnational corporations. *Transnational Corporations, 4*(1), 44–67.

Nehrt, C. (1996). Timing and intensity effects of environmental investments. *Strategic Management Journal, 17,* 535–547.

Roome, N. (1992). Developing environmental management systems. *Business Strategy and the Environment, 1,* 11–24.

Rugman, A., & Verbeke, A. (1998). Corporate strategy and environmental regulation: An organizing framework. *Strategic Management Journal, 19*(4), 363–375.

Rugman, A., & Verbeke, A. (2001). Environmental policy and international business. In: A. Rugman & T. Brewer (Eds), *The Oxford Handbook of International Business* (pp. 537–557). Oxford: Oxford University Press.

Russo, M. V., & Fouts, P. A. (1997). A resource-based perspective on corporate environmental performance and profitability. *Academy of Management Journal, 40,* 534–559.

Schmidehiny, S. (1992). *Changing course.* Cambridge, MA: MIT Press.

Schot, J., & Fischer, K. (1993). Introduction: The greening of the industrial firm. In: K. Fischer & J. Schot (Eds), *Environmental Strategies for Industry* (pp. 3–33). Washington, DC: Island Press.

Sharma, S., & Vredenburg, H. (1998). Proactive corporate environmental strategy and the development of competitively valuable organizational capabilities. *Strategic Management Journal, 19,* 729–753.

Shrivastava, P. (1995a). Environmental technologies and competitive advantage. *Strategic Management Journal, 16,* 183–200.

Shrivastava, P. (1995b). Ecocentric management for a risk society. *Academy of Management Review, 20,* 118–137.

Shrivastava, P., & Hart, S. (1992). Greening organizations. *Academy of Management Best Paper Proceedings, 52,* 185–189.

Starik, M., & Rands, G. P. (1995). Weaving an integrated net with multilevel and multisystem perspectives of ecologically sustainable organizations. *Academy of Management Review, 20,* 908–935.

Teece, D. (Ed.) (1987). *The competitive challenge.* Cambridge, MA: Ballinger.

Wartick, S. L., & Cochrane, P. L. (1985). The evolution of the corporate social performance model. *Academy of Management Review, 4,* 758–1169.

Welford, R., & Gouldson, A. (1993). *Environmental management and business strategy.* Pitman: London.

ENVIRONMENTAL ASPECTS OF DANISH FOREIGN DIRECT INVESTMENT IN DEVELOPING COUNTRIES: THE ROLE OF HOME COUNTRY FACTORS IN SHAPING THE GLOBAL ENVIRONMENTAL PRACTICES OF DANISH MULTINATIONALS

Michael W. Hansen

ABSTRACT

The literature on foreign direct investment (FDI) and the environment has paid little attention to the role of home country factors in shaping the global practices of multinational enterprises (MNEs). By analyzing the interface between FDI and the environment from a Danish perspective, this chapter seeks to cast light on this issue. Denmark is a small, highly open economy dominated by small and medium-sized enterprises servicing specialized niche markets for consumer products or large industrial customers. What makes the case of Danish FDI in developing countries interesting from an environmental perspective is that environmental issues for the past three decades have

Multinationals, Environment and Global Competition
Research in Global Strategic Management, Volume 9, 65–94
© 2004 Published by Elsevier Ltd.
ISSN: 1064-4857/doi:10.1016/S1064-4857(03)09004-1

had an exceptionally strong position on the Danish political agenda and have earned Danish environmental regulation a reputation as among the toughest in the world. The question is whether and how this strong environmental home base has spilled over into the environmental practices of Danish MNEs in developing countries. The chapter describes how the issue of corporate environmental responsibility in developing countries reached the Danish agenda with great force in the late 1990s, embroiling a number of Danish MNEs in damaging public battles. The chapter then moves on to review the – embryonic – literature on environmental practices of Danish MNEs. The chapter concludes by discussing whether and how the environmental practices of Danish MNEs may be traced back to distinct aspects of the Danish home country context.

1. INTRODUCTION

The role of home country factors in shaping the foreign environmental practices of multinational enterprises (MNEs) is rarely analyzed in the growing literature on Foreign Direct Investment (FDI) and the environment. Typically, MNE environmental practices are seen as functions of multinationality as such (Royston, 1985), of industry and technology (Dasgupta et al., 1998; Jenkins, 1999), of market orientation (Jenkins, 1999; Santos et al., 1998), of ownership (Hansen, 2002), or of size (Jones, 1997). This apparent lacuna in the literature may be caused by several factors, including a propensity for viewing MNEs as more global than they actually are or a propensity to assume that all MNEs have home bases like the United States (U.S.). However several empirical studies have suggested that home country factors significantly impact the foreign environmental practices of MNEs (Hansen, 2002; Perry & Singh, 2001; UNCTAD, 1993), although none of these studies actually explain, what the nature of this influence may be. By taking up a small country case – Denmark – and analyzing the environmental practices of Danish MNEs in developing countries, this chapter provides a preliminary insight into the question of how home country factors may affect foreign environmental practices. The chapter starts out with a presentation of the particular Danish context in terms of FDI and environmental protection. It proceeds by presenting a number of cases illustrating how issues related to FDI and environment in developing countries won prominence on the Danish political as well as corporate agendas in the 1990s. The chapter then moves on to review the – highly embryonic – literature on environmental practices of Danish MNEs. The chapter concludes by discussing if and how home country factors have shaped the environmental practices of Danish MNEs.

2. THE INTERNATIONALIZATION OF DANISH INDUSTRY

Denmark is a small country of 5 million inhabitants and among the 10 richest countries in the world. Denmark has no particular natural endowments and its wealth is therefore largely built on strong positions in manufacturing and services. Essentially Danish industry consists of companies and organizations, which cross sectors to form five networks: foods, construction, maritime, healthcare, and the "welfare industrial" network. These networks are characterized by certain strengths and synergy effects, which give them a comparative advantage over inward foreign investors (Lindholm, 1994). Apart from shipbuilding, no large-scale industrial activity exists in Denmark, and most Danish companies can be classified as small or medium-sized; only nine companies make it to the Financial Times list of Europe's 500 largest companies – and even these appear comparatively small.[1]

The Danish economy is highly open: While foreign trade for most OECD countries accounts for less than 10% of GDP, Danish exports as percentage of total GDP were 21% in 1970, 29% in 1984, 34% in 1995 and 43% in 2000.[2] However, Danish firms are international traders rather than international producers: As proportion of GDP, outward FDI stocks are relatively modest compared to other small and middle-sized European countries (see Fig. 1), and there are no Danish firms among the world's 100 largest multinationals (UNCTAD, 2001). The low level of international production in the otherwise highly internationally oriented Danish industry can be explained by the relative absence of large companies with sufficient market power to organize international production. Another explanation is that internationally oriented sectors such as oil and electronics historically have been relatively absent in the Danish economy. Third, Danish firms are rarely involved in

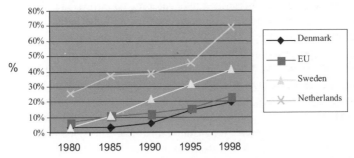

Fig. 1. Outward FDI Stock as Percentage of GDP. *Source:* The Danish National Bank.

the production of standardized goods which traditionally has driven much FDI, but are instead suppliers to large MNEs or producers for specialized niche markets.

Nevertheless, Danish direct investment has followed the international trend and Danish industry is increasingly engaging in international production; direct investment has increased from DKK 20 billion in the early and mid-1990s to more than 180 billion. And where there was approximately 1000 Danish MNEs in the mid-1990s (Hansen, 1996), there are now an estimated 2000.[3] The recent surge in FDI is to a large extent driven by small and medium sized enterprises (SMEs); two thirds of all foreign direct investment projects are made by SMEs, defined as firms with less than 250 employees (DI, 1998).

2.1. Investment in Developing Countries

Danish FDI patterns largely follow those of trade, with the European Union (EU) countries accounting for approximately 70% of outflows and 65% of stock. Danish FDI to developing countries and Eastern Europe as proportion of total outward Danish FDI has been between 5 and 10% throughout the early 1990s, a level that is modest compared to global patterns.[4] In the second half of the 1990s however, the share of developing countries and Eastern Europe increased to 15–20%, and especially in the year 2000 a notable increase in FDI in these countries took place in absolute terms. The firms investing in developing countries are relatively big; where 1 of 25 SME subsidiaries are located in developing countries, it is 1 of 10 subsidiaries of large companies (DI, 1998).

Danish investors with operations in developing countries are essentially driven by four motives: First, there are investments made to access natural resources. Traditionally, investment into developing countries was driven by a need to get access to natural resources, and already in the 19th century Danish MNEs, like the East Asian Company (trading and plantations) or Christian Hansen (inputs to dairy production), engaged in investment in developing countries. In a recent survey of 200 investments in developing countries conducted by the Industrialization Fund for Developing Countries (IFU, 2002), 23% of the respondents cited access to natural resources as an investment motive.

Second, there are investments made to obtain a low cost export platform. These are investments where high production costs in Denmark drive relocation of especially labor-intensive activities. This type of investment is dominant in the textile and furniture industries, but also the Danish software industry has undertaken labor cost saving investment, for instance in India. The same survey, involving 200 projects in developing countries found that only 19% were motivated by low labor costs in host countries (IFU, 2002). However, such investments have risen significantly in recent years due to more liberal trade regimes and improved production conditions in many developing countries (IFU, 2002).

Third, there are investments made to access local markets. This is undisputedly the dominating investment motive of Danish investors; in IFU's survey, 74% of the 200 projects cited this investment motive. However, the term "market access" covers several specific motives:

(a) In the 1970s and 1980s many Danish MNEs (e.g. producers of food-products and producers in the metals and machinery industry) invested in especially Latin American import substituting countries (such as Brazil and Mexico) to circumvent trade barriers;

(b) Some products need to be produced locally because they are too expensive to export (e.g. wind turbines or cement production) or because they cannot be exported at all (some food products and services in general);

(c) Servicing the local market sometimes demands the presence of a local (service) organization (wind turbines, for example);

(d) A large number of Danish firms have in recent years extended their supply relationships into developing country markets, establishing affiliates close to their major industrial customers. Examples of firms involved in such follow-my-leader strategies are producers of enzymes, producers of ingredients for food production, producers of auto parts, and producers of certain business services;

(e) A final important type of market seeking investment is investment made in order to organize transport and logistic services in host countries (e.g. investment by the large Danish shipping and transport service MNEs such as A. P. Møller or the Laurizen Group).

Fourth, some Danish investment in developing countries is motivated by the delivery of equipment for turnkey projects and/or BOOT (Build, Own, Operate, Transfer) arrangements, but where the sale of equipment requires equity involvement by the Danish supplier. A relatively large number of Danish firms are undertaking such investment.[5] IFU estimates that approximately 5% of Danish investment projects are of this type.

3. DANISH ENVIRONMENTAL REGULATION

Since the 1970s, environmental issues have had a very strong position on the Danish political agenda. This is partly explained by strong environmental sentiments in the population,[6] amplified by a peculiar parliamentary situation. During much of the 1980s, the conservative minority government was able to get support from liberal center parties for its policy of economic austerity, but failed to generate support from those parties on environmental and security issues. Environment (and security) therefore provided an opportunity for the left wing opposition to create a split in the government coalition (Skou-Andersen et al., 1998). When power in the 1990s shifted to a center-left minority government, its majority was dependent on a green leftwing party as well as a greenish center party, which gave environmental issues a privileged position on the political agenda. Furthermore, the maverick Minister for the Environment and Energy – Mr. Auken – was among the most popular and influential politicians in Denmark, and he transformed the Ministry for Energy and Environment into one of the most powerful ministries.

The main objective of the Environmental Protection Act of 1972 was to deal with problems related to industrial pollution, and it was designed as a legislative framework with broad competencies delegated to the environmental administration at the state, regional, and local level. Since its inception, the legislation has evolved in several ways. First, the focus has changed from concentrated and often highly dangerous pollution to diffuse and multi-source pollution, such as that generated by households and agricultural production. Second, the focus on production related emissions has been replaced by a focus on product related issues. Third, the instruments have undergone a transformation from command-and-control regulation, end-of-pipe solutions and large-scale infrastructure projects, to pollution prevention measures, life cycle approaches, mandatory environmental reporting, clean technology programs, voluntary agreements, and environmental taxes (Skou-Andersen et al., 1998). Green taxes and levies[7] have, next to income tax, become the main source of revenue for the state, accounting for DKK 63.5 billion of a state budget of DKK 400 billion in 2001, more than funding the public expenditures for the environment (DKK 25.2 billion) (Danish Economic Council, 2002). The state has promoted the development of alternative energy through generous subsidies and supportive regulation, e.g. investment support, production subsidies, tax exemptions, and preferential payment (Danish Economic Council, 2002, p. 192). The combination of huge investment in environmental protection, extensive green taxation, and regulatory activism, has earned Denmark a reputation as being among the environmental leaders in the EU (Holzinger, 1997; Sbragia, 1996) and as having an environmental standard significantly above the OECD average (OECD, 1999).

While Danish environmental regulation undoubtedly is characterized by state activism, it is also characterized by close co-operation and consultation between regulators and industry (Christensen, 1996). The 1972 Environmental Protection Act institutionalized the practice that the most important interest groups within trade and industry should be consulted in all matters regarding the law. Thus, the Government consults trade and industry associations before new legislation is adopted and these have endorsed most of the numerous amendments to the Environmental Protection Act. The legislation is implemented through extensive consultation with the firms concerned and industry is directly represented in the administrative courts deciding environmental disputes (Skou-Andersen et al., 1998). All in all, Danish environmental regulation is in many respects an illustration of the neo-corporatist model (Schmitter, 1974) that has often been employed to characterize Scandinavian politics.

The regulatory activism paired with the huge investments has lead to the development of a sizable Danish environment industry. The industry directly employs 30,000 people. This number does not include additional employment among suppliers; e.g. is it estimated that the wind turbine industry's 3,000 directly employed generate an additional 10–12,000 jobs (Danish Economic Council, 2002, p. 224). The environmental goods and services industry has grown significantly more than other industries; where this industry grew 5.4% per year between 1993 and 1999, industry in general grew 2.3% (Danish Economic Council, 2002, p. 228). Furthermore, the Danish environmental goods and services industry has an export performance above the OECD average, and significantly above that of other small OECD countries (Ministry for Trade and Industry, 2000). In fact, in terms of export growth vis-à-vis other OECD countries, this was the best performing Danish industry in the period 1988–1996 (Ministry for Trade and Industry, 2000, p. 29). The strongest performing sector within the environmental goods and services industry is the wind turbine industry; in 1999, this industry exported DKK 7 billion in goods and services and controlled 51.1% of the rapidly growing world market for wind turbines. Also the water treatment goods and services is a major export industry, exporting DKK 2 billion in 1999 (Danish Economic Council, 2002, p. 230). Other activities with a strong export performance are the production of filters for power plants and waste management services.

3.1. The Internationalization of Danish Environmental Regulation

Throughout the 1980s and 1990s, Danish environmental regulation has increasingly been driven by EU-directives and it is estimated that 50% of Danish environmental legislation now is initiated by the EU.[8] The growing importance of EU legislation has – as seen in connection with the 1986, 1992 and 1993 EU referendums – caused much concern and debate in Denmark. Environmentalists have feared that the perceived tough Danish standards would be undermined by EU driven harmonization of environmental and technical standards. Industry has feared that unilateral Danish regulation in an integrated European market would undermine the competitiveness of Danish industry. In particular, the unilateral Danish CO_2 tax stirred strong resentment in industry; as the chairman of the Danish Manufactures Association said to the Financial Times when the Danish CO_2 tax was launched in 1995:

> It will certainly save energy but only because . . . industries will move abroad.[9]

The Danish EU debate illustrates a dilemma endemic to Danish trade and environment policy. On the one hand, Denmark has, due to its huge trade dependence, been a staunch supporter of trade liberalization in the OECD, in the EU, and in the World Trade Organization (WTO). On the other hand, the growing environmental activism in Danish politics has lead to calls for Danish unilateralism in environmental affairs, even if this infringes free trade principles. Danish governments have sought to resolve this dilemma partly by promoting international harmonization of environmental standards towards high standards in the EU, the WTO and in Multilateral Environmental Agreements (MEAs), and partly by using subsidies drawn from the vast Danish development assistance program[10] to support efforts to resolve environmental conflicts in connection with trade and investment.

Concerning the first strategy, Danish governments have actively supported and promoted the establishment of international environmental agreements – including the Montreal Protocol, the Basel Convention, and the Climate Change Convention – and promoted the inclusion of trade measures in those agreements. Moreover, the state has called for the integration of environmental minimum standards in international trade and investment agreements, including the EU, the Energy Charter Treaty, the Multilateral Agreement on Investments (MAI) and the WTO (Eriksen & Hansen, 1999).

Concerning the second strategy, Danish governments have used the vast development assistance as a leverage to gain influence on the environmental conduct of Danish firms in developing countries. A significant proportion of Danish development assistance is channeled into private sector programs, typically programs where Danish firms, through linkages to local industry in developing countries, are mobilized for private sector development. These are programs like the Private Sector Program,[11] the Mixed Credit Scheme[12] and the Danish Investment Funds (see Box 1). Through these and other programs, the state has ample opportunity to impact the environmental performance of Danish industry abroad.[13] Other programs have directly supported the export of environmental goods and services[14] or direct investments in environmental improvements in developing countries and Eastern Europe.[15]

Box 1: The Industrialization Fund for Developing Countries

Like other OECD countries, Denmark has a state sponsored facility to support Danish direct investment in developing countries, the Industrialization Fund for Developing Countries (IFU). Having invested in 449 projects and dispersed DKK 4.8 billion for projects with a total project investment of DKK 50 billion, IFU participates in the majority of Danish investment projects in developing countries, and may therefore have an opportunity to significantly impact Danish investors' environmental performance. IFU's influence is exerted partly through its representation on the boards of projects, and partly through various guidelines and policies that partners must observe. For instance, IFU has an environmental policy, which requires Danish partners to implement environmental, health and safety standards in accordance with IFU guidelines, guidelines that encourage firms to work toward Danish standards in international operations. IFU further offers opportunities for financial support for environmental investment through its Environment and Training Fund.

---

4. THE ENVIRONMENTAL PRACTICES OF DANISH MNEs IN DEVELOPING COUNTRIES

With a time lag of 10–15 years compared to the U.S., the issue of environmental responsibilities of MNEs arrived at the Danish political as well as corporate agenda by the mid-1990s. As Danish firms increasingly became involved in developing countries, media stories on apparent misconduct of Danish MNEs started surfacing. These stories were fuelled – if not created – by Danish Non-Governmental Organizations (NGOs)[16] initiating campaigns on issues related to global business responsibilities. In the following, a number of case stories involving Danish MNEs will be presented. Further, the case stories will be placed in context through a review of the limited research on the global environmental practices of Danish MNEs.

4.1. Industrial Flight to Pollution Havens

The classical FDI and environment issue – and an issue that has dominated much of the economic literature since the 1970s – concerns the question of whether polluting industries are moving their production to developing countries to escape tough regulations in home countries. Leonard (1988) coined this phenomenon "Industrial flight" to "Pollution havens." This issue has played a prominent role in Danish political debates due to the perceived high Danish environmental standards.

4.1.1. Cases

The following quotation from the 1996 annual report of the Danish Steel Mill – one of the largest energy consumers in Danish industry and a company that has been forced to make very large environmental investments – serves as an illustration of how large parts of trade and industry perceive Danish environmental unilateralism:

> We do not understand why the Danish government, at the same time as it imposes a series of environmental standards on the company, does not as a natural thing ensure that the company's competitors should meet the same standards.

The company warns that it will

> actively explore the options for establishing production abroad in order to allow for the future expansion which is prevented in Denmark because of environmental restrictions and costs.

The Steel Mill never moved, however the fact that the production was closed down in 2002 due to inability to compete with cheap steel from Eastern Europe could indicate that the warnings were not unfounded.

A clear case of industrial flight from Denmark is the Proms case. Proms Chemical Factory was a company that was notorious for its repeated violations of Danish environmental regulation throughout the 1970s and 1980s. In 1986, the company moved part of its production to Teesside, England, citing Danish environmental regulation as the main reason for movement. The U.K. activity was located in an area where it could obtain EU-grants as well as regional development funding, something that further fuelled the public outrage in Denmark (Nielsen, 1996). In addition to this well documented case of flight, there are several examples where industry and trade unions have warned against flight, in particular in foot-loose industries. For instance, it has been alleged that the textile industry would move to Poland due to Danish health and safety rules;[17] that production of certain impregnated tree products would move to Eastern Europe due to Danish taxes on toxic waste;[18] that the Danish fruit industry would be wiped out due to a Danish pesticide tax;[19] or that electricity production would move to Eastern Europe due to CO_2 taxation.[20]

In an interesting twist of the industrial flight issue, it was recently revealed that the Danish refrigeration company Gram had been bought up by the Polish Amica. Up until the early 1990s, Gram was a leading and prosperous company within the large Danish refrigeration industry.[21] However, where other Danish producers of refrigerators responded to political pressures for phasing out of ozone depleting coolants by undertaking huge investments in alternatives to ozone depleting gases and by developing more energy efficient refrigerators, Gram embarked on a political strategy, lobbying for longer phasing out periods and less stringent requirements for energy efficiency. By the late 1990s, Gram had a technology that was outdated and its market share started collapsing. Eventually, it was acquired by Amica which – ironically – could provide the environmentally friendly technology now demanded by the market.[22]

4.1.2. Studies

While the industrial flight hypothesis has generated much research in other OECD countries,[23] very little examination of this issue has taken place in Denmark. There are exceptions though. Hoffman (1996) concludes that fear of relocation of Danish production due to environmental regulation is exaggerated. Examining the profile of Danish investment flows toward developing countries he detects no evidence that polluting industries are over-represented. And comparing the import and export flows between Denmark and developing countries he sees no signs of increasing imports of polluting products from developing countries over the past decade. Hansen (1996) finds – based on a survey of 153 Danish manufacturing companies with operations in Eastern Europe or developing countries – that Danish MNEs typically invest to access new markets and that only one fifth cite favorable cost conditions as the main motivating factor behind investment.[24] Even among these firms, it was lower labor costs that motivated investment, and only in one case did environmental factors appear to have impacted the investment. Consistent with this, a more recent study of 89 Danish investment projects in India and Poland found that 76% were motivated by "market access," and that only 20% were motivated with lower production costs. No examples of projects citing variations in environmental control costs as a decisive or even contributing investment motive were identified in this study (Danish Investment Funds, 2000).

Overall the existing evidence suggests that the widespread concerns for industrial flight to developing countries in the form of direct investment are largely unfounded in the case of Denmark. However, it is still possible that Danish industry will exploit variations in environmental regulation through sourcing strategies. Based on case studies of the Danish textile, leather and furniture industries, a report by the Danish Parliament's Technology Assessment Council from 1999 warned against such sourcing. The report found that certain environmentally sensitive or costly activities within the textile, leather and furniture industries had been out-sourced to producers in emerging economies (Technology Assessment Council, 1999). The evidence on environmentally motivated sourcing presented in this report rests on case studies in selected industries and more research on this issue is therefore called for.

4.2. Managing Foreign Subsidiaries

While there is little evidence that Danish MNEs invest in developing countries to escape environmental regulation in Denmark, they may exploit the opportunity to pollute once they get there for instance by applying inferior environmental management standards and by using technologies that are more polluting or more dangerous than what would be acceptable in Denmark. The issue of corporate "double standards" has been debated in the U.S. at least since the 1984 Bhopal catastrophe and numerous studies have examined the international practices of MNEs (Castleman, 1985; Clark, 1993; Dasgupta, 1998; Gladwin, 1987; Hadlock, 1994; Hansen, 2002; Jenkins, 1999; Perry & Singh, 2001; Rappaport, 1991; UNCTAD, 1993). However not before the second half of the 1990s did the issue reach the Danish political as well as research agenda.

4.2.1. Cases

In the mid-1990s several media stories surfaced about Danish subsidiaries in developing countries operating with inferior standards. In 1996, the Malaysian government exposed 50 foreign investors in the media, listing them as environmental "sinners" – among those the Danish brewery Carlsberg which allegedly was failing to meet Malaysian waste water standards. Due to the exposure, Carlsberg undertook measures to reduce wastewater emissions and the Malaysian government concluded that

> Carlsberg did not meet the requirements for waste water, but after their name was listed in public they have got a hold of things.[25]

In 1997, a documentary described the Danish MNE GN Batteries as a laggard in Poland, not observing basic safety rules and exposing workers to unacceptable risks. An undercover TV footage vividly demonstrated the lack of safety precautions of the plant in question. As a result of the public exposure, the state sponsored Investment Fund for Eastern Europe, which was a partner in the project, sold its shares. A number of other cases of alleged inappropriate practices of subsidiaries of Danish MNEs have surfaced in the public debate (see also report from Technology Assessment Council, 1999).

4.2.2. Studies

A number of studies provide insight into the state of environmental management at affiliates of Danish MNEs: Hansen (1998) argues that environmental management of foreign subsidiaries is an underdeveloped policy area within Danish MNEs. Among the 153 companies surveyed in 1995–1996, only 17% had formalized cross border reporting and control procedures and only 12% pledged to employ the same environmental standards regardless of location.[26] Among those Danish corporations having ighly integrated global management systems are most of the leaders of Danish industry, e.g. Grundfoss and Danfoss (producers of pumps); Rockwool (a producer of stone-wool); Hartman (a producer of packaging material);

Danisco (a producer of food stuff and ingredients); DLH (a wood trading company); and Novo Nordic (An insulin and enzyme producer) (see Box 2).

Box 2: Novo Nordic Global Environmental Strategy

Novo Nordic (NN) is a leading Danish MNE involved in pharmaceutical and enzyme production. The company has an annual turnover equaling more than 2% of Danish GDP. NN has 41 foreign affiliates including 10 in developing countries. Already in the late 1980s, NN formulated an environmental strategy in response to consumer boycott of its enzyme products. In the early 1990s NN developed elaborate environmental reporting systems and has recently expanded this reporting into social dimensions, so-called triple bottom line accounting/reporting.

In 1996 and 1997 external reviews by the British verification agency Sustainability against the 16 points in the ICC Business Charter for Sustainable Development pointed to the need for a greater focus on the international coordination of Novo Nordic's environmental activities. In response, NN expanded its environmental management system to include foreign activities. It formulated goals for the entire corporation, created comparable standards internationally, and sought to encourage the diffusion of NN standards to suppliers and subcontractors. Moreover, it established a network of environmental managers from its nine largest sites, which meets annually to discuss shared environmental challenges and to formulate targets and measures. In addition to the environment, NN has established a system for the collection and comparison of data from foreign subsidiaries on workers health and safety issues.

NN's plant in Tiajin, China illustrates NN's high environmental profile. At this plant, opened in 1997, operations are according to NN state-of-the-art with regard to technology, management and environmental performance. The Chinese Government has according to NN expressed satisfaction with Novo Nordisk investment because of its contribution in terms of improving local environmental conditions, providing infrastructures as well as educating local employees and communities. This may according to NN have provided NN with advantages vis-à-vis other investors. (Author's own interviews in Tienjin, 1999).

These companies are all comparatively large and are highly internationalized. The study by Hansen found that a pledge to operate with uniform standards clearly was a function of the size of the company; whereas 11% of multinationals with less than 50 employees pledged to operate with uniform standards, the number was 23% for MNEs with more than 1500 employees. However, an even better prediction of the scope and content of global environmental management

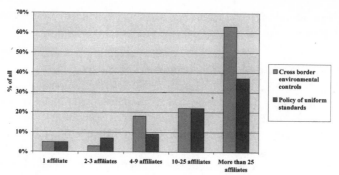

Fig. 2. Multinationality and Cross Border Environmental Management. *Source:* Hansen (1998).

practices is caused by "international orientation of the corporation": 36% of the MNEs with more than 25 foreign affiliates pursued policies of uniform standards but only 5% of the MNEs with one foreign affiliate, and the correlation was even stronger in the case of cross border environmental controls (see Fig. 2).

While environmental management in Danish MNEs may be relatively underdeveloped, it cannot necessarily be concluded that the performance of Danish MNEs in terms of impacts on the environment also is inferior. This is demonstrated by a unique study from 1999 of 89 Danish investment projects in India and Poland (Danish Investment Funds, 2000). Each of the 89 projects was visited by external environmental consultants who through their observations, interviews, and information collected from questionnaires, assessed the environmental status of projects. In line with Hansen (1998), the study found that relatively few projects (approximately one third) had formal management systems in place at affiliates, and only 9% had obtained certification according to international environmental management standards[27] (see Fig. 3). However, in spite of the lack of formalization of environmental management, almost all projects were, according to the environmental consultant's best judgement, operating fully in accordance with local laws and regulations. In fact, consultants assessed that 55% of the projects could obtain environmental approvals in Denmark; 60% of the projects in Poland and 44% of the projects in India.

The study of the 89 projects also provided insights into the driving and inhibiting forces of environmental management at Danish affiliates. The project managers were asked to assess a list of factors potentially motivating improved environmental performance and to report whether they considered these factors to be "very influential." With 50%, "regulatory pressures of the host country" was the most frequently cited "very influential" factor behind environmental improvements

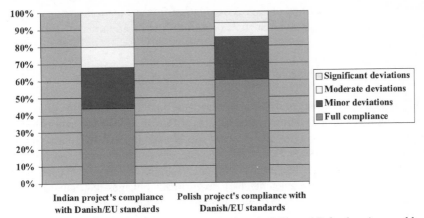

Fig. 3. The Status of 89 Danish Investment Projects in India and Poland as Assessed by External Consultants. *Source:* The Danish Investment Funds (2000).

(see Fig. 4). "The parent company policies and procedures" were the number three motivating factor; in the case of India it was the most frequently cited "very influential" factor. This suggests that especially in developing countries with widespread regulatory failure there is a strong influence from the home country on environmental practices. Finally, 16% reported that the Danish Investment Funds' policies and procedures had been "very influential," 36% among projects with less than 25 employees. Relatively few projects cited consumer pressure as a main motivating factor behind environmental improvements. However, some of

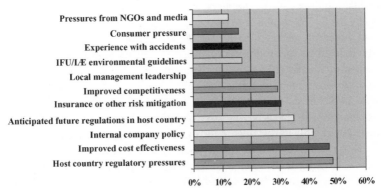

Fig. 4. Ranking of Factors Motivating Environmental Improvements (*n* = 89). *Source:* The Danish Investment Funds (2000).

largest Danish MNEs find pressures from industrial customers as among the main motivations behind measures such as ISO 14001 certification.[28]

4.3. Environmental Concerns Related to Non-Equity Relations

In addition to environmental concerns related to equity involvement, there has been growing focus on the environmental aspects of Danish MNEs' non-equity links in developing countries. First, the growing use of sourcing and subcontracting has raised the question of how Danish firms manage the environmental aspects of their supply chain. Another non-equity issue increasingly challenging Danish MNEs is the environmental management of downstream linkages, e.g. environmental management of customers, franchise holders or vendors.

4.3.1. Cases
A number of highly publicized cases of problems with managing suppliers have surfaced in recent years. These cases typically involved firms in industries that in large measure source activities in developing countries, in particular the wood and furniture industry and the textile industry (Technology Assessment Council, 1999).

Trip Trap, a provider of high quality garden furniture and a company that seeks to maintain a high environmental profile was in 1999 criticized for using Asian suppliers operating with environmental and health and safety standards way below Danish standards. The company responded that it would become uncompetitive if it insisted on high standards at its suppliers since "the customers are not willing to pay the premium." Moreover, the company stated that it was too small to set environmental requirements for suppliers, which typically were larger than the Danish company itself.[29] A similar case involved the large Danish wood trading company Dalhorf Larsen & Horneman (DLH). This company has since the early-1990s marketed itself as environmentally friendly, e.g. by subscribing to the Forest Stewardship Council (FSC) certification scheme, and by promoting sustainable forestry in developing countries through various programs. However, in 2002 Danish media revealed that DLH, in spite of its supplier requirements and environmental policy, was buying large quantities of tropical hardwood which was harvested in a highly unsustainable and in fact illegal manner (Mørkedal & Hedeby, 2002). Responding to the revelations (see also Box 3), DLH argued that one of the problems of setting demands to suppliers is that customers in Europe are unwilling to pay a price premium for certified tropical wood, and that local suppliers of tropical wood have alternative outlets, e.g. in the rapidly growing Asian markets where no environmental screening takes place (Mørkedal & Hedeby, 2002).

Box 3: Dalhorf Larsen Supply Chain Management

DLH is a Danish owned corporate group, which has traded in timber since it was established in 1908. The company is present world-wide and has subsidiaries in Africa, Latin America and Asia. The company has an annual turnover of DKK 4.5 billion. DLH has initiated sustainable forestry projects in important supply countries – e.g. in Ghana – in collaboration with local producers and the Danish aid agency DANIDA. Through the projects, DLH wishes to build knowledge about sustainable forestry that can be transmitted to suppliers, customers, authorities and educational institutions. In response to recent critique, the company has designed and implemented a "good supplier project," which has five components: (1) Thorough assessment of suppliers based on information not only from suppliers but also from NGOs and local authorities and consolidation of this information in databases; (2) A supplier agreement where suppliers pledge to meet a number of minimum requirements regarding human rights and the environment; (3) More careful selection of suppliers; (4) Systematic monitoring of suppliers; and (5) Promotion of the FSC certification scheme among suppliers (Mørkedal & Hedeby, 2002).

Also downstream activities in developing countries have caused concern in the Danish public. In 1997, it was revealed that the largest Danish chemical manufacturer, Cheminova, produces and exports a pesticide – methylparathion – to Nicaragua and Guatemala that is banned for sale in Denmark and that workers allegedly had been injured using the pesticide. The case created an outrage in the public and had serious repercussions for Cheminova's image; in spite of large efforts to repair the damaged image (see Box 4), a 1998 survey rated Cheminova "the most unethical" Danish company.[30] Almost simultaneously another case was revealed involving the diversified company the East Asian Company (EAC). Among EAC's extensive activities in South East Asia, it produced and distributed the pesticide "Paraquat" in Thailand in co-operation with the British chemical manufacturer Zeneca. It was revealed that farmers allegedly had died as a consequence of using the pesticide. As was the case with the Cheminova case, the pesticide was already banned in Denmark. The CEO for EAC reacted to the critique by expressing regrets that people in Thailand were hurt because they had failed to follow the safety precautions provided by the EAC, but that

> Paraquat on balance does more good than bad.

The CEO added:

> We can not control how farmers use the pesticide in remote farming districts. That is just the way it is (Politiken, 1/6 1997 and 4/6 1997).[31]

This company had a few years earlier been involved in another incident because it attempted to sell to a Pakistani consortium old production equipment from a chlorine factory in Copenhagen that was shut down by the Danish environmental authorities.[32]

Box 4: Cheminova Changes Policy

In the wake of the media campaign, Cheminova sought to improve its damaged image by withdrawing methylparathion in liquid form from its markets in Nicaragua and Guatemala, and instead selling the product in new safer microcapsules. Furthermore, Cheminova pledged to make information public about pesticides sold in all foreign markets as well as complying fully with the PIC-Convention (Prior Informed Consent Convention). Moreover, Cheminova decided that it would no longer co-operate with distributors, who cannot accept full openness about pesticides. Finally, Cheminova pledged to use the same environmental standards all over the world. In January 1998, it took over the Indian company, Lupin Agrochemicals, which is among the 10 largest manufacturers of agricultural pesticides in India. This was Cheminova's first overseas production site and Cheminova declared that it would implement EU Best Available Technology (BAT)-standards for the chemical industry at the Indian production site, hence setting higher standards than what the Indian government requires. This objective would according to the company be very costly to implement, and the Indian investment would for that reason not show positive results the first couple of years (Børsen, 4/2, 1998).

A final case that shaped the Danish public's perceptions of Danish MNE's practices in developing countries involved the shipping company Scandlines, which has the Danish state as a major shareholder. In 1997, this company sold a number of ferries through a British dealer to the Indian scrap industry. A TV documentary[33] vividly demonstrated how the Danish ferries – like old ships from all over the world – were sailed to a beach in India, where they were chopped up in pieces for scrap under appalling environmental, health and safety conditions; four workers died per month at the site, and oil, chemicals and asbestos were discharged directly into the ocean. In response, Scandlines argued that it had no stake in the affair as the sale to India was solely the responsibility of the British dealer, however it was revealed that Scandlines in fact had known about the end destination of the ships.

4.3.2. Studies

There are very few systematic studies of the environmental aspects of Danish firms' non-equity linkages in developing countries. One exception is a report from the Danish Parliament's Technology Assessment Council from 1999, which documented that a number of firms within the Danish furniture, leather and textile industries were sourcing heavily in developing countries and Eastern Europe without having adopted appropriate environmental management tools. The industry that was most closely scrutinized in the report was the furniture industry. Here the report found that in spite of the growing linkages to producers in developing countries, none of seven examined furniture companies were setting direct environmental and health and safety requirements to their suppliers, and six declared that they had no environmental strategy or policy for their supply links (Technology Assessment Council, 1999).

That supply chain environmental management is relatively embryonic in Danish industry is supported by at least two studies. A survey of 153 Danish MNEs conducted in 1995 and 1996, found that only approximately 20% of Danish MNEs with operations in developing countries had adopted environmental supply chain measures such as screening procedures or setting environmental standards. Only in exceptional cases did the Danish MNEs discontinue using suppliers that failed to meet environmental standards and requirements (Hansen, 1998, see also Andersen, 1999). A more recent onsite assessment of 89 investment projects in India and Poland conducted by external consultants found that one third of the projects were setting environment and health and safety requirements for suppliers and sub-contractors. This was typically the case for projects in the food and beverages industry and projects in the textile industry. In most cases the requirements were product related, and only rarely did Danish MNEs set demands to processes. A handful of projects however, were reported to contribute to an upgrading of suppliers' ability to address environmental challenges through technical collaboration (Danish Investment Funds, 2000).

4.4. Summary

Summing up, it is evident that issues related to the environmental responsibilities of foreign investors arrived at the Danish political and corporate agendas relatively late compared to what was the case in the U.S. However, with Danish firms' growing presence in developing countries in the 1990s, the environmental responsibilities of Danish MNEs were increasingly being debated. By the late 1990s this issue had become highly salient on the political and corporate agendas and a number of firms became embroiled in damaging public battles with the media, politicians and NGOs. The growing focus on the environmental responsibilities of Danish MNEs prompted a limited number of studies of the environmental practices of Danish MNEs. While it is difficult to generalize this research – for that the studies are too few and methodologically heterogeneous – it seems that there are two apparently conflicting characteristics of Danish MNEs' practices in developing countries. On the one hand, parts of Danish industry have a very high environmental profile in developing countries, either because Danish firms are involved in the provision of environmental goods and services, or because Danish firms have evolved into industry leaders in terms of environmental management and technology. On the other hand, there is a large undergrowth of Danish firms that are merely environmental followers, if not outright laggards. These have rarely formalized/formulated environmental strategies for their global operations and are addressing environmental issues in a piecemeal and ad hoc fashion. It is among this latter group that we find those MNEs that ran into problems when the media and NGOs directed attention to their activities during the 1990s.

5. HOME COUNTRY DETERMINANTS OF FOREIGN ENVIRONMENTAL PRACTICES

We started out by hypothesizing that Danish firms' response to the environmental challenges of international production might be partly explained by factors specific to the Danish home country context. The question to be examined in this section is whether and to what extent the nature of the Danish home base in general and the Danish environmental activism in particular has spilled over into foreign operations of Danish MNEs?

5.1. Home Country Pressures and Competitiveness

The most obvious link between the Danish home base and the foreign environmental practices of Danish MNEs concerns competitiveness. Tough Danish environmental regulation may have undermined the competitiveness of domestic firms and driven them to invest in developing countries and Eastern Europe. However, the limited existing research on this issue suggests that it is unlikely that Danish MNEs have invested to escape tough Danish environmental standards. There may be many reasons, why this is the case, among those that differences in current and especially anticipated standards between developing and OECD countries may not be that great after all,[34] or that damages in terms of tarnished image may exceed the economic benefits of relocation. However, to the extent that the lack of corroboration of the industrial flight hypothesis is mainly due to a lack of internalization advantages from direct investment in the pollution haven, it could be predicted that Danish firms instead will exploit the pollution haven through foreign sourcing. In fact, there is evidence – albeit anecdotal – that certain activities within Danish industries with low asset specificity are increasingly being sourced from suppliers in locations with less stringent EH&S standards.

The competitiveness issue can also be turned around. Thus, the particular Danish regulatory context may have enhanced the competitive position of Danish industry and led to increased FDI in areas where Danish firms have gained environmental competitive advantage. In fact, it could be argued that the Danish case is that of Porter-inspired regulators (Porter & van der Linde, 1995) providing Danish industry with a competitive advantage by adopting tough but smart environmental standards and regulations that encourage Danish firms to innovate and provide them with first-mover advantages.[35] This argument may be valid in several ways.

First, Danish environmental regulation and large public investments in environmental infrastructure have led to the emergence of a sizeable Danish environmental goods and services industry. This industry has had a very strong export performance, has displayed higher growth rates than other industries, and has obtained growing shares of the world market. The environmental goods and services industry has furthermore become an important player in Danish direct investment in developing countries and Eastern Europe, e.g. wind turbine firms investing in India to be present in the expanding Indian market for wind-energy, or waste and water-treatment firms as well as consultant firms investing in Eastern Europe to exploit the market opportunities offered by these countries' accession to the EU (Danish Investment Funds, 2000).[36]

Second, firms outside the environmental goods and services industry proper may have developed an environmental competitive advantage due to 30 years of relatively intense regulation, advantages that they can exploit in their internationalization process. For instance, the Danish machinery and equipment industry may have obtained an edge in regard to obtaining contracts, due to their knowledge of environmental solutions. One example is FLS industries, a major Danish provider of turn-key cement plants in developing countries. This company has obtained an edge in some emerging markets due to its environmental competencies, in particular where there are international finance and aid institutions involved in the projects (Hansen, 1998). Another example could be the pharmaceutical and enzyme producing company Novo Nordic, which may have obtained an advantage in emerging markets due to its excellent environmental and social reputation.

Third, unilateral Danish environmental regulation may have provided Danish firms with first-mover advantages if and when international standards approach Danish standards. While it can be debated how much influence Danish regulation has on international standards, it has at least been argued that EU regulation has tended to converge around the highest standards within the EU rather than the lowest common denominator (Ministry for Environment and Energy, 1998), and that Danish environmental regulation in some cases has provided the blue print for EU regulation (Skou-Andersen & Liefferink, 1997).

Fourth, in certain industries, like breweries and energy production, Denmark has invoked unilateral requirements with reference to environmental benefits, but with the important intended or unintended side effect of protecting Danish industry. The best-known example involves the Danish recycling requirements for bottles. This regulation prohibits the sale of beer in cans and mandates recycling of bottles meeting specific requirements, a system that undoubtedly has produced environmental benefits, but that also has effectively closed the Danish market for foreign beer producers.[37] While some have argued that the Danish recycling regulation is an example of industry capture of regulation (Murphy & Oye, 1998), the direct link between industry interests and legislation has not been firmly established.

The above examples suggest that environmental regulation in some cases may have improved the competitiveness of Danish industry, thereby also strengthening the FDI performance of Danish industry. Nevertheless, it can be questioned whether the net effect on the competitiveness of Danish economy has been positive. As argued earlier, Danish industry is exceptionally export-oriented, and Danish firms are highly integrated in international production chains as suppliers. In this situation, it makes much more sense for Danish industry to invest in adaptation to the standards and technologies prevalent in their major markets, or among their major industrial customers, than to allocate large resources for adapting specifically to Danish regulation (Rugman & Verbeke, 1997). Thus, Danish firms would probably have been better off focussing on industry developments such as the formulation of technical standards in international standards organizations (Goldschmidt, 1995), or developments in the German and EU markets. Moreover, even if tough Danish environmental regulation has led to the emergence of a large environmental goods and services industry, this is not necessarily a proof of success, as the labor and capital engaged in that industry may have earned higher rents in other sectors (Palmer et al., 1995). In line with this, an estimate from 2002 suggests that the Danish environmental goods and services industry generated less revenue on investment than a number of reference industries (Danish Economic Council, 2002, p. 240).

5.2. Home Country Pressures and Environmental Performance

Apart from furnishing Danish industry with competitive advantages or disadvantages, Danish environmental regulation may affect the environmental practices of Danish firms in developing countries in at least two additional ways. First, an environmentally hyper-sensitive Danish public may scrutinize Danish MNEs to a larger extent than is the case with MNEs from other OECD countries, thus forcing Danish MNEs into high standards in international operations. Second, Danish regulation may have pressured Danish industry to develop environmentally more sound technologies and management systems that they bring with them to their international operations.

The chapter demonstrated how the Danish media, NGOs and politicians took a very strong interest in the global environmental responsibilities of Danish MNEs from the mid 1990s and onwards, and how many MNEs became embroiled in damaging media battles as a consequence. This apparently had a major impact in the boardrooms of the largest Danish MNEs, and a notable turn-around on environmental issues took place in the 1990s, from a reactive toward a proactive approach to global environmental challenges. Some of the large Danish MNEs, e.g. Grundfoss, Danisco and Novo Nordic, even became industry leaders with regard to the environmental management of their global portfolio.

However, apart from a small group of leading MNEs, corporate self-regulation still appears to be relatively underdeveloped among Danish investors in developing countries. Three explanations related to the Danish home country context could be offered. First, SME enterprises figure relatively prominently in Danish industry. Small MNEs may due to their inferior ownership advantages, their relative invisibility and their lack of scale advantages have fewer incentives to provide environmental management measures for their developing country operations. In particular, it can be argued that the transaction cost advantages of integrated management systems and uniform standards are smaller for companies with low multinational asset specificity than for companies with high multinational asset specificity (Murphy & Oye, 1998). Second, in spite of being highly international, Danish industry only recently engaged in international production. Due to the lack of internationalization experience, Danish firms are only now learning how to manage the environment in an international context. Third, the regulatory activism of the Danish state combined with the tradition for close collaboration between state and industry, may have caused self-regulation in the form of environmental management and voluntary industry initiatives to have a relatively weak standing on the Danish corporate agenda. This lack of self-regulation may have backfired when Danish firms during the 1990s became increasingly engaged in global operations, and in particular in operations in locations with widespread regulatory failure, that is, developing countries.

While it appears that the environmental management performance of especially small Danish MNEs is relatively low, it should be noted that environmental management is but one indicator of environmental performance. Domestic regulation may have impacted environmental practices of Danish MNEs by altering their technology, organization, and culture. A testimony in support of this hypothesis is the finding that even if most Danish MNEs do not have environmental management systems in place in their developing country operations, they still appear to achieve performance levels close to Danish standards. This could indicate that Danish environmental regulation has spurred technological upgrading to cleaner production and the development of a culture of environmental protection, which while not formalized in management systems, still leads to high environmental performance in developing countries.

5.3. Home Country Measures for Foreign Operations

Due to the growing openness of the Danish economy and the obligations made in international fora like the WTO and the EU, the options for unilateral environmental Danish action are severely constrained, including the options for regulating the foreign environmental conduct of Danish MNEs. However, the Danish state has not entirely surrendered its abilities to influence the foreign practice of Danish firms. The Danish state has actively used its vast development assistance to promote the internationalization of Danish industry through export and investment promotion programs. Through such programs the state has a strong point of leverage to affect the environmental practices of Danish MNEs. In particular, the state-sponsored investment promotion agency IFU is a central player in Danish FDI, accounting for 5–10% of all Danish FDI in developing countries, and participating in 50% of all investment projects in those countries. Through its involvement on the boards of projects, through environmental guidelines, and through its privileged access to funds that can support environmental improvements, this finance institution may have an important catalytic effect with regard to the environmental performance of Danish investors, particularly for the smaller MNEs.

6. CONCLUSIONS

This chapter portrayed the interface between FDI and the environment from the perspective of a small MNE home country, Denmark. The objective was to examine whether and to what extent home country factors have shaped the foreign environmental practices of Danish firms.

It was argued that in particular two characteristics of the Danish home country context have exerted a significant impact on the foreign environmental practices of Danish MNEs:

First, the Danish state has throughout the 1980s and 1990s been exceptionally active in environmental matters in terms of regulation, in terms of environmental taxation, and in terms of funding allocated to domestic and international environmental protection. This environmental activism appears to have spilled over into the international activities of Danish firms, partly by forcing some firms to outsource activities with high pollution abatement costs, partly by providing parts of industry with a competitive advantage that has been exploited in foreign locations, and partly by encouraging some Danish firms to build corporate cultures and technological competencies that are carried to foreign locations. Moreover, in search for outlets for its environmental activism under globalization, the Danish Government has actively used the vast Danish development assistance funds to promote environmental improvements in trade and investment, something that has further shaped the global environmental practices of Danish MNEs.

The second home country characteristic relevant to explaining the foreign environmental practices of Danish MNEs is the particular internationalization path of Danish industry. Being dominated by SME enterprises involved in specialized niche production, Danish industry is a latecomer to FDI, and only recently have Danish firms engaged in investment in the developing world in earnest. One implication of this particular internationalization path appears to have been that Danish industry was relatively unprepared to address environmental concerns related to operations in developing countries when NGOs and the media in the 1990s directed their focus toward this issue. Consequently, many Danish MNEs became embroiled in damaging media battles throughout the second half of the 1990s. A contributing factor to this lack of preparedness could be that the tradition for corporate self-regulation is relatively weak in Danish industry due to the corporatist nature of Danish environmental regulation.

All in all, the Danish case indicates that home country factors may significantly influence the global environmental practices of MNEs, especially small and medium-sized MNEs, and that the role of home country factors in shaping global practices of MNEs therefore deserves continued scrutiny in future research on FDI and the environment.

NOTES

1. Measured by market capitalization the nine Danish companies are: (1) A. P. Møller, shipping and diversified industrial activity (ranks no. 93); (2) The Danish Bank (116); (3) Novo Nordisk, a pharmaceutical and enzyme producing company (146); (4) TDC, a telecom company (163); (5) Lundbeck, a pharmaceutical company (274); (6) GN Store Nord, producer of cables and telecommunication infrastructure (348); (7) Carlsberg, a brewery (356); (8) ISS, a cleaning company; and (9) Danisco, a sugar, food ingredients and beverage corporation (473).

2. Source: Danmarks Statistik Homepage (http://www.dst.dk).

3. Status based on extract from Købmandstandens Database, February 2002.

4. In the 1990s, between 20 and 40% of global FDI inflows were in developing countries (UNCTAD, 2001).

5. For example Niro (delivering equipment for dairy and meet production), APV Pasilac (delivering equipment for the food and beverage industry) FLS (delivering turn key cement factories), or Sabroe (delivering industrial cooling equipment).

6. Throughout the 1980s and 1990s environmental issues ranked among the top ten issues of concern in the Danish population and at levels significantly higher than the neighboring countries Sweden, Finland and Norway (Skou-Andersen et al., 1998, p. 47).

7. For instance on CO_2 emissions, on pesticides, on PVC, on water consumption, on waste, and on petrol.

8. The 50% estimate is provided by the Environmental Protection Agency and includes all areas. In legislative areas such as physical planning (forestry and landscape) legislation is mainly driven by domestic rules, and EU directives account for only approximately 20%. Conversely, EU-directives influence more than 50% in other areas (Author's own interviews, 1999).

9. Financial Times, 21/2, 1995.

10. Allocating 1% of its GNP for development assistance, Denmark is the world's largest provider of aid per capita. To this should be added the Danish environmental assistance and emergency relief in developing countries and Eastern Europe, which is projected to grow to 0.5% of GNP by 2004.

11. The Danish aid agency Danida has since 1992 established private sector programmes in selected countries. These programs offer a wide range of support facilities on a concessionaire basis to Danish and local companies wishing to develop a joint business concept. The aim of the programs is to mobilize Danish know how and expertise in the private sector development of these countries. Furthermore, Danida has established an Environment and Training Fund, which may be used to finance a training and management component in connection with the establishment of new IFU projects in those countries where there are no private sector programmes.

12. The Mixed Credit Scheme was established in 1993 and annually allocates DKK 300 million in the form of credits and guarantees. The scheme finances Danish firms' deliveries of goods and services to development projects in the poorest developing countries, provided there is a request from the host country. Over the years, the state has allocated DKK 3.9 billion in credits and DKK 1.6 billion in interest rate guarantees (Danida, 2002).

13. An interesting observation is that while internationally FDI flows to developing countries surpass aid flows many times over (UNCTAD, 2001), the DKK 10 billion in Danish official development assistance has throughout the 1990s been significantly higher than Danish direct investment in developing countries.

14. For example the "Green Mixed Credit Scheme" or the "Partnership Facility."

15. For example the MIØ (The "Environmental Investment Fund for Eastern Europe"). See Krut et al. (1999) for more examples of programs supporting the environmental efforts of Danish industry in developing countries.

16. Such as the MS (Mellemfolkeligt Samvirke), Ibis and Greenpeace Denmark.

17. According to the Textile and Garment Labor Union Danish regulation of "the neck and shoulder syndrome" imposed large costs on Danish textile firms, and made some of them move production to Poland (Nielsen, 1996). According to the same union, the unilateral CO_2 tax could lead to flight of more than 1000 textile jobs (Politiken, 25/2, 1995, p. 12).

18. Weekend Avisen, 18/10, 1996, p. 7.

19. B.T., 27/5, 1997, p. 14.

20. The Danish electricity producers warn that a pending liberalized EU market for electricity makes it possible for providers of electricity to move production to locations where there is no CO_2 tax, and where requirements regarding sulfur emissions and energy efficiency are inferior to Danish standards (Politiken, 1/2, 1995, p. 6).

21. The refrigeration industry is a significant industry in Denmark, having a turnover of DKK 15 billion and employing 15000 people. The main companies are Danfoss, Sabroe, Gram, Vestfrost, Caravel and Gramskov producing everything from industrial and household refrigerators to components (Jensen, 2001).

22. Politiken, 29/9, 2002, p. 5.

23. For reviews of that research, see Chudnovsky et al. (1999), Zarsky (1999), Jaffe et al. (1995) and Dean (1992).

24. Pedersen et al. (1993) reach similar conclusions in their analysis of the motives behind Danish foreign direct investment.

25. Børsen, 20/11, 1997.

26. This argument is supported by another study from 1999 of 163 mainly European TNC affiliates in Malaysia, India and China (Hansen, 2002). This study found that 60% had environmental management ties between HQ and affiliates and 30% had an explicit policy of operating with similar standards internationally. Among the 18 Danish projects taking part in the study however, only 40% had formalized management relationships between affiliates and parents in the environmental field.

27. Although it should be noted that a further 31% were considering certification.

28. In the case of Novo Nordic in China, pressures from Procter & Gamble; in the case of Roulund India, GM and Volvo; in the case of Danisco Ingredients in China, pressures from McDonald's (Authors own interviews, 1999).

29. Mandag Morgen No. 43, December 1999.

30. Børsen, Guldnummeret, 1998.

31. Nevertheless, the EAC in the spring of 1998 announced changes in its business strategy to accommodate the critique. The Ministry of Environment and Energy made an arrangement with Zeneca and the EAC with the aim of reducing the amounts of pesticides being used in Thailand as well as ensuring greater safety for the farmers using it. According to this arrangement, Zeneca and EAC would be responsible for carrying out an educational campaign to assure that the farmers using pesticides will use smaller amounts under safer conditions, and the Thai and Danish governments would be responsible for promoting ecological production among Thai farmers (Politiken & Information, 18/4, 1998).

32. The environmental authorities had closed down the Copenhagen Chlorine factory because this extremely dangerous production was located in a densely populated area within the Danish capital. The planned sale stirred a row in Denmark as well as in Pakistan because the production equipment sold was outdated and highly dangerous. Eventually, the deal was canceled, because the Pakistani buyer withdrew. Nevertheless the case led to an amendment to the Danish Environmental Protection Act, requiring Danish companies to notify countries receiving used production equipment of the permits and restrictions issued by Danish environmental authorities.

33. "Operation White Wash."

34. This argument is particularly relevant in regard to Danish investment in the EU accession countries in Eastern Europe.

35. That Danish authorities indeed believe that they have improved the competitiveness of Danish industry through environmental regulation, see Ministry of Trade and Industry (1998).

36. Important as these investments may be, there are no estimates of outward FDI in the environmental goods and services industry. In a recent ambitious analysis of the Danish environmental goods and services industry (Danish Economic Council, 2002) FDI is not even mentioned.

37. For instance the brewery Carlsberg (United Breweries) controls 80% of the Danish beer market, a position that undoubtedly has been strengthened due to the Danish recycling requirements.

REFERENCES

Andersen, M. (1999). *Med Blikket mod Øst*. Unpublished Doctoral Dissertation, Copenhagen Business School, Denmark.

Castleman, B. J. (1985). The double standard in industrial hazards. In: J. Ives (Ed.), *The Export of Hazard: Transnational Corporations and Environmental Control Issue*. Boston: Routledge and Kegan Paul.

Christensen, P. M. (1996). Denmark. In: P. M. Christensen (Ed.), *Governing the Environment*. Copenhagen: Nordic Council of Ministers.

Clark, G. (1993). Competition and environmental performance of Australian mineral companies. Is the race to the bottom inevitable? *International Environmental Affairs*, *3*, 147–172.

Danida (Danish Development Assistance) (2002). Årsberetning 2002, Copenhagen: Udenrigsministeriet.

Danish Economic Council (Det Økonomiske Råd) (2002). Vurdering af 90ernes miljø og energi politik. Dansk Økonomi Forår 2002, Copenhagen: Det Økonomiske Råd.

Danish Investment Funds (2000). *The environmental status of investment fund projects in India and Poland*. Copenhagen: IFU.

Dasgupta, S., Hettige, H., & Wheeler, D. (1998). What improves environmental performance? Evidence from the Mexican industry. Policy Research Working Paper, No. 1877. Washington, DC: World Bank.

Dean, J. M. (1992). Trade and the environment: A survey of the literature. In: P. Low (Ed.), *International Trade and the Environment*. Washington: World Bank Discussion Papers.

DI (Dansk Industri) (1998). *Danske virksomheders etableringer i udlandet*. Copenhagen: DI.

Eriksen, J., & Hansen, M. W. (1999). Environmental aspects of Danish FDI to developing countries. UNCTAD/CBS: Occasional Paper, No. 1. Copenhagen Business School.

Gladwin, T. (1987). Environment and development and multinational enterprises. In: C. Pearson (Ed.), *Multinational Corporations, Environment and the Third World*. Duke University Press.

Goldschmidt. L. (1995). Internationalt standardiseringsarbejde: En udfordring for miljøadministrationen. In: P. Lubcke (Ed.), *Miljøet, Markedet og Velfærdsstaten*. København: Fremad.

Hadlock, C. R. (1994). Multinational corporations and the transfer of environmental technology to developing countries. *International Environmental Affairs*, *6*(2).

Hansen, M. W. (1996). Danish foreign direct investment in less developed countries and eastern Europe. A survey of the international operations of Danish companies. Working Paper, No. 9. Copenhagen Business School.

Hansen, M. (1998). *Transnational corporations in sustainable development. An appraisal of the environmental implications of foreign direct investment in less developed countries.* Unpublished Doctoral Dissertation, Copenhagen Business School, Denmark.

Hansen, M. W. (2002). *Managing the environment across borders.* Copenhagen: Samfundslitteratur.

Hoffman, H. (1996). *Danske Investeringer i udlandet, handel og sektorforskydninger i beskæftigelsen.* Copenhagen: Arbejderbevægelsens Erhvervsråd.

Holzinger, K. (1997). The influence of the new member states on EU environmental policy making: A game theoretic approach. In: Lieffering & Skou-Andersen (Eds), *The Innovation of EU Environmental Policy.* Denmark: Scandinavian University Press.

IFU (The Industrialization Fund for Developing Countries) (2002). An assessment of the IFU emphasizing the 1996–2000 capital injection. Confidential Report to the Board. Copenhagen: IFU.

Jaffe, A. B., Peterson, S., & Portney, P. R. (1995). Environmental regulation and the competitiveness of U.S. manufacturing: What does the evidence tell us? *Journal of Economic Literature, XXXXIII*(March), 132–163.

Jenkins, R. (1999). Trade, investment and industrial pollution: A Malaysia case study with some Mexican comparisons. IKMAS Working Paper, Malaysia.

Jensen, K. J. (2001). *Finding the drivers of the CFC phase out.* Thesis submitted at Copenhagen Business School.

Jones, M. T. (1997). *The institutional determinants of social responsibility.* Auckland: University of Auckland.

Krut, R. I., & Moretz, A. (1999). Home country measures for encouraging sustainable FDI. Occasional paper cross border environmental management project, No. 8. Copenhagen: CBS.

Leonard, H. J. (1988). *Pollution and the struggle for world product: Multinational corporations, environment and international comparative advantage.* Cambridge: Cambridge University Press.

Lindholm, M. (Ed.) (1994). *Danmark i verdensøkonomien.* Copenhagen: Samfundslitteratur.

Ministry for Environment and Energy (1998). *Til folketingets miljøudvalg.* Copenhagen: Miljø- og Energiministeriet.

Ministry for Trade and Industry (1998). *Erhvervsredegørelse 1997.* Copenhagen: Erhvervsministeriet (Oktober).

Ministry for Trade and Industry (Erhvervsministeriet) (2000). *International benchmarking af dansk erhvervsliv – en statistisk analyse af de danske ressource.* Copenhagen: Erhvervsministeriet.

Murphy, D. M., & Oye, K. A. (1998). Comparative regulatory advantage: Firm state relations in the global economy. Paper presented at ISA Conference in Minneapolis (March).

Mørkedal, I., & Hedeby, Z. (2002). Can Northern corporations save the rainforest. Thesis submitted at Copenhagen Business School.

Nielsen, J. (1996). *Eksport af farligt arbejde: Et studie i flytning af arbejdsmiljø og miljøproblemer indenfor EU og globalt.* Køge: SID.

OECD (1999). *Environmental performance review – Denmark.* Paris: OECD.

Palmer, K., Oates, W. E., & Portney, P. (1995). Tightening environmental standards: The benefit cost or the no cost paradigm. *Journal of Economic perspectives, 9*(4), 119–132.

Pedersen, T. et al. (1993). *Danske virksomheders etableringer i udlandet – hovedresultater fra en empirisk undersøgelse.* Copenhagen: Handelshøjskolens Forlag.

Perry, M., & Singh, S. (2001). *Corporate environmental responsibility in Singapore and Malaysia: The potential and limits of voluntary initiatives.* Geneva: UNRISD.

Porter, M. E., & van der Linde, C. (1995). Green and competitive. *Harvard Business Review* (September–October), 120–134.

Royston, M. B. (1985). Local and multinational corporations. *Environment, 27*(12–20) (January–February), 39–43.

Rugman, A., & Verbeke, A. (1997). Global strategies for multinational enterprises. In: Islam & Shepherd (Eds), *Current Issues in International Business*. Cheltenham, UK: Edward Elgar.

Santos, R. et al. (1998). Environmental regulations, firm strategies and market behavior. In: Faucheux et al. (Eds), *Sustainability and Firms*. Northampton, MA: Edward Elgar.

Sbragia, A. (1996). Environmental policy: The push-pull of policymaking. In: Wallace & Wallace (Eds), *Policymaking in the European Union*. Oxford: Oxford University Press.

Schmitter, P. (1974). Still the century of corporatism. *Review of Politics, 36*, 85–131.

Skou-Andersen M., Christensen, P. M., & Winther, S. (1998). Denmark: Consensus seeking and decentralization. In: K. Hanf & A. Jansen (Eds), *Governance and Environment in Western Europe*. UK: Addison Wesley.

Skou-Andersen, M., & Liefferink, D. (1997). Strategies of the green member states in EU environmental policy making. *Journal of European Public Policy, 5*(2), 254–270.

Technology Assessment Council (Teknologirådet) (1999). *Farlig teknologi: Miljøregulering ved samhandel med udviklingslande*. Copenhagen: Teknologirådet.

UNCTAD (2001). *World Investment Report 2001: Fostering linkages*. Geneva: UNCTAD.

UNCTAD (United Nations Conference on Trade and Development) (1993). *Environmental Management in Transnational Corporations*. NY: United Nations.

Zarsky, L. (1999). Havens, halos and spaghetti: Untangling the evidence about FDI and the environment. Paper presented to OECD conference on Foreign Direct Investment and the Environment, 28–29 January 1999. Paris: OECD.

INTERNATIONALIZATION AND ENVIRONMENTAL REPORTING: THE GREEN FACE OF THE WORLD'S LEADING MULTINATIONALS

Ans Kolk and Rob van Tulder

ABSTRACT

This chapter examines the green face of the world's one hundred largest firms from developed economies by linking degrees of internationalization to (pro)activity on environmental reporting. A bargaining approach, emphasizing intrinsic and extrinsic motivations, is applied to understand why the most international firms show the greenest face. Bargaining relations within the home country appear to be most important. Country characteristics explored include size, openness and the nature of business-society relationships.

INTRODUCTION

The 1990s witnessed the re-emergence of the debate on multinationals' environmental impact, which originated in the 1970s from concern with the negative effects of "industrial flight" on so-called "pollution havens." Recent attention has focused on assessing whether evidence can be found for their more positive, even "leading edge" role in developing more environmentally friendly processes (Christmann & Taylor, 2001; Gentry, 1999; Kahn, 2000; Low, 1982;

Multinationals, Environment and Global Competition
Research in Global Strategic Management, Volume 9, 95–117
Copyright © 2004 by Elsevier Ltd.
All rights of reproduction in any form reserved
ISSN: 1064-4857/doi:10.1016/S1064-4857(03)09005-3

Mani & Wheeler, 1999; OECD, 1997; Tsai & Child, 1997; UNCTAD, 1999, pp. 289–312; Zarsky, 1999). Although overall, no clear evidence exists in favor of the pollution haven hypothesis or for systematic performance differences between multinationals and domestic firms, cases have been found of usually large, highly visible multinationals that underline their positive environmental influence. At the same time, negative examples also continue to receive attention.

The inconclusiveness of the evidence on the overall relationship between internationalization and firms' environmental behavior is due to several factors. Firstly, it has been difficult to establish a significant relationship due to problems of data availability, measurement and the generally relatively low level of environmental costs (Kolk, 2000). Secondly, generalization has proved impossible because of the peculiar characteristics of existing research in this field: most studies have been quantitative assessments on the macro-level that do not consider firms, surveys, which are frequently limited to the United States (U.S.) context, or individual case studies.

In this situation, how can we draw more generally applicable conclusions about the environmental aspects of internationalization? In other words, are multinationals, in the current absence of international regulation that prescribes their environmental behavior abroad – or confronted with rival regulatory requirements in the countries where they have invested most, i.e. the Triad – inclined to diminish their activities in this field, as a skeptical view would suggest? Or are they, as the "leading edge" proposition holds, instead becoming more active with increasing degrees of internationalization? The answers to these questions are particularly relevant in view of steadily rising degrees of internationalization – the more internationally these large firms operate, the higher their influence on other firms and on societies will be.

This chapter focuses on the green face of internationalization, investigating the extent to which firms' activities on environmental communication increase with internationalization: are higher levels of internationalization accompanied by more and more elaborate environmental reporting? If so, multinationals' greater inclination to engage in a societal dialogue on their environmental impact might give opportunities for increased transparency, and for addressing the effects of international investments in an era of privatization and deregulation.

To facilitate generalization of the results on the relationship between internationalization and multinationals' green face, the largest one hundred industrial firms worldwide have been selected for the current study. The approach of systematically scrutinizing all the firms in this set, differs fundamentally from most studies on multinationals and environmental management, where data originates from surveys or from the U.S. context only. The analysis in this chapter thus enables a comparison between multinationals from different home countries/regions. An institutional approach might assume isomorphic pressures on firms' strategies, leading to convergence (DiMaggio & Powell, 1983), also in the case of emerging environmental issues (Hoffman, 1999). When multinationals are involved, however, the country-of-origin effect (COE) in which firms from different institutional backgrounds are supposed to behave differently, is expected to lead to divergent responses (cf. Rugman & Verbeke, 1998). This COE, or institutional context, involves cultural values and institutional norms, government policies and countries' resources (Sethi & Elango, 1999).

This chapter is organized as follows. The first three sections analyze the insights that can be derived from previous research on internationalization, environmental reporting and bargaining relations. Next, the choice for one hundred so-called "core firms" is elucidated, which, subsequently, should facilitate a systematic assessment of the relationship between internationalization and environmental reporting practices, thereby identifying patterns and links to national regulatory differences. The final section offers conclusions and reflects on the latest developments.

TWO THEORETICAL PERSPECTIVES

To understand the linkages between environmental and internationalization strategies, theoretical insights from both international business and political economy are valuable. Whereas political economists in the 1960s and 1970s stressed extrinsic motivations for internationalization, international business studies in the 1980s and 1990s focused primarily on the intrinsic motivations (see Table 1). The "first-generation" studies on the multinational enterprise (MNE) thus prioritized

Table 1. Strategic Motivations.

	Internationalization	Environmental (Reporting) Strategies
Intrinsic motivation → transaction costs and efficiency approaches	Market-seeking Efficiency-seeking Resource-seeking Asset-seeking	Increase transparency Increase performance (competitive advantage) Increase coordination
Extrinsic motivation → bargaining and game theoretical approaches	Home: Escape from home country Host: Barriers to entry Sector: Bandwagon effects, e.g. in country selection	Home: Environmental flight Host: Pollution haven, adaptation to stricter regulation Sector: Follow the leader in most polluting sectors

bargaining and game-theoretical approaches, particularly in business relationships with host governments, studying effects on host economies (cf. Vernon, 1971). The "second generation" used a transaction cost approach, focusing on minimizing costs, maximizing efficiency and/or competitiveness, while internalizing markets. Gomes-Casseres (1990) aptly summarized this as the tension between what the firm "wants" and what the firm "can get."

In the 1990s, the "want" of the internationalizing firm became habitually summarized by four motives introduced by Dunning (1993): market-seeking, efficiency-seeking, resource-seeking and (strategic) asset-seeking. What this firm "can get," however, is determined by negotiations with governments and stakeholders. Regulatory barriers to entry in the host country ("voluntary" export restraints, taxation regimes, industrial policies) influence the internationalization process. In addition, firms may also internationalize in order to escape from domestic (home) regulations. This latter issue, of "rent-seeking" behavior of firms to evade home government regulation or to move towards company-friendly regulatory environments (havens), has been much less addressed in the International Business (IB) literature, however. The host-country perspective (which takes the internationalization strategy of the MNE as an independent variable) has usually received more attention than the home-country perspective (with the internationalization strategy of the MNE as the dependent variable). In addition to home and host country factors, a third category of extrinsic motives can be mentioned, which relates to "bandwagon" effects. Triggered by oligopolistic competition, firms can internationalize primarily to "follow the leader."

It must be noted that the extrinsic motivations, as distinguished in Table 1, are much more difficult to "prove" than the internal ones. Therefore, it is not surprising that most IB studies have concentrated on intrinsic motivations and the *effects* of internationalization strategies on the host economy. Reflecting this general direction in the 1990s, research on environmental strategies has also tended to pay considerable attention to intrinsic aspects, with a particular interest in performance-enhancing implications. A number of studies on the impact of home/host regulation have been conducted, but without conclusive evidence. Bandwagon dynamics can be seen with regard to environmental management and reporting, where the activities of early adopters are followed by competitors in some sectors, sometimes influenced by international industry associations.

One of the problems with regard to studies on the relationship between internationalization and environmental regulation is that investment decisions are rarely taken on the basis of only environmental criteria. Environmental costs are generally of minor importance in location decisions, hampering the delineation of the positive or negative effects of specific home/host country regulation. The overall institutional context is generally assumed to play an important role, but difficult to assess and disentangle with regard to the environment. If we abstain from trying to assess the overall impact of the environment on international locations decisions, however, but focus instead on MNE behavior concerning specific environmental aspects such as environmental reporting, insights on the relationship between internationalization and the environment, and firms' motivations can be obtained. In view of increasing MNE activity and home-country attention to environmental reporting, this is an area where both firm behavior and extrinsic motivations can be studied.

CATEGORIZING HOME-COUNTRY EFFECTS AND INSTITUTIONS

The Country-of-Origin Effect (COE) involves cultural values and institutional norms, government policies and countries' resources (Sethi & Elango, 1999). Only a limited number of studies have systematically tried to link national institutions to different "styles" or "trajectories" of internationalization: in general (Pauly & Reich, 1997), as influenced by stakeholders (Rugman & D'Cruz, 2000; Wartick & Wood, 1998), mediated by national business systems (Whitley, 1999), governance structures (Halme & Huse, 1997), industrial complexes (Ruigrok & van Tulder, 1995) and national cultures (Hofstede, 1980). No identifiable links between different national institutions and styles or degrees of internationalization have been established. Comparable deficiencies exist in environmental research.

In order to consider the (developed) home country of origin as a "bargaining arena" from which to internationalize, and within which firms bargain over common rules and institutions for environmental management, the following indicators have been selected to classify the nature of the home bargaining arena (cf. Kolk, 2000; Ruigrok & van Tulder, 1995; Whitley, 1999): relative size and closedness or openness of the economy, institutional linkages with neighboring countries, centralized or decentralized governance structures, and the position of societal stakeholders (state and civil society). Table 2 distinguishes three groups of economies of different size, within which six national trajectories are explored, and their characteristics.

The *larger economies* have the most closed bargaining arenas, although the precise peculiarities exhibit differences per country as well. The possibilities of larger economies such as the United States and Japan to externalize the negative effects (for example, with regard to environmental pollution) of restructuring strategies are greater than for smaller economies (cf. Katzenstein, 1985). Leading firms have the bulk of their activities in the home market. Japan is more closed than the U.S.,

Table 2. Home-Country Bargaining Characteristics.

	Large Economies		Medium-Sized Economies			Small Economies (e.g. Netherlands)
	U.S.	Japan	France	Germany	U.K.	
Dominant governance style	Shareholder	Stakeholder	Stakeholder	Stakeholder	Shareholder	Mixed
Bargaining arenas	Decentralized	Decentral	Central	State/region	Decentral	Central
Civil society	Strong	Weak	Weak	Strong	Strong	Strong
State	Medium	Medium	Strong	Strong	Medium	Strong
Host/home MNEs	Home	Home	Home	Home	Home/host	Home/host
Bargaining relations	Antagonistic	Firm dominated	State dominated	Corporatist	Antagonistic	Corporatist
Closed/open arena	Closed	Closed	Semi-closed	Semi-closed	Semi-open	Open

with less than 1% of FDI (as % of GDP) foreign-owned, compared to almost 10% for the U.S. (UNCTAD, 2000). In Japan home firms prevail, in the United States, the influence of host firms has been growing since the mid-1980s – albeit remaining at a relatively low level. Japan has a stakeholder system, while the U.S. can be considered a shareholder economy. In Japan most ("collaborative") relations are dominated by the interests of the firms, in the absence of a manifest civil society. Japanese firms do not face formal regional integration initiatives, while U.S. firms are involved in NAFTA. As regional integration agreement, NAFTA is much more "shallow" than the European Union (it has, for instance no regional competition or trade policy), and thus has a less pervasive effect on firm strategies. In the U.S., civil society and the state represent prominent actors. However, the separation of powers between the various segments of society has induced antagonistic bargaining relations. In both the U.S. and Japan, industrial bargaining is relatively decentralized. In theory, a more closed national arena should facilitate bargaining, because positive and negative externalities are confined to the same territory, whereas the players are likewise more attached and loyal. Whether or not firms adopt a (re/pro)active strategy then depends on the relative strength of domestic stakeholders.

Smaller economies share an extremely open bargaining arena. Most leading firms have larger interests abroad. Smaller countries – like the Netherlands or Belgium at the downstream end of major European rivers – are faced with more than average environmental problems due to their international geographical location, thus triggering considerable interest in environmental regulation as well as substantial activities in environmental protection. Differently located and more sparsely populated Nordic countries with large territories might, nevertheless, still be classified amongst the "small countries" due to the particular institutional challenge posed by the greater internationalization of their economies. Small and open economies share smaller populations, a lower GDP, a higher concentration of employment in production with a few large companies, but also a higher propensity towards national consensus-building. With the increasing importance of technology for economic growth, some authors have hinted at the existence of a "small-country squeeze" (Kristensen & Levinson, 1983; van Tulder, 1989), pointing at the size-related problems that small countries face when confronted with the choice for particular technological paradigms. Small and open economies have institutionally been faced with the challenge of internalizing external (political, economic and cultural) effects, whereas larger economies have often been able to externalize some of their internal problems (cf. Katzenstein, 1985) thus creating all sorts of negative externalities for smaller (neighboring) countries. The internalization of the effects of these negative externalities spurred compensatory governmental policies and a larger claim of the public sector on the national economy (cf. Cameron's classic 1978 study). This, in turn, created extrinsic motivations for larger firms to try to escape national regulation, or threaten to do so. Small economies have the most centralized and corporatist bargaining institutions of all developed countries. Relevant actors (firms, state, civil society) are permanently represented. In small countries such as the Netherlands, Switzerland and Sweden, home and host multinationals are well represented, and in some instances responsible for approximately 50% of the sizable stock of domestic FDI.

European *medium-sized* economies have bargaining arenas that fall in between large and small economies. In Germany and France, the bargaining arena is semi-closed. In the United Kingdom (U.K.), the impact of host and home multinationals is comparable to that of smaller countries, making it the most open of all medium-sized economies. At the same time, the U.K. also replicates U.S. (antagonistic) shareholder orientation. Bargaining relations are relatively decentralized. In France, civil society is weakly organized, whilst the central state still dominates most of the bargaining relations with firms. Many leading firms in France are still (partly) state-owned. The bargaining arena in France is highly centralized. Both the French and German economies have had relatively limited inroads of foreign multinationals. The German setting resembles smaller countries' institutions, but organized at a relatively decentralized level. Tripartite bargaining relations between the government, employers and employees have created (neo)corporatist institutions, which have also included environmental lobbying groups. In Germany, like in smaller countries, green parties have become part of government.

ENVIRONMENTAL REPORTING

Environmental reporting, which can stem from both extrinsic and intrinsic motivations, has received extensive scholarly interest. Considerable attention has been paid to multinationals, although most research consists of nationally-oriented surveys or case studies. In the accounting literature, studies on environmental reporting and disclosure practices are frequently confined to firms from one country (cf. Deegan & Gordon, 1996; Gray et al., 2001; Neu et al., 1998). The firms studied are often large, but it is not clear whether they are really THE largest firms in the countries concerned – obscuring their relationship with national institutions. Finally, research covers the period up to the mid-1990s, analyzing annual reports rather than environmental reports. A number of studies on environmental reporting have made a systematic analysis of sets of large firms, such as the U.S. *Fortune* 50 or 500 (Davis-Walling & Batterman, 1997; Lober et al., 1997), or the global *Fortune* 100 or 250 (Kolk, 2003; Kolk et al., 2001; KPMG/UvA, 2002; KPMG/WIMM, 1999; Krut & Moretz, 2000; Line et al., 2002). Even in these studies, however, internationalization was excluded as explanatory variable.

The majority of studies on environmental reporting merely analyze the contents or "quality" of reports, rather than assessing underlying factors that influence reporting behavior. A skeptical view seems to predominate: environmental reporting either obfuscates negative environmental effects, because they will rarely disclose poor performance (Chan & Milne, 1999), or is only a response to external stakeholder pressure, and therefore tends to be event-dependent, temporary and public relations oriented (cf. Neu et al., 1998; Walden & Schwartz, 1997). The "external pressure" argument – and the re-active nature of reporting – seems to be primarily based upon North American samples.

Existing research underlines sector and country characteristics, and occasionally also size, for explaining reporting behavior. Sector peculiarities are not just relevant for "benchmarking" reports, but also explain frequencies of reporting. Firms from more polluting and visible sectors publish more reports (Kolk et al., 2001; KPMG/WIMM, 1999; Krut & Moretz, 2000). One study found that large firms in so-called sensitive industries disclose more information, whereas this relationship did not apply to smaller firms (Adams et al., 1998). Substantial national reporting differences have been observed, but not many studies have tried to assess – let alone understand – the determinants of this effect. Halme and Huse (1997), who searched for the impact of national governance of smaller countries on environmental disclosure in annual reports, found some support for this thesis.

Reporting as part of the bargaining dynamics with external and internal stakeholders relates to the discursive power of firms – the power to "frame debates." Multinationals – confronted with a variety of discursive and cultural contexts (cf. Haas, 1990; Litfin, 1994) – can use environmental reports as a means of influencing or responding to society. According to Levy and Egan (1998), U.S. firms, in exercising their discursive power, preferred the national over the international environmental bargaining arena. The discursive dimension of environmental reports could consist of two functions: the expression of relative bargaining positions in the home economy (extrinsic motivation: towards governments and pressure groups), and as an indication of the impact of internationalization on the environmental strategy and organization of the firm (intrinsic motivation). It is also an indication of what prevails in firm's environmental strategies – sector or country characteristics.

Different strategies for environmental reporting can be distinguished: none, tentative, active and pro-active. The "none" category means that firms do not show attempts at environmental communication. In the case of "tentative" reporting, firms release environmental brochures, other public information or refer to environmental matters in their annual reports. Both "active" and "pro-active" firms publish an environmental report, but the latter represent a distinct category.

Pro-active reports are externally verified and include more far-reaching information in their reports (particularly on supplier requirements and financial implications of the environment). There is some supporting evidence that advanced reporting mirrors good environmental performance as well (Al-Tuwaijri & Christensen, 1999). Pro-active reporting requires the installation of elaborate management systems throughout the organization. OECD-analyses of European and Asian (including Japanese) firms also showed that, in all cases, implementation rates of environmental management systems were substantially higher than environmental reporting percentages (OECD, 2000). Moreover, the bargaining dynamics in which reporting develops increases the likelihood of comparable behavior. Stakeholders will urge firms to live up to their promises, and firms run the risk of severe damage to their image and brands if they fail to do so. In case of more antagonistic bargaining relations – in "litigation societies" such as the U.S. – firms share an interest in not initiating too clear reports. An accelerator effect exists: the more information an organization discloses, the more stakeholders can question the validity and credibility of the disclosed information, which could lead to a new round of bargaining (cf. Kolk, 2000).

It is likely that firms that have an integrated and intrinsically motivated environmental strategy (perhaps due to more internal coordination problems) are the most interested in pro-active reporting practices. Firms that are primarily extrinsically motivated by pressure groups would probably prefer tentative (re-active) reporting styles, whereas firms that are extrinsically motivated by governments are interested in active reporting styles. Firms that do not disclose information are clearly not influenced by pressure groups or national regulation, while also lacking any intrinsic motivation to communicate their environmental strategy, if they even have one.

CORE FIRMS: CONCEPT AND DATA COLLECTION

To assess the relationship between internationalization and environmental reporting, the world's one hundred largest so-called "core" firms have been examined. Like in other definitions of leading firms, such as "focal firms" or "flagship firms" (Rugman & D'Cruz, 2000), core firms are characterized by their size and importance in networks of supply and distribution, as "spiders in an industrial web," and by their relative importance in national bargaining arenas, where core firms shape home institutions (Ruigrok & van Tulder, 1995). The one hundred largest core firms from developed countries have been selected from the

1995 *Fortune* global 500 list (van Tulder et al., 2001).[1] The category excludes financial services firms, in order to focus on firms that directly or indirectly cause most environmental problems and also have the largest research facilities to work on possible solutions. The environmental face that the 100 largest core firms show towards society therefore matters. They represent a significant category for studies on the bargaining dynamics in environmental issues.

The degree of internationalization of these core firms is calculated from the ratio between foreign assets (total fixed and current assets outside the home country) and total assets. The figures are derived from company sources, usually annual reports. The data have been complemented by and checked with the firms. Assets were selected as indicator because they directly relate to environmental impact. Other indicators of internationalization are sales and employees, or the combination of the three – the transnationality index (TNI) as calculated in UNCTAD's annual World Investment Report. In studies on internationalization and (financial) performance, the Degree of Internationalization (DOI) is almost always based on sales data (e.g. Sullivan, 1996), usually because of their relatively good availability. Internationalization of sales is a less relevant indicator for environmental strategies: the international spread of sales has a more indirect bearing on environmental issues, for example, through increased transport. Environmental problems (and their solutions) relate in the first place to firms' production strategies, exemplified by the international distribution of assets and production sites.

To obtain data on environmental disclosure, all 100 core firms were requested to send their most recent corporate environmental report, corporate health, safety and the environment report, or another publication with the same kind of information.[2] All reports were analyzed following the logic explained in the preceding section, to identify the four types of environmental reporting strategies.

PATTERNS OF INTERNATIONALIZATION AND ENVIRONMENTAL REPORTING

Overall, the percentage of core firms with an environmental report (the active and pro-active categories) is extremely high with 70%, exceeding by far the numbers found in other recent research on large multinationals from different nationalities (Kolk, 2003; Kolk et al., 2001; KPMG/WIMM, 1999; KPMG/UvA, 2002; Krut & Moretz, 2000; Line et al., 2002). This can partly be explained by the selection criteria of core firms, particularly the exclusion of financial firms. Even compared to the results of only industrial firms from the *Fortune* 500, however, the outcome still remains exceptional. Apparently, these largest firms have a particular profile

Table 3.   Average Degrees of Internationalization, Different Environmental
Reporting Strategies.

Reporting Strategy	Internationalization (%)
No strategy ($n = 5$)	10.29
Tentative ($n = 25$)	22.07
Active ($n = 51$)	29.57
Proactive ($n = 19$)	49.90

that encourages them to show a green face. It is plausible that this is related to
the fact that core firms are the least able to ignore societal debates on important
questions such as the environment, and that their societal "license to operate"
depends on their willingness to make public statements on environmental issues.

The data on environmental reporting strategies have been linked to those on
internationalization. Table 3 shows that pro-active reporters have the highest
degree of asset internationalization, followed respectively by firms with active
and reactive reporting strategies; firms without a reporting strategy are least
internationalized. This means that the most international core firms clearly show a
greener face than the least international firms, i.e. those firms that are still chiefly
operating in their home country.

Having found this overall relationship, the question is what further patterns
can be distinguished. To this end, the characteristics of internationalization and
environmental reporting strategies will be examined in more detail. Table 4
presents the data for the average degrees of asset internationalization (DOI)
for various sectors with considerable numbers of top 100 core firms, grouped
according to home-country differences.

Table 4.   Average Degrees of Internationalization of the Largest 100 Core Firms.

	Total ($n = 100$)	Autos ($n = 15$)	Oil ($n = 11$)	Electronics ($n = 16$)	Food ($n = 14$)
Europe (total) ($n = 38$)	42.31	44.48	53.49	61.93	57.28
Small[a] ($n = 6$)	65.32	51.51	67.75	80.92	58.21
Medium ($n = 32$)	36.18	48.91	49.92	42.94	54.48
Japan ($n = 33$)	20.16	33.68	7.25	21.51	8.04
U.S. ($n = 28$)	27.12	22.29	50.91	42.91	2.32
Total ($n = 100$[b])	30.60	39.70	48.11	36.96	19.25

[a] Includes 1 Swiss; 1 Swiss/Swedish; 1 Swedish; 1 Dutch; 2 Anglo-Dutch firms.
[b] Includes 1 Venezuelan firm (PDVSA).

The average degree of asset internationalization is 30.60%, but there is considerable country variance. European firms score particularly high, consecutively followed by U.S. and Japanese firms ($N = 38, 29$ and 33 respectively). On average, the European DOI is 42.31%; multinationals from smaller economies are highly internationalized. Medium-sized European countries are characterized by higher DOIs than both Japan and the U.S. Core firms from smaller countries had intrinsic motivations to internationalize related to the small size of the domestic markets. They also had extrinsic motivations in escaping home government pressure. Most multinationals from smaller countries adopted a multi-domestic style, highly adaptive to local circumstances, but also creating sizable coordination problems.

The U.S. is characterized by core firms with the widest variety in DOI. Multinationals from the United States internationalized relatively early and were intrinsically motivated. Neither home nor host governments (initially) created major barriers to enter or exit, whereas foreign interests never prevailed over domestic interests. Many U.S. multinationals adopted a centralised, geo-centric style of internationalization aiming at uniform markets and products (globalization). Japanese firms internationalized much later, primarily triggered by extrinsic motivations. U.S. and European impositions of export restraints, trade quotas and currency agreements formed prime triggers for the internationalization of assets by leading Japanese firms. Consequently, Japanese firms adopted a strategy of *glocalization* – being locally-adaptive, but based on hierarchical, geo-centric structures (Ruigrok & van Tulder, 1995).

U.K. core firms internationalized earlier and more outside the European continent than firms from other medium-sized countries. The U.K. resembles the U.S. experience, but stems from a more open domestic bargaining arena. Some of the U.K. multinationals developed multi-domestic strategies and are thus equally interested in the potential of environmental management for increased international company-internal coordination as multinationals from the smaller economies are. French and German firms internationalized relatively late – and primarily within Europe. German firms shared the motive to "escape" the domestic arena – with its high wages and strong interest representation. French firms lacked comparable extrinsic motivations in either home or host economies. French and German firms adopted relatively centralized internationalization styles.

Table 5 summarizes core firms' reporting strategies using the same format as Table 4. It shows that different national/regional contexts are also important in this regard. Using the division into four reporting strategies, European core firms show the greenest face (3.08), followed by Japanese (2.82) and U.S. firms (2.55). Firms from smaller countries are more (pro)active than firms from medium-sized countries, while those in Germany (and the U.K.) are considerably more pro-active than the French.

Table 5. Average Environmental Reporting Strategies of the Largest 100 Core
Firms (1 = No; 2 = Tentative; 3 = Active; 4 = Proactive).

	Total (n = 100)	Autos (n = 15)	Oil (n = 11)	Electronics (n = 16)	Food (n = 14)
Europe (total) (n = 38)	3.08	3.50	3.40	3.25	3.00
Small (n = 6)	3.63	4.00	4.00	3.50	3.33
Medium (n = 32)	2.93	3.43	3.25	3.00	2.00
Japan (n = 33)	2.82	3.25	3.00	3.10	3.00
U.S. (n = 28)	2.55	2.67	3.20	2.75	1.57
Total (n = 100[a])	2.84	3.30	3.27	3.06	2.29

[a] Includes PDVSA (Venezuela).

Sector differences can be noted as well. Generally speaking, the most polluting sectors have the highest propensity for publishing environmental reports. This applies particularly to sectors such as chemicals, cars, oil and (energy) utilities. Their production characteristics (initially) inhibit firms from showing a pro-active green face, but a bandwagon effect takes place once important multinationals have started to publish reports and hire third parties to verify the contents. Reporting is considerably less common in sectors with lower pollution levels, such as postal services, telecommunications, food stores, trade and retail. This also holds for the banks and insurance firms that have been excluded from this study.

An exception to this overall relationship between pollution levels and environmental reporting is computers/electronics. Although the direct environmental impact is relatively low compared to heavy industry sectors, many firms publish environmental reports. Peculiar to computers and electronics is that the international environmental management standard ISO 14001 has become a market requirement, originating from Japan (U.S.AEP, 1997). Although this standard does not require the publication of an environmental report, it seems likely that it has been an incentive for showing a greener face. In addition, (regulatory) attention to take-back and recycling has been relatively high in computers and electronics.

A sector-based perspective also provides additional characteristics of the largest core firms in terms of their internationalization patterns. Overall, firms operating in process industries such as oil and chemicals show high degrees of asset internationalization. Their markets are often separated from their resource bases. Core firms in batch-good sectors such as cars, trade and computers share medium to high degrees of internationalization. They have more often engaged in an international division of labor between their suppliers and assembly facilities. Core firms in utilities are least internationalized: their national background still matters most, due to the relatively recent start of privatization processes in their sector.

Both Tables 4 and 5 indicate that the country factor seems more important than sector differences in determining internationalization and environmental reporting.[3] Table 4 shows for the sectors with the largest numbers that European firms are in all cases more internationalized than their Japanese and U.S. counterparts; in addition, the spread of DOIs is greater for U.S. than for Japanese firms. The overview in Table 5 reveals that the differences between the reporting strategies of the Triad apply generally, regardless of the sector, with Europe ranking highest and the U.S. lowest. The exception to this rule is the oil industry, where U.S. firms show a greener face than the only Japanese firm in the sector. Of all industries, environmental reporting strategies of European versus U.S. oil multinationals are also least different. This sector is peculiar in general in that U.S. firms started to publish environmental reports much earlier (Chevron, Exxon, Texaco in 1990, Amoco in 1992) than European oil multinationals (ENI, BP, both 1995, Shell, 1997). The Exxon Valdez oil spill and the U.S. context at the time were important factors (cf. Kolk & Levy, 2001). Although relative late-comers, the three European oil majors from smaller countries and the U.K. have published more elaborate, externally verified environmental reports. The two French multinationals have followed with more (re)active disclosure practices. The overall picture means, however, that attention must be paid to the institutional context of environmental reporting, especially regulatory developments and societal pressures. These different bargaining arenas provide the context in which firms' strategies are developed.

UNDERSTANDING CHANGES IN NATIONAL REGULATION

Although none of the firms' home countries legally required the publication of environmental reports in the period under investigation, regulatory requirements on disclosure are gradually increasing, particularly in the smaller countries with more open bargaining arenas. In the Netherlands and the Scandinavian countries, legal developments have reflected societal concerns about environmental issues. Many of them suffer from more environmental problems than other countries due to their geographical location (the Netherlands, for example, as a low-lying country, adjacent to the North Sea, with estuaries of three major European rivers, bringing in pollution from neighboring countries such as Germany and France), and sometimes also their levels of industrialization.

From fiscal year 1999 onwards, Dutch law requires firms with a so-called "significant impact" to publish an environmental report; this applies to 250 plants. Denmark, which has no large domestic multinationals, was the first country to adopt comparable legislation (though applicable to many more firms and already in place since fiscal year 1996). In Norway and Sweden, government regulations obligate firms to include environmental information in their financial reports, starting with fiscal year 1999. Multinationals from the smaller countries have the strictest reporting practices with high degrees of verification, but also include more "soft" and qualitative strategies on the environment, including pleas for covenants and other forms of stakeholder management.

Core firms from smaller economies were already actively reporting *before* they became subject to legal obligations. Environmental management tools had been helpful in facilitating better coordination for firms following a multi-domestic strategy. At the same time they could present themselves as "good citizens" in host countries – lacking the backing of strong home governments. In the Netherlands and Scandinavia, legal developments reflected societal concerns about environmental issues. Because these concerns are more institutionalized in smaller (corporatist) countries, core firms have identified a pro-active strategy as the best way to create a "level-playing field" in their home economies, supporting government attempts to arrive at more international regulation.

Medium-sized countries did not adopt comparable regulation on environmental reporting. The European Union (EU) *voluntary* Eco-Management and Audit Scheme (EMAS) does, however, require participating sites to produce an annual environmental statement, which is comparable to an environmental report, though always at the site level. EMAS-registrations are particularly high in Germany, and much less common in the U.K., the Netherlands and France (Kolk et al., 2001). In Germany, the government explicitly supports EMAS, sometimes offering relaxation of other environmental requirements in return.

In the U.K., there is more outspoken societal pressure to report on environmental and social issues. This is apparent from the relatively high percentage of verified (pro-active) environmental reports, in which firms in the U.K. by far exceed those in other countries (KPMG/WIMM, 1999). Verification is particularly notable in the utilities' reports; the most likely explanation for this phenomenon is the requirement of public transparency that formed a precondition for the privatization of these firms. According to Adams et al. (1998), who found relatively high levels of social disclosure in the U.K., possible explanations might be the strong ethical investment community, the relatively greater importance of reporting to shareholders in view of dispersed share ownership, and firms' preemptive attempts to show that regulation is not needed. Moreover, the strong presence of host multinationals shaped a bargaining dynamics comparable to smaller countries. In 1998, the U.K. environment minister warned firms about introducing regulation if they did not voluntarily publish better-quality environmental information. This threat has been repeated since then, and supported by the Prime Minister as well.

France is typical for its lack of clear societal pressures on environmental disclosure, and for relatively high government involvement in strategic sectors such as oil, electricity, telecommunications and water utilities. The strategic relevance for national industrial policy is likely to make these firms less sensitive to consumer pressures. Consequently, French core firms merely follow the reporting practices of their main competitors. While we have seen that environmental reporting practices in the U.K. and Germany are due to societal pressure, the lack of this pressure in France explains the weak spread of environmental reporting practices. The largest French multinationals are more active on environmental reporting than shown by a greater sample of French firms (KPMG/WIMM, 1999). It must be noted, though, that the situation has changed after the current study was carried out: the French government adopted a law in 2002 which obliges reporting on social and environmental issues (see the concluding section).

The largest countries have a different bargaining situation in connection with environmental reporting. The U.S. in particular requires firms to report on emissions for a national pollutant or toxic release inventory, and to make information on environmental liabilities available to the Securities and Exchange Commission. These quantitative, strict requirements have a relatively long tradition in the U.S.; emission registration is still about to start in the EU. U.S. firms started relatively early with "voluntary" environmental management, particularly in response to environmental incidents such as the 1984 Bhopal explosion and the 1989 Exxon Valdez oil spill, and the societal concerns that these aroused (see the example of the oil industry given in the preceding section). Since then, however, the strict imposition of standards, coupled with the litigious tradition in the U.S., seems to have had a deterrent effect. U.S. firms have shown little interest in voluntary standards such as ISO 14001, even openly resisting it through the Coalition on ISO 14000 Implementation for fear that it might become a regulatory requirement (Kolk, 2000; see also Delmas, 2000).[4] U.S. firms currently have less (pro)active reporting strategies than European multinationals, and especially those originating from smaller economies.

In Japan there were, in the period under investigation, neither regulatory requirements on environmental reporting nor substantial societal pressure in this direction, but government incentives on environmental accounting and reporting practices started to emerge (and resulted in government guidelines from 2001 onwards). Overall, Japanese firms score higher than U.S. firms. Many Japanese multinationals embraced ISO 14001, which is likely to have encouraged reporting on environmental management, as explained earlier. MITI actively stimulated certification to the standard by supporting registration agencies (Kurasaka, 1997). An important incentive was the suspicion that ISO 14001 would become a condition for entering the European market (a worldwide reality for electronics). Such a development occurred earlier in the case of the ISO 9000 quality system, to which Japanese firms initially objected because it did not conform to their internal approach to quality management. For Japanese multinationals that are part of vertical *Keiretsu*, such as Toyota, Nissan, NEC and Canon, stricter supplier requirements also fit in their strategies to coordinate their supply chain.

CONCLUSIONS AND DISCUSSION

This chapter has shown that, firstly, (pro-)activity on environmental reporting increases with internationalization. The most international core firms show a greener face than those that are more nationally-oriented. This means that the likelihood increases that these multinationals spread this practice "internally" worldwide to reduce coordination costs and that they influence other firms' behavior on environmental communication. Firms might also profit from reporting if it helps to gear their management system towards providing correct and relevant information, thus forming an additional control on efficiency and effectiveness. Governments and NGOs can use pro-active reporters as examples to raise standards and encourage other firms to do the same, thus perhaps even furthering the emergence of a new "market morality" (cf. Bowie & Vaaler, 1999). Moreover, multinationals can be requested to live up to their promises and perform as they declare publicly.

As such, environmental reporting in and of itself does not necessarily mean that firms behave accordingly. Communication can differ substantially from performance; one might even state that multinationals have discovered environmental reporting as a good public relations' tool. It must be noted, however, that the reports of the most pro-active multinationals contain quantitative information that can be checked, and a considerable number have been verified by third parties. Although these outsiders have been paid to perform this task, their status can be damaged if their assurance proves wrong. Moreover, verified reports contain details about data collection and aggregation, and the assessment of performance. All this offers some guarantees that the information is reliable, and firms that offer detailed information make themselves more vulnerable to outside monitoring and criticism than those that do not – although they also take the lead in choosing the issues.

A second finding of the research in this chapter is that there is a clear distinction between multinationals from different institutional contexts as far as internationalization and reporting practices are concerned. National origins and institutions matter, contradicting the assumption of isomorphic pressures. Firms from smaller/open economies in Europe in particular combine high degrees of internationalization with the most proactive environmental reporting strategies. The degree of divergence with the U.S. and Japan varies between sectors, but holds in all cases. In turn, these firms also operate with different approaches, perceptions of accountability, and "discursive power" in their home countries.

Hence, nationality still matters, but it is unclear whether it matters as much as it did in the past. It is not appropriate, however, to conclude that it matters less, *because* multinationality of firms matters more. Nationality is a fleeting concept as well. National institutional settings are also dynamic, different than the dominant "national business system" literature suggests (cf. also Casson & Lundan, 1999), which has been one of the reasons why this chapter adopted a slightly different typology than is used in mainstream institutional literature. The national and international bargaining situation is part of a dynamic process, as ongoing developments with regard to environmental reporting legislation demonstrate. After the finalization of the study included in this chapter, new initiatives have been taken in both Japan and Europe, but not in the U.S. (Kolk, 2003). In Japan, the government has developed a range of guidelines on environmental accounting, performance indicators and environmental reporting in general. Japanese firms very rapidly adopted these recommendations (published by both the ministry of the environment and MITI), resulting in an increase in the frequency and conformity of reporting. The particular characteristics of the Japanese bargaining arena, as explained in this chapter, have facilitated domestic policy makers in developing relatively coherent policies (in the usual consultation with Japanese core firms) with specific environmental regulation geared towards the (closed) Japanese context.

In France, the government has adopted a law in 2002 which requires publicly-quoted companies to start with reporting on environmental and social issues. This development, which fits in the state-dominated bargaining situation in this country, will lead to a convergence of environmental reporting practices in Europe, where France used to be exceptional compared to other medium-sized, and more particularly the smaller, countries. With their relatively open bargaining arenas, smaller countries have more actively adopted environmental reporting legislation, reflecting domestic societal concerns and sometimes also higher levels of environmental vulnerability. National environmental regulation has been put in place in spite of the fact that home multinationals are characterized by high degrees of internationalization, and thus have the largest stakes abroad. By this influence on their multinationals' environmental strategies (at home, but most likely also in host countries), and their attempts to have comparable legislation accepted at the international/regional level, small countries have had more political leverage on international environmental regulation than could be expected on the basis of their size.

At the same time, multinationals from smaller countries were already active on environmental reporting before they became subject to legal obligations. This may have resulted from adequate anticipation of regulation, but other factors seem to have played a role as well. Multinationals from smaller countries generally internationalized relatively early, usually adopting multi-domestic strategies that proved to be good entry strategies, but created sizeable coordination problems in later stages. Implementing management tools such as environmental reporting seemed to have been helpful in this regard. So far, it is merely anecdotal information from several firms that can support this claim. Moreover, firms from smaller countries have experienced a greater impetus to present themselves as "good citizens" in host countries because they lacked the backing of strong home governments. Large multinationals thus created a "level playing field" in the bargaining arenas of their home countries, in which they supported government attempts – stimulated by civil society pleas – to arrive at relatively strict national and international environmental rules.

In view of the fact that European firms internationalize mostly within the region, there is ample room for further development of initiatives at this level. This is facilitated by the adoption of legislation in France, and reflected in some recent recommendations by the European Commission, in which disclosure on environmental and social issues (and the "triple bottom line") is encouraged. The absence of developments with regard to environmental reporting in the U.S. means that there are no signs that the current divergence will diminish.

NOTES

1. List as published on 5th August 1996; firms from outside the Triad were excluded for purposes of this study.

2. The firms were first approached in June 1998, with a second mailing in November 1998, and subsequent telephone contact in the first half of 1999. As the number of firms with an environmental or HSE report is increasing rapidly, we did a final check on the non-reporters in May 2000.

3. A statistical test of the five indicators specified in this chapter (size, sector, degree of internationalization, country of origin and nature of environmental reporting) is difficult due to the limited number of observations and the ordinal scale used for classifying environmental reporting. Taking these limitations into account, an exploratory test shows a statistically significant correlation between degree of internationalization and environmental reporting (correlation coefficient of 0.41, with an R-square of 0.17, which might appear not very high but is nevertheless acceptable, also because both the one- and two-tailed T-value is 0.00 – implying a very significant association). Correction for "size" does not lead to major alterations. A univariate regression analysis shows that "country" is more significant in explaining the correlation between internationalization and environmental reporting than "sector." So even when we take into account that countries consist of different mixes of sectors, the country factor seems more dominant than the sector origins of firms. These results are nevertheless provisional. More research on reporting strategies, using a continuous rather than an ordinal scale, is under way.

4. There is, however, a relatively recent EPA initiative to reward firms with a good environmental system with a friendlier approach by regulators.

ACKNOWLEDGMENTS

We gratefully acknowledge Douglas van den Berghe for supporting the data collection on internationalization of core firms, Susanne van de Wateringen for analyzing environmental reporting of core firms and Fabienne Fortanier for statistical support with previous versions of the paper.

REFERENCES

Adams, C. A., Hill, W., & Roberts, C. B. (1998). Corporate social reporting practices in western Europe: Legitimating corporate behaviour? *British Accounting Review*, *30*(1), 1–21.

Al-Tuwaijri, S. A., & Christensen, T. E. (1999). The relation between environmental disclosure and environmental performance: A simultaneous equations approach. Paper, 1999 Financial Economics and Accounting Conference, Austin.

Bowie, N., & Vaaler, P. (1999). Some arguments for universal moral standards. In: G. Enderle (Ed.), *International Business Ethics: Challenges and Approaches* (pp. 160–173). Notre Dame: University of Notre Dame Press.

Cameron, D. (1978). The expansion of the public economy: A comparative analysis. *American Political Science Review*, *LXXII*(4), 1243–1261.

Casson, M., & Lundan, S. (1999). Explaining international differences in economic institutions: A critique of the national business system as an analytical tool. *International Studies of Management and Organization*, *29*(2), 25–42.

Chan, C. C. C., & Milne, M. J. (1999). Investor reactions to corporate environmental saints and sinners: An experimental analysis. *Accounting and Business Research*, *29*(4), 265–279.

Christmann, P., & Taylor, G. (2001). Globalization and the environment: Determinants of firm self-regulation in China. *Journal of International Business Studies*, *32*(3), 439–458.

Davis-Walling, P., & Batterman, S. A. (1997). Environmental reporting by the fortune 50 firms. *Environmental Management*, *21*(6), 865–875.

Deegan, C., & Gordon, B. (1996). A study of the environmental disclosure practices of Australian corporations. *Accounting and Business Research*, *26*(3), 187–199.

Delmas, M. (2000). *Globalization of environmental management standards: Barriers and incentives.* Bren School of Environmental Science and Management, University of California, Santa Barbara.

DiMaggio, P., & Powell, W. W. (1983). The iron cage revisited: Institutional isomorphism and collective rationality in organizational fields. *American Sociological Review*, *48*, 147–160.

Dunning, J. (1993). *Multinational enterprises and the global economy.* Workingham: Addison-Wesley.

Gentry, B. (1999). Foreign direct investment and the environment: Boon or bane? In: OECD, *Foreign Direct Investment and the Environment* (pp. 21–46). Paris: OECD.

Gomes-Casseres, B. (1990). Firm ownership preferences and host government restrictions: An integrated approach. *Journal of International Business Studies*, *21*(1), 1–22.

Gray, R., Javad, M. J., Power, D. M., & Sinclair, C. D. (2001). Social and environmental disclosure and corporate characteristics: A research note and extension. *Journal of Business Finance & Accounting, 28*(3), 327–356.

Haas, E. (1990). *When knowledge is power: Three models of change in international organizations.* Berkeley: University of California Press.

Halme, M., & Huse, M. (1997). The influence of corporate governance, industry and country factors on environmental reporting. *Scandinavian Journal of Management, 13*(2), 137–157.

Hoffman, A. J. (1999). Institutional evolution and change: Environmentalism and the U.S. chemical industry. *Academy of Management Journal, 42*(4), 351–371.

Hofstede, G. (1980). *Culture's consequences.* London and Beverly Hills: Sage.

Kahn, M. E. (2000). United States pollution intensive trade trends from 1972 to 1992. Paper, Columbia University.

Katzenstein, P. (1985). *Small states in world markets: Industrial policy in Europe.* Ithaca and London: Cornell University Press.

Kolk, A. (2000). *Economics of environmental management.* Harlow: Financial Times Prentice Hall.

Kolk, A. (2003). Trends in sustainability reporting by the Fortune Global 250. *Business strategy and the environment, 12*(5), 279–291.

Kolk, A., & Levy, D. (2001). Winds of change: Corporate strategy, climate change and oil multinationals. *European Management Review, 19*(5), 501–509.

Kolk, A., Walhain, S., & van de Wateringen, S. (2001). Environmental reporting by the fortune global 250: Exploring the influence of nationality and sector. *Business Strategy and the Environment, 10*(1), 15–29.

KPMG/UvA (2002). KPMG International Survey of Corporate Sustainability Reporting. De Meern.

KPMG/WIMM (1999). KPMG International Survey of Environmental Reporting. The Hague/Amsterdam.

Kristensen, P.-H., & Levinson, J. (1983) *The small country squeeze.* Forlaget for Safundsokonomi og Planlaegning, Roskilde, 336.

Krut, R., & Moretz, A. (2000). The state of global environmental reporting: Lessons from the global 100. *Corporate Environmental Strategy, 7*(1), 85–91.

Kurasaka, T. (1997). Attitudes and experiences of the Japanese business community vis-à-vis EMS standards. In: C. Sheldon (Ed.), *ISO14001 and Beyond. Environmental Management Systems in the Real World* (pp. 155–168). Sheffield: Greenleaf Publishing.

Levy, D., & Egan, D. (1998). Capital contests: National and transnational channels of corporate influence on the climate change negotiations. *Politics and Society, 26*(3), 337–361.

Line, M., Hawley, H., & Krut, R. (2002). The state of global environmental reporting: Lessons from the global 100. *Corporate Environmental Strategy, 9*(1), 69–78.

Litfin, K. (1994). *Ozone discourses: Science and politics in global environmental cooperation.* New York: Columbia University Press.

Lober, D. J., Bynum, D., Campbell, E., & Jacques, M. (1997). The 100 plus corporate environmental report study: A survey of an evolving environmental management tool. *Business Strategy and the Environment, 6*(3), 57–73.

Low, P. (Ed.) (1982). *International trade and the environment.* Discussion Paper, No. 159. Washington: World Bank.

Mani, M., & Wheeler, D. (1999). In Search of Pollution Havens? Dirty Industry in the World Economy, 1960–1995. Room document presented to the OECD conference on FDI and the Environment, The Hague.

Neu, D., Warsame, H., & Pedwell, K. (1998). Managing public impressions: Environmental disclosures in annual reports. *Accounting, Organizations and Society, 23*(3), 265–282.

OECD (1997). *Foreign direct investment and the environment: An overview of the literature.* Paris.

OECD (2000). *Corporate responsibility: Results of a fact-finding mission on private initiatives.* Paris, DAFFE/IME(2000)/15.

Pauly, L. W., & Reich, S. (1997). National structures and multinational corporate behavior: Enduring differences in the age of globalization. *International Organization, 51*(1), 1–30.

Rugman, A. M., & D'Cruz, J. (2000). *Multinationals as flagship firms: Regional business networks.* Oxford: Oxford University Press.

Rugman, A. M., & Verbeke, A. (1998). Corporate strategies and environmental regulations: An organizing framework. *Strategic Management Journal, 19*, 363–375.

Ruigrok, W., & van Tulder, R. (1995). *The logic of international restructuring.* London and New York: Routledge.

Sethi, S. P., & Elango, B. (1999). The influence of "country of origin" on multinational corporation strategy: A conceptual framework. *Journal of International Management, 5*, 285–298.

Sullivan, D. (1996). Measuring the degree of internationalization: A reply. *Journal of International Business Studies, 27*(1), 179–192.

Tsai, T., & Child, J. (1997). Strategic responses of multinational corporations to environmental demands. *Journal of General Management, 23*(1), 1–22.

Tulder, R. van (Ed.) (1989). *Small industrial countries and economic and technological development.* The Hague: NOTA.

Tulder, R. van, Berghe, D., & van den Muller, A. (2001). *The Erasmus (S)coreboard of core companies. The world's largest multinationals.* Rotterdam: EUR.

UNCTAD (1999). *World investment report 1999. Foreign direct investment and the challenge of development.* New York and Geneva: United Nations.

UNCTAD (2000). *World investment report 2000. Cross-border mergers and acquisitions and development.* New York and Geneva: United Nations.

U.S.AEP (1997). *Candid views of Fortune 500 companies.* U.S.-Asia Environmental Partnership.

Vernon, R. (1971). *Sovereignty at bay: The international spread of U.S. enterprises.* New York: Basic Books.

Walden, W. D., & Schwartz, B. N. (1997). Environmental disclosures and public policy pressure. *Journal of Accounting and Public Policy, 16*, 125–154.

Wartick, S., & Wood, D. (1998). *International business and society.* Malden: Blackwell.

Whitley, R. (1999). *Divergent capitalisms: The social structuring and change of business systems.* Oxford: Oxford University Press.

Zarsky, L. (1999). Havens, halos and spaghetti: Untangling the evidence about foreign direct investment and the environment. In: OECD, *Foreign Direct Investment and the Environment* (pp. 47–74). Paris: OECD.

ENVIRONMENTAL SELF-REGULATION IN THE GLOBAL ECONOMY: THE ROLE OF FIRM CAPABILITIES

Petra Christmann and Glen Taylor

ABSTRACT

Globalization increases concerns about national governments' ability to regulate firms' environmental conduct because firms can avoid complying with stringent environmental regulations by locating polluting operations in countries with low regulations. Business self-regulation is increasingly seen as a force that can counterbalance the decreasing power of governments in the global economy. Previous research identified external stakeholder pressures as an important determinant of business self-regulation. In this chapter we explore how firm capabilities affect the likelihood that firms self-regulate their environmental conduct by adopting ISO 14000 environmental standards. Our findings show that firm capabilities are indeed an important determinant of self-regulation in the global economy. We discuss implications of this finding for governments, other stakeholders, and business decision makers.

INTRODUCTION

Globalization can be seen as a relatively new phenomenon that is made possible by vastly improved and expanded global communications and transportation infrastructure combined with falling barriers to international trade and foreign

Multinationals, Environment and Global Competition
Research in Global Strategic Management, Volume 9, 119–145
© 2004 Published by Elsevier Ltd.
ISSN: 1064-4857/doi:10.1016/S1064-4857(03)09006-5

investment. Globalization results in an increasingly complex system of interdependent markets and sources of supply for goods and services. It also brings societal expectations in countries around the world into direct contact with one another, and gives rise to concerns about an increasing inability of national governments to regulate firm conduct in areas such as environmental protection. The phenomenon of globalization poses new challenges for firms. Firms participating in the global economy are experiencing pressures from a variety of national and international stakeholders to address social concerns such as environmental conduct. Capabilities that allow firms to effectively self-regulate their environmental conduct by controlling the environmental impact of their operations worldwide to secure a good reputation for environmental management with customers and other stakeholders are becoming more important as a source of competitive advantage in the global economy.

A rapidly growing number of firms self-regulate their environmental conduct by adopting various international standards. Firm self-regulation can be expected to play an important role in reducing firms' environmental impact in developing countries, because many of these countries are characterized by low levels of environmental regulations and/or weak enforcement. At the same time, firms in developing countries can be expected to face particular challenges in implementing international standards for environmental conduct, because these firms frequently have lower capabilities to address environmental management challenges. Many environmental standards are difficult to implement without an educated workforce, participatory management, and capabilities to make changes in products and production processes. In this chapter, we examine how a firm's capabilities affect the likelihood that it will self-regulate its environmental conduct by adopting a particular international voluntary environmental standard – specifically, the *ISO 14000* series of environmental management system standards.

The successful implementation of *ISO 14000* requires systemic changes to a firm's management processes that may be particularly difficult to implement in developing countries in which factors such as the level of education of the workforce impose important organizational constraints. We suggest that a firm's ability and likelihood to self-regulate its environmental conduct by adopting *ISO 14000* environmental standards depends on complementary assets and capabilities (Teece, 1986). These complementary assets are developed in the normal course of business and can be leveraged in the implementation of firms' environmental policies (Christmann, 2000). We identify four complementary assets that we expect to facilitate the implementation of *ISO 14000*: The level of innovative capability of the firm (Christmann, 2000); the level of education of the firm's employees; the firm's capabilities to implement a management system, and the participation of employees in environmental management processes. We empirically test whether these three complementary assets contribute to adoption of *ISO 14000* standards for a sample of firms in China – a rapidly growing developing country.

PERSPECTIVES ON THE EFFECTS OF GLOBALIZATION ON THE ENVIRONMENT

Critics of globalization stress the potential for multinational enterprises (MNEs) to undermine national systems of government regulation by stressing the vulnerability of developing countries when bargaining with MNEs for foreign direct investment (Korten, 1995). It is argued that developing countries attract MNE investment in polluting industries by lowering their environmental standards and easing enforcement of environmental regulations, because these actions lower firms' production costs. One of the concerns frequently raised is that the global economy offers new avenues for MNEs to circumvent stringent environmental regulations in developed countries by locating polluting operations in developing countries with low levels of environmental regulation (Leonard, 1988). To remain competitive in global markets, all MNEs would have to adopt similar approaches. To attract foreign direct investment, all countries would be forced to compete by lowering their environmental standards. These competitive pressures would then create a downward spiral, sometimes called a "race to the bottom," in which countries continually lower their standards and MNEs move production capacity to low regulation countries to reduce their costs and improve competitiveness (Spar & Yoffie, 2000). As a result, in a race to the bottom situation, countries with low regulation would be expected to become production and export platforms for polluting industries.

An alternative "self-regulation" view of globalization has recently emerged based on the observation that many MNEs and firms in their global supply chains choose to operate according to global standards that exceed local government regulations in many developing countries (Christmann & Taylor, 2001; Rugman & Verbeke, 1998a; Spar & Yoffie, 2000). The critique of globalization is focused on the role of government regulations and assumes that firms do just enough to comply with local environmental regulations. For firms participating in the global economy however, local environmental regulations are only one consideration in designing environmental strategies (Rugman & Verbeke, 1998a). Various stakeholders pressure MNEs to design environmental strategies that go far beyond local government regulations and enforcement standards. Non-governmental organizations (NGOs) represent a wide range of stakeholders and special interest groups seeking to influence public policy and MNE decision makers. NGOs extend their reach beyond national borders by drawing attention to issues in foreign countries that have an impact on their home constituencies, and by focusing on areas of special international interest such as the environment (Lundan, 2001). NGOs can appeal to the values and interests of consumers in developed countries that represent the largest markets for products from developing countries. MNEs can be pressured by their developed country customers to adopt effective environmental management systems and to improve the transparency of their operations by more accurately reporting their environmental performance (Christmann, 1998). NGOs can also influence investors by encouraging them to consider the global environmental performance of MNEs as an investment criteria (Christmann & Taylor, 2002). Pressures from NGOs, customers, and investors constrain the range of choices available to firms by forcing them to legitimize their behavior and conform to social norms (DiMaggio & Powell, 1983; Oliver, 1997). Thus, even where national government regulations are low, other stakeholders may exert pressures on MNEs to "self-regulate" their environmental impact by taking actions that exceed the requirements of national government regulations. Business self-regulation has come to be seen as an important element in overcoming the problems caused by ineffective and poorly enforced government regulations in many developing countries. Many participants in the United Nations Conference on Environment and Development (UNCED) held in Rio de Janeiro in 1992 expressed the opinion that business self-regulation was an essential element in improving environmental performance of firms.

The self-regulation view suggests that globalization shifts the focus in developing countries from national governments as regulators of environmental conduct to NGOs and other stakeholders as advocates of higher international standards. While globalization erodes the power of national governments to regulate firm conduct as falling barriers to trade and investment allow firms to exploit cross-country differences in environmental regulations, other stakeholders such as international NGOs are becoming more influential in shaping the environmental conduct of firms participating in the global economy. One of the ways in which NGOs extend their influence is by conducting public relations campaigns to gain leverage over firms that rely on building brand reputations. NGOs pressure companies by targeting firms whose customers might vote with their wallets unless high standards of conduct are promised and delivered. Because NGOs closely scrutinize and publicize the environmental conduct of MNEs, poor environmental conduct in foreign countries has the potential to negatively affect an MNE's global reputation for environmental responsibility and legitimacy (Christmann, 1998). In response to these pressures, MNEs will find it very difficult to adopt lower standards in one country than they adopt in another. NGOs also insist that a firm's environmental responsibilities include responsibility for the conduct of its suppliers (Gereffi, Garcia-Johnson & Sasser, 2001). By targeting firms at the retail end of the supply chain, such as the Home Depot, Lowe's, and Staples, NGOs exploit the vulnerability of MNE corporate reputations and brand images in order to influence purchasing practices. NGOs used this tactic to criticize the forest product purchasing practices of these companies with the hope that this would force them to require firms in their international supply chains to adopt more responsible environmental practices. Thus, environmental damage caused by suppliers can threaten the social legitimacy of their foreign customers, and as a result, customers from developed countries are increasingly concerned about the environmental performance of the firms in their supply chains. Many firms, such as Ford, Shell, and Toyota include environmental performance as a criterion for selecting suppliers. What begins as customer expectations for higher environmental performance in one country can end with environmental self-regulation being adopted by suppliers wherever they are located in the global economy.

Empirical evidence supports the view that national environmental regulations are not a major determinant of MNEs' location decisions and of firms' environmental policies in developing countries. Studies of foreign direct investment flows found no evidence that variations in environmental regulations across countries affected the location choices of MNEs (Duerksen & Leonard, 1980; Leonard, 1988; Walter, 1982). Empirical studies have also analyzed whether countries with low levels of environmental regulations turn into pollution havens and become production and export platforms for dirty industries (for a review of studies see Jaffe, Peterson & Portney, 1995). While these studies found that developing countries attracted more pollution intensive industrial sectors when environmental regulation in industrialized countries increased in the 1970s and 1980s (Low & Yeats, 1992; Lucas, Wheeler & Hettige, 1992), it is not clear whether this is due to a normal pattern of industrial development in which pollution intensive industries such as steel are associated with early stages of industrialization. Studies that have tried to estimate whether countries with low environmental regulations become exporters of pollution-intensive goods have so far failed to detect any significant relationship (Tobey, 1990).

While the empirical evidence does not support the hypothesis that MNEs relocate their polluting activities to low regulation countries, there is evidence showing that MNEs are increasingly moving towards adopting 'global environmental standards' – standards set for all their worldwide operations that exceed the regulatory environmental standards that are imposed and enforced in developing countries (Christmann, 1998; Dowell, Hart & Yeung, 2000). One of the reasons for this finding may be that MNEs adopt standards that reflect the demands for more responsible environmental conduct in developed countries even if local governments in developing countries do not impose and enforce stringent environmental regulations (Christmann & Taylor, 2001). Another reason for the adoption of global environmental standards by MNEs is that such standards may contribute to firm performance (Dowell, Hart & Yeung, 2000). These reasons suggest that the cost savings from locating operations in low regulation countries are not as large as differences in environmental government regulations suggest.

The fact that manufacturing plants in developing countries vary widely in their environmental performance further supports the view that government regulations are not the main determinant of firms' environmental conduct in countries with low environmental regulations. In Thailand and Mexico, studies found large variations in the environmental performance of firms even when all firms are subject to the same level of environmental regulations and enforcement (Dasgupta, Hettige & Wheeler, 2000; Hettige et al., 1996). While some plants were found to violate local standards, other plants had environmental performance that far exceeded local standards, and some even complied with environmental regulations equivalent to industrialized country standards.

THE ROLE OF VOLUNTARY INTERNATIONAL ENVIRONMENTAL STANDARDS

Various stakeholders have become involved in efforts that seek to codify and simplify conflicting and competing stakeholder expectations into widely adopted global standards. MNEs and their suppliers are major beneficiaries from these efforts. The need to harmonize standards to facilitate global trade is one of the key driving forces behind the emergence of global environmental standards and other international voluntary environmental initiatives. From a corporate perspective, a consistent set of internationally harmonized requirements for environmental conduct offers substantial advantages over competing and often contradictory expectations and requirements imposed by various stakeholders. The interplay of MNEs seeking simplified standards and NGOs seeking to have their particular area of interest enshrined in a global code of conduct or standard has produced a small but rapidly growing set of international voluntary environmental initiatives, the adoption of which is not required by government regulations (Christmann & Taylor, 2002). By adopting these standards and initiatives, MNEs and other firms assume some degree of responsibility for environmental self-regulation.

There is a wide range of voluntary initiatives for environmental self-regulation, ranging from broad statements of management principles, to corporate governance "codes-of-conduct" as well as to far more specific standards for the implementation of environmental management systems and environmental disclosure.

For example, the United Nation's (UN) *Global Compact* simply lists broad environmental, labor, and human rights principles for firms to follow, whereas the Global Reporting Initiative's (GRI) *Sustainability Reporting Guidelines* provide a reporting structure for environmental, economic, and social performance. The *ISO 14001* standard lays out specific requirements for the implementation of an environmental management system. Voluntary environmental initiatives also differ in the way that compliance with requirements is monitored. Some initiatives do not have external verification requirements, while others require external monitoring of compliance. For example, firms participating in the UN *Global Compact* are required to submit progress reports that are not externally audited. In contrast, *ISO 14001* requires independent third-party certification of compliance.

Voluntary environmental initiatives are advocated as a modification of corporate governance that compensates for the potential failure of national governments to implement and enforce environmental regulations. The UNCED recommendations on Sustainable Development set forth in *Agenda 21*, which was adopted by the participants of the Rio Conference, encouraged the development and adoption of voluntary initiatives. International voluntary initiatives that are particularly effective in counterbalancing the shortfall of government regulations are initiatives with specific requirements that make it possible to verify firms' adherence to the initiative's requirements combined with independent compliance monitoring (Christmann & Taylor, 2002). Without these characteristics voluntary environmental initiatives are often little more than statements of good intentions with little or no impact on firm behavior.

The increasing prevalence of global standards for environmental conduct that exceed national government regulations suggests that a firm's ability to implement such standards may become an important factor in determining its competitiveness in the global marketplace. The willingness of a firm to adopt a voluntary environmental initiative and assume responsibility for environmental self-regulation is influenced by the extent to which the firm already has a good foundation of related capabilities. Some NGOs and governments view MNEs and firms in their supply chains as essential participants in the search for solutions to environmental problems. MNEs have the financial, technical, and organizational resources and capabilities to do something about environmental issues in developing countries. MNEs can transfer their environmental capabilities from their operations in more developed countries with more stringent environmental regulations to developing countries with lower levels of environmental regulations (Porter & van der Linde, 1995). Knowledge transfers by MNEs to subsidiaries provide access to better environmental technologies in developing countries than are available to local firms. In addition, firms transfer capabilities to their suppliers through conscientious supplier development activities (Wolf & Taylor, 1991) as well as through other contacts between the customers and suppliers (Kraatz, 1998). In this chapter, we examine the relationship between the development of a firm's capabilities and its adoption of a particular international voluntary environmental initiative – the *ISO 14001* management system.

THE *ISO 14000* ENVIRONMENTAL MANAGEMENT SYSTEM

A Tool for Self-Regulation

To effectively counterbalance potential failures of government regulations to protect the environment in the global economy, voluntary initiatives need to have specific criteria along with independent third-party monitoring. The *ISO 14000* series of environmental management standards meets these criteria. *ISO 14000* is a series of voluntary international standards covering environmental management tools and systems developed by the International Organization for Standardization (ISO). ISO, a Swiss-based worldwide organization of national standards bodies from 111 countries, is perhaps best known for developing the *ISO 9000* series of quality management system standards. ISO develops its standards through a process of expert consensus-building in which member countries nominate representatives to develop and ratify new standards. The *ISO 14000* series was officially launched in September 1996. The intent of the *ISO 14000* series is to provide all industries with a structure for an environmental management system that will ensure that all operational processes are consistent and effective and will achieve the stated environmental objectives of a given organization. The foundation for *ISO 14000* is the *ISO 14001* Environmental Management System (EMS), which can be certified by passing an independent third-party audit. EMS implementation does not guarantee that all environmental problems are solved, just as the implementation of an accounting system does not ensure that a company will be profitable. Despite the limitations, empirical evidence suggests that EMS implementation improves environmental performance (Montabon et al., 2000).

Determinants of ISO 14000 Adoption: Existing Research
Research on the adoption of management system standards has used a variety of theoretical perspectives to explain which firms are more likely to adopt these standards. Researchers have found that isomorphic pressures operating across borders are an important force contributing to the international diffusion of *ISO 9000* and *ISO 14000* certification (Christmann & Taylor, 2001; Corbett & Kirsch, 2001;

Guler, Guillen & MacPherson, 2002). These cross-border isomorphic pressures include trade ties and pressures from foreign customers (Christmann & Taylor, 2001; Corbett & Kirsch, 2001; Guler, Guillen & MacPherson, 2002, concluded that customer pressures from export markets or foreign customers are an important determinant of the likelihood of *ISO 14000* adoption in China. Similarly, Corbett and Kirsch (2001) found that countries with higher export propensity had higher *ISO 14000* certification counts and Terlaak and King (2001) found that exports were a significant determinant of *ISO 9000* adoption for facilities located in the United States. Increased adoption by rival firms was found to lead to mimetic isomorphism in *ISO 9000* adoption (Guler, Guillen & MacPherson, 2002). Only a few studies have focused on the role of firm capabilities as a determinant of ISO adoption. King and Lenox (2001) found that certain firm characteristics facilitated early adoption of *ISO 14001* in the United States. Some of the firm characteristics that they included in their study, such as R&D intensity and *ISO 9000* certification, are indicators of firm capabilities and both of these were found to contribute to *ISO 14001* adoption. This review of the existing research suggests that so far not much attention has been paid on the role of internal capabilities as determinants of *ISO 14000* adoption, especially for firms in developing countries.

Determinants of ISO 14000 Adoption: The Role of Firm Capabilities
The presence of external pressures for environmental self-regulation and the availability of globally recognized standards for EMS are, by themselves, not sufficient to predict whether or not firms in developing countries will embrace *ISO 14000*. The resource-based view of the firm (RBV) (Barney, 1986, 1991; Dierickx & Cool, 1989; Penrose, 1959; Rumelt, 1991; Teece, 1986; Wernerfelt, 1984) suggests that firm capabilities are an important determinant of firm behavior and that differences in firm performance are primarily the result of resource heterogeneity between firms. We draw on the RBV to examine the role of firm capabilities as a determinant of self-regulation by *ISO 14000* adoption in developing countries.

Christmann and Taylor (2002) suggested that internal firm capabilities are an important factor that firms need to consider in their decision-making framework to evaluate alternative approaches to self-regulation. A firm should only adopt proactive or accommodative approaches to self-regulation regarding a specific environmental issue if it possesses capabilities that allow it to address the environmental issue effectively. Environmental management practices are often difficult to separate from a firm's other activities (Hart, 1995). Thus, capabilities that firms have developed in the normal course of business are frequently required to successfully implement environmental policies and to self-regulate environmental conduct. Firms can leverage the capabilities they have developed in the normal course of their business to implement their environmental policies and adopt more effective environmental practices at lower relative cost (Christmann, 2000). The existing capabilities that can be leveraged are thus complementary assets (Teece, 1986), i.e. assets that are required to capture the benefits associated with the implementation of certain environmental practices.

Thus, existing firm capabilities may be important determinants of a firm's ability and willingness to implement environmental self-regulation. Empirical studies have found that firm capabilities affect the likelihood of adoption of *ISO 14000* in the United States (King & Lenox, 2001), that firm characteristics affect the implementation of environmental programs (Aragon-Correa, 1998), and that capabilities affect firms' ability to gain competitive advantage from environmental strategies (Christmann, 2000). We identify four firm capabilities that are likely to affect a firm's ability and/or cost of self-regulating their environmental conduct by implementing the *ISO 14000* environmental management system: Innovative capabilities, the level of education of the workforce, the organizational dispersion of environmental responsibilities, and the firm's ability to implement management system standards.

Christmann (2000) identified innovative capabilities as an important moderating variable in the relationship between the implementation of certain "best practices" of environmental management and resulting cost advantages. Firms were able to leverage innovative capabilities in the implementation of their environmental practices, which led to higher cost advantages from the implementation of environmental "best practices." King and Lenox (2001) found that the R&D intensity of a firm, which can be expected to be related to the firm's innovative capabilities, was positively related to *ISO 14000* adoption for facilities in the United States. This suggests that innovative capabilities may be complementary assets (Teece, 1986) that facilitate the implementation of *ISO 14000*. While *ISO 14000* is primarily an organizational innovation rather than a technological innovation, firms that have the capability to innovate in their production processes and products are more likely to have a better understanding of their existing processes and can use this knowledge to facilitate *ISO 14000* implementation. An *ISO 14001* environmental management system requires firms to evaluate the environmental aspects and impacts of their operations, document the processes and control the parameters that affect their environmental impacts, as well as to monitor and measure the critical environmental parameters and take corrective actions when problems occur. Firms that possess innovative capabilities, particularly capabilities for process innovation, can be expected to have a better understanding of their production processes than other firms, which facilitates the documentation, monitoring, and measurement of environmental impacts, as well as the implementation of corrective actions. In addition, firms that are innovative in their products and their implementation of new technologies may also have better capabilities to implement organizational innovations such as *ISO 14000*. Thus, we can develop the following hypothesis:

Hypothesis 1. The higher a firm's innovative capabilities, the more likely the firm will be to adopt *ISO 14000*.

An additional complementary asset that can be expected to affect the ease of implementation of the *ISO 14000* standards is a firm's absorptive capacity (Cohen & Levinthal, 1990), i.e. the firm's ability to successfully assimilate and implement the knowledge embodied in the *ISO 14000* standards. *ISO 14000* is a codified set of standards that has been designed to be implemented by firms worldwide, and numerous consultants offer services to help firms with *ISO 14000* implementation. Thus, the knowledge necessary to implement *ISO 14000* is easily available and not tacit. However, a firm may not have the capability to absorb this knowledge and implement the *ISO 14000* system in its own operations. While previous research has analyzed the absorptive capacity in the context of knowledge transfer and identified endowments of relevant technologies and R&D investments as important determinants of a firm's absorptive capacity (Cohen & Levinthal, 1990; Mowery, Oxley & Silverman, 1996; Szulanski, 1996), the absorptive capacity required to successfully implement *ISO 14000* can be expected to reside in the firm's workforce. This is because *ISO 14000* requires extensive involvement of employees and documentation of procedures in written documents. In developing countries, firms may face special challenges in implementing *ISO 14000*. Frequently, large proportions of the workforce lack the basic levels of literacy and numeric ability that is required for successful implementation and use of *ISO 14001* as an environmental management system. Thus, the level of education of a firm's workforce can be expected to become an important determinant of the absorptive capacity in developing countries.

Hypothesis 2. The higher the education level of a firm's workforce the more likely the firm will be to adopt *ISO 14000*.

A third capability that affects a firm's ability to successfully implement *ISO 14000* standards is the firm's management system implementation capability. A "management system" refers to what the organization does to manage its processes or activities. A management system requires the definition of goals and objectives and the establishment of policies, defined processes and an organizational structure to support these goals. Management system standards, such as the *ISO 14001* EMS, provide the organization with a model to follow in setting up and operating the management system. A firm's capability to implement management systems can be expected to be an important determinant of the firm's decision to adopt the *ISO 14001* EMS, which is the central element of the *ISO 14000* standards. Firms that have already implemented management systems with similar requirements, such as standards within the *ISO 9000* series of quality management systems are likely to have developed capabilities of management system implementation that they can leverage in their implementation of the *ISO 14001* environmental management system. This is supported by the findings of previous studies that have found a positive relationship between *ISO 9000* certification and *ISO 14001* adoption (Corbett & Kirsch, 2001; King & Lenox, 2001).

Hypothesis 3. Firms that possess superior management system implementation capabilities are more likely to adopt the *ISO 14001* EMS.

Innovative capabilities, educated employees, and management system implementation capabilities provide a good basis for the adoption of *ISO 14000*. To leverage these complementary assets in the development of an environmental management system requires broad participation by employees throughout the organization. The *ISO 14001* EMS requires firms to define the roles and responsibilities for environmental management. Firms that do not yet have broad employee involvement in the implementation of their environmental policies can expand participation by gradually extending involvement to include all employees working within the system. This can be time consuming. Alternatively, a firm can implement major changes in the organization of their environmental responsibilities rapidly, which has the potential to cause disruptions in the firm's operations. In both cases there are costs associated with the organizational changes required to achieve broad involvement. This suggests that firms that have already dispersed the responsibility for the implementation of their environmental policies throughout the organization are in a better position to implement the *ISO 14001* EMS.

Hypothesis 4. The more dispersed a firm's environmental responsibilities are the more likely the firm will be to adopt *ISO 14000*.

RESEARCH DESIGN

Research Setting

We test these hypotheses using data from multinational and domestic firms in China, the world's most populous country. China has experienced high economic growth and rapid industrialization since the economic reforms of 1978. At the same time, China's regulatory system has not been effective in protecting the environment. Despite a complex system of environmental laws and regulations and a network of environmental officials throughout China, compliance with environmental regulations remains low. Two factors account for low compliance rates. First, China's environmental regulations are relatively flexible. Emissions that exceed official standards are not considered legal violations (Wang & Chen, 1999), but are instead subject to a compensation fee charged for these emissions according to the quantities and concentrations of pollutants released. Estimates suggest that the compensation fee charge only amounts to 20% of the costs that firms would incur if they were to reduce pollution to the levels required by regulation (Wang, 2000). This makes pollution more profitable for firms than compliance, so that many enterprises prefer to pay the fines rather than reduce pollution. As a result, approximately 500,000 factories have been charged for their emissions since the compensation fee system was implemented nationally in 1982 (Wang, 2000). Second, the enforcement of regulations is relatively arbitrary (Qu, 1991). The vagueness of standards in many laws and regulations, coupled with the lack of a comprehensive enforcement regime, has led to a situation where many environmental laws still reflect deals cut between the local environmental protection agencies, the National Environmental Protection Agency, other ministries, local government bodies, and the polluting enterprises. In addition, local regulators have considerable discretion in judging both compliance and appropriate penalties for non-compliance (Dasgupta, Huq & Wheeler, 1997) so that enforcement differs across provinces (Wang & Wheeler, 1996). Rapid growth and industrialization combined with ineffective environmental regulation have contributed to serious environmental problems. China is home to at least half of the world's ten most polluted cities and environmental pollution is expanding into the countryside (NEPA, 1997). Levels of particulate air pollution in several of China's cities such as Shanghai and Shenyang are among the highest in the world, contributing to associated problems such as lung disease. Environmental problems are also seriously affecting overall social and economic development in the country. Chinese government estimates of the economic costs associated with ecological destruction and environmental pollution have reached as high as 14% of the country's gross national product (GNP) (Chen, 1997). The Government of China has identified environmental factors as one of the four leading factors influencing the morbidity and mortality of China's people today (NEPA, 1997). China also has the potential to seriously impact the global environment. Within 25 years, China is expected to overtake the United States as the world's largest emitter of greenhouse gases, a major cause of global warming.

Despite recent efforts of the Chinese Government to increase the stringency and enforcement of environmental regulations (World Resources Institute, 1998), this situation clearly indicates that environmental self-regulation can play a critical role in improving the environmental quality in China. Firms in China have started to adopt *ISO 14000*. But as of June 1999 when data was collected for this study, only 81 facilities in China had received *ISO 14001* certification (ISO World, 1999).

Data Collection and Survey Design

We collected data through a survey of Chinese managers participating in two seminars on standards-based management practices conducted by Asia Pacific Economic Cooporation (APEC). These seminars were held in Shenzhen and Shanghai in May 1999. Shenzhen and Shanghai were selected as data collection sites because they are both located in Special Economic Zones in which the Chinese Government promotes openness to foreign direct investment (FDI). These provinces might thus be a good illustration for what will happen in other provinces now that China has joined the World Trade Organization (WTO). However, we also recognize that firms in provinces with less FDI may have lower levels of capabilities to implement *ISO 14000*.

We designed the survey in three steps. First, we designed a preliminary version, translated it into Chinese, and pre-tested it with several Chinese managers in Beijing in March 1999. We also discussed the survey with employees of the China Quality Certification Center (CQC), the largest ISO certifying agency in China, and with APEC experts and officials. Second, we revised the survey based on comments obtained in the first step and discussed the new version again with APEC experts and officials. Third, we created a final English version of the survey incorporating their feedback. This version was professionally translated into Chinese and back-translated into English in order to assure the accuracy of the translation.

Common method bias can pose problems for survey research that relies on self-reported data (Campbell & Fiske, 1959) by artificially inflating observed relationships between variables. In order to diminish if not avoid the effects of consistency artifacts, the dependent variables were placed after the independent variables in the survey (Salancik & Pfeffer, 1977).

Surveys were administered to seminar participants before each seminar to avoid potential response biases resulting from information obtained in the seminar. Seminar participants had one hour to complete the survey. To assure a high response rate and to obtain truthful answers, the survey was administered anonymously and respondents were asked not to identify themselves or their company. Most respondents were high-level executives (president, CEO, vice president) or quality assurance managers. Because participants could see for themselves that the survey was completely anonymous, there was no incentive to inflate responses or overstate their capabilities.

Sample

Potential seminar participants in Shenzhen and Shanghai were identified and invited by CQC. We asked that the invitees come from a representative group of industries, and that they differ in country of firm ownership. These selection criteria were met by our sample of 118 firms, of which 27% were wholly Chinese owned, 38% were partially foreign owned, and 36% were wholly foreign owned. Foreign ownership included Europe, North America, Japan, and other countries. Of the Chinese and partially Chinese-owned firms 38% were state-owned enterprises. Sample firms range in size from small firms with under 50 employees to large ones with more than 5,000 employees, with the majority having between 500 and 1,000 employees.

Of the 118 survey responses 87 were usable for this study. The other responses had incomplete information possibly because some firms had not yet decided on a strategy towards *ISO 14000*.

Measures

Some measures are adopted from existing surveys, while others are original to this study. The definition of all of the measures is shown in Appendix (but none is named in the text).

Dependent Variables
In our sample, only 12 firms (10%) reported they had a certified facility and only 19 other firms (16%) had started the *ISO 14000* implementation process in China. Because most firms had not yet started the implementation process we used the likelihood of *ISO 14000* adoption in China reported by the respondents as a dependent variable. While this is a measure of intentions and not of actual behavior a recent study of recycling (Boldero, 1995) has shown that intentions significantly predict the focal behaviors. We created a measure to capture whether the firm had already been *ISO 14000* certified, or whether it had started the implementation process, or if it had not started the process how likely it was to start the process within the next year.

Independent Variables
We used maximum likelihood factor analysis with varimax rotation to construct measures of three of our firm capability variables – innovative capabilities, the level of employee education, and the dispersion of environmental management – based on ten of our survey items. The survey items for the construction of the

measure of innovative capabilities had been used previously (Christmann, 2000), while the other two scales were originally constructed. A summary of the scales and Cronbach Alpha coefficients for all measures is provided in the Appendix. All Cronbach Alpha coefficients except one exceeded 0.70, indicating sufficient reliability of the measures. While the reliabilities of the scale representing the employee education did not quite meet the 0.70 criterion suggested by Nunnally (1978), it came relatively close to this guideline.

We measure capabilities for management system implementation by using a dummy variable that takes the values of one if the firm has already been *ISO 9000* certified and zero otherwise.

Control Variables

Because multinational companies have the ability to transfer innovative and organizational capabilities across countries, subsidiaries of multinational companies and joint venture companies can be expected to have higher levels of these capabilities than locally-owned firms. In addition, multinational companies and joint ventures may attract more qualified workers because of their ability to pay higher salaries than locally-owned firms. The relationships between firm capabilities and *ISO 14000* adoption may thus differ between MNEs, joint-ventures and locally-owned firms. We control for this effect by including a variable measuring the percentage of multinational ownership on a five-point scale.

Firm size has been found in previous studies to have positive effects on *ISO 14000* adoption (Christmann & Taylor, 2001; Hartman, Huq & Wheeler, 1997), which may be due to economies of scale in ISO implementation. We use the number of employees to control for the effects of firm size.

Because the levels and types of capabilities required to compete successfully differ across industries, we need to control for industry effects. We identified three industries for which the level of at least one capability differed significantly from other industries – electronics, apparel, and toys – and included three industry dummy variables in all equations.

Method and Preliminary Data Analysis

The hypotheses were tested using OLS regression analysis. Before testing the hypotheses we analyzed the likely extent of multicollinearity in the data by analyzing the correlations between the independent variables. Most of the correlations are below 0.3 indicating no problems of multicollinearity (see Table 1). We also evaluated the presence of multivariate multicollinearity using several diagnostic tests suggested by Belsley, Kuh and Welsh (1980). An examination of variance

Table 1. Descriptive Statistics and Correlation Matrix.

	Mean	S.D.	1	2	3	4	5	6	7	8	9	10	11
1. Innovative capabilities	0.00	1.08	1.00										
2. Level of employee education	0.00	1.26	0.03	1.00									
3. Dispersed environmental management	0.00	1.26	−0.04	−0.01	1.00								
4. ISO 9000 certification	0.65	0.48	0.13	0.02	0.00	1.00							
5. MNE ownership	2.10	1.63	0.19†	0.26*	0.02	0.24**	1.00						
6. Customer pressures for ISO 14000 adoption	2.45	1.34	0.18†	−0.02	0.27*	0.15	0.05	1.00					
7. Firm size	5.00	1.04	0.27*	0.02	0.03	0.10	−0.06	0.34**	1.00				
8. Electronics	0.34	0.48	0.16	0.01	−0.01	0.32**	0.16	0.18	0.15	1.00			
9. Toys	0.11	0.31	−0.00	−0.20†	−0.06	−0.05	−0.13	−0.12	0.02	−0.27*	1.00		
10. Apparel	0.10	0.29	−0.22**	−0.02	0.11	−0.12	0.04	0.01	0.17	−0.23*	−0.10	1.00	
11. Likelihood of ISO 14000 adoption	4.38	2.12	0.37***	0.21**	0.26**	0.18†	0.31***	0.49***	0.21**	0.27***	−0.21†	−0.06	1.00

† $p < 0.10$.
* $p < 0.05$.
** $p < 0.001$.
*** $p < 0.001$.

inflation factors and condition indexes revealed that only mild multicollinearity was present in the data.

RESULTS

Our regression results can be seen in Table 2.

Hypothesis 1 stated that firms with higher innovative capabilities are more likely to adopt *ISO 14000* than other firms. This hypothesis is supported by the data. The coefficient for this variable is positive and significant ($p < 0.01$).

Hypothesis 2 stated that firms with higher educated workforces are more likely to adopt *ISO 14000* than other firms. This hypothesis is supported by the data. The coefficient for this variable is positive and significant ($p < 0.10$).

Hypothesis 3 stated that firms that have already obtained *ISO 9000* certification are more likely to adopt *ISO 14000* than other firms. This hypothesis is not supported by the data. While the correlation coefficient between the likelihood

Table 2.   Regression Results.

	Dependent Variable (Likelihood of *ISO 14000* Adoption, $N = 87$)
Intercept	3.27^{**} (1.00)
Explanatory variables	
Innovative capabilities	0.50^{**} (0.19)
Level of employee education	$0.29^{\dagger}$ (0.17)
Dispersed environmental management	0.29^{*} (0.15)
ISO 9000 certification	0.00 (0.41)
Control variables	
Firm size	0.00 (0.20)
MNE ownership	$0.22^{\dagger}$ (0.12)
Customer pressures for *ISO 14000* adoption	1.71^{***} (0.47)
Electronics	0.55 (0.43)
Toys	-0.46 (0.65)
Apparel	-0.00 (0.75)
R^2	0.45
Adjusted R^2	0.38

Note: Standard errors are in parentheses.
$^{\dagger}p < 0.10$.
$^{*}p < 0.05$.
$^{**}p < 0.01$.
$^{***}p < 0.001$.

of *ISO 14000* adoption and *ISO 9000* certification is positive and significant ($p < 0.10$) the regression coefficient is very small and not significant.

Hypothesis 4 stated that firms with more dispersed environmental responsibilities are more likely to adopt *ISO 14000* than other firms. This hypothesis is supported by the data. The coefficient for this variable is positive and significant ($p < 0.05$).

DISCUSSION OF RESULTS

Our results indicate that, in addition to external pressures and multinational ownership, firm capabilities are an important determinant of firm self-regulation such as *ISO 14000* adoption. We identified three firm characteristics that contribute to the likelihood of *ISO 14000* adoption by firms in China: Innovative capabilities, the education level of the firm's employees which is related to the absorptive capacity of the firm, and the dispersion of environmental responsibilities throughout the organization. In contrast to expectations and findings in prior studies, firms that already had obtained *ISO 9000* certification were not found to be more likely to adopt *ISO 14000* than other firms in our regression even though the correlation between the two variables is positive and significant. A possible explanation for this surprising finding may be found in the composition of our sample, which included a high proportion of *ISO 9000* certified firms. Many of the *ISO 9000* certified firms in our sample are MNEs, indicating that MNEs might have higher management system implementation capabilities than other firms in developing countries. MNE ownership is also a significant determinant of the likelihood of *ISO 14000* adoption. Other studies that have found significant effects of *ISO 14000* certification in emerging economies have not included multinational ownership as an explanatory variable. One of the reasons for the insignificant effect in this study may be that multinational ownership partly explains the higher capabilities.

Our correlation results show that MNEs have significantly higher levels of three of the four complementary assets that facilitate *ISO 14000* adoption than other firms. MNEs have higher innovative capabilities, higher absorptive capacity through a better-educated workforce, and higher management system implementation capabilities. This suggests that MNEs can pursue self-regulation strategies more easily than other firms and may be less likely to take advantage of lax environmental regulations. This also suggests that stakeholder pressures for environmental self-regulation imposed on MNEs are more likely to lead to actions by firms not only because MNEs tend to be more visible and have more reputation to loose than other firms, but also because of their capabilities for environmental self-regulation.

The finding that MNE ownership contributes significantly to *ISO 14000* adoption even after including firm capabilities in the regression is interesting. This suggests that the capabilities we have included in the study do not completely explain why MNEs are more likely to adopt *ISO 14000* than other firms. Other capabilities, such as specific environmental management capabilities that MNEs can transfer across countries might contribute to the higher likelihood for MNEs to adopt *ISO 14000*. In addition, MNEs might also face different stakeholder pressures than other firms. While we control for customer pressures in our regression, MNEs are likely to face pressures from a variety of other stakeholders such as NGOs and investors, which may lead them to be more likely to self-regulate their environmental conduct.

CONCLUSIONS

Globalization significantly alters the role of national government regulations as a determinant of firms' environmental strategies. In theory, firms could adopt standards in developing countries that are substantially lower than standards in developed countries. In practice, many MNEs and firms in global supply chains have strategic and operational reasons to adopt global standards that may be higher than required by local governments – an outcome that we call "self-regulation." Part of the motivation for self-regulation is defensive. MNEs self-regulate their environmental conduct to protect their public image and to sustain the value of their branded products and services. Firms in global supply chains adopt self-regulation to fulfill customer requirements. In this study we found that firms are also internally driven towards self-regulation, although external pressure might well be needed initially to motivate commitment to self-regulation. However, in addition to responding to these external pressures, firms appear to develop other internal motivations based on a desire to fully utilize complementary assets, resources and capabilities developed within the firm in the course of implementing their business strategies.

Voluntary environmental initiatives that set standards for global environmental conduct are emerging as an important tool for firm self-regulation in the global economy. Adhering to global environmental standards allows firms to achieve two inter-related objectives. On the one hand, it allows firms to respond to stakeholder demands for environmentally responsible firm behavior. On the other hand, it provides a sound basis for managing global operations and global supply chains with a harmonized approach to environmental management. Instead of reacting on a local level to opportunities to exploit varying levels of government regulation and enforcement, firms involved in the global economy can benefit substantially from a strategy based on global self-regulation.

Adopting environmental management system standards such as *ISO 14000* is one of the ways in which MNEs and their suppliers respond to global pressures. *ISO 14000* adoption allows firms to leverage existing capabilities. Our findings support the proposition that the adoption of *ISO 14000* is more likely to be embraced by organizations that already possess complementary assets such as capabilities to innovate, to assimilate the *ISO 14000* system, and to engage the whole organization in the implementation of the system.

Our findings further suggest that companies that are seriously pursuing global self-regulation and company-wide implementation of an EMS need to focus on leveraging complementary assets within the firm. Firms that have a capacity for innovation, an absorptive capacity through an educated workforce, and well-dispersed involvement of employees in the implementation of an environmental management system are in a much better position to adopt strategies of environmental self-regulation. The development and transfer of "best practices" and firm-level management capacity for self-regulation is one of the most important consequences of globalization. MNEs can use their environmental management capabilities developed in countries with high regulations and as the basis to exceed standards set in developing countries by applying their own superior global standards for environmental self-regulation. Our findings on self-regulation can also be linked to transnational strategy in which firms make dual use of both firm-specific advantages such as proprietary know-how, and country-specific advantages such as differences in regulation (Rugman & Verbeke, 1998b). However, rather than moving toward countries with the lower environmental standards, MNEs can gain a competitive advantage by leveraging their non-location-bound firm-specific advantage to become global leaders in environmental management. In addition, firms in global supply chains benefit from capability transfer by their customers through supplier-development activities. Even if the capabilities transferred are not originally intended specifically to address environmental issues, suppliers may be able to leverage these capabilities in their environmental policies and may be in a better position to self-regulate their environmental conduct.

An important implication of our findings is that the lack of firm capabilities is an important obstacle for the diffusion of environmental self-regulation in emerging economies. This suggests that institutions interested in promoting self-regulation, such as NGOs and global customers can further their goals by focusing on the development and transfer of capabilities to firms in emerging economies. Thus, in addition to establishing global standards and pressuring firms to adopt them, stakeholders can play an important role in promoting the development of firm capabilities through means such as the dissemination of information, and education of management decision makers.

The importance of firm self-regulation does not suggest that government regulatory capability by individual nation states is no longer important. National regulations continue to provide an indispensable context for firm-level decision-making. Our findings do, however, suggest an additional role for national governments besides establishing and enforcing environmental regulations. This role is to develop incentives for innovation and education that complement their regulatory efforts. Developing country governments can benefit from working more closely with MNEs as these firms play an increasingly important role as a source of environmental management capability (Lundan, 2001).

In conclusion, self-regulation arises from the interplay of market and political forces that are an intrinsic feature of globalization. Rather than merely providing an incentive to MNEs to locate in countries with lax environmental standards, globalization provides an opportunity for firms to leverage their strategic capabilities to gain a global advantage. This does not by any means eliminate the need to force some companies to comply with minimum standards. But contrary to the most pessimistic interpretation, globalization does have the potential to force firms to respond to global competitive and stakeholder pressures by raising their standards rather than lowering them. Firms with innovative capabilities, that focus on developing their workforce, and that disperse responsibilities to employees throughout the organization are in the best position to respond positively to these pressures.

ACKNOWLEDGMENTS

We would like to thank the Asia Pacific Economic Cooperation (APEC) and the China Quality Certification Center (CQC) for their help with the data collection for this study. We gratefully acknowledge the financial support for completing the research leading up to this chapter received from the Darden Foundation and the Batten Institute of the Darden School of Business Administration, University of Virginia.

REFERENCES

Aragon-Correa, J. A. (1998). Strategic proactivity and firm approach to the natural environment. *Academy of Management Journal, 41*, 556–567.

Barney, J. B. (1986). Strategic market factors: Expectations, luck, and business strategy. *Management Science, 32*, 1231–1241.

Barney, J. B. (1991). Firm resources and sustained competitive advantage. *Journal of Management, 17*, 99–120.

Belsley, D. A., Kuh, E., & Welsh, R. E. (1980). *Regression diagnostics.* New York: Wiley.

Boldero, J. (1995). The prediction of household recycling of newspapers: The role of attitudes, intentions, and situational factors. *Journal of Applied Social Psychology, 25,* 440–462.

Campbell, D., & Fiske, D. (1959). Convergent and divergent discriminant validation by the multitrait-multimethod matrix. *Psychological Bulletin, 56,* 81–105.

Chen, Q. (1997). Improve the eco-environment and rebuild the beautiful mountains and rivers. *China Environment News, 13*(September), A.

Christmann, P. (1998). *Environmental strategies of multinational companies: Global integration or national responsiveness?* CIBER Working Paper 98–16. Anderson School at UCLA.

Christmann, P. (2000). Effects of 'best practices' of environmental management on cost advantage: The role of complementary assets. *Academy of Management Journal, 43,* 663–680.

Christmann, P., & Taylor, G. (2001). Globalization of the environment: Determinants of firm self-regulation in China. *Journal of International Business Studies, 32*(2), 439–458.

Christmann, P., & Taylor, G. (2002). Globalization and the environment: Strategies for international voluntary initiatives. *Academy of Management Executive, 16*(3), 121–135.

Cohen, W., & Levinthal, D. (1990). Absorptive capacity: A new perspective on learning and innovation. *Administrative Science Quarterly, 35,* 128–152.

Corbett, C., & Kirsch, D. (2001). International diffusion of ISO 14000 certification. *Production and Operations Management, 10*(3), 327–342.

Dasgupta, S., Hettige, H., & Wheeler, D. (2000). What improves environmental performance? Evidence from Mexican industry. *Journal of Environmental Economics and Management, 39,* 39–66.

Dasgupta, S., Huq, M., & Wheeler, D. (1997). *Bending the rules: Discretionary pollution control in China.* Policy Research Working Paper, No. 1761. Washington, DC: World Bank.

Dierickx, I., & Cool, K. (1989). Asset stock accumulation and the sustainability of competitive advantage. *Management Science, 35,* 1504–1514.

DiMaggio, P. J., & Powell, W. W. (1983). The iron cage revisited: Institutional isomorphism and collective rationality in organization fields. *American Sociological Review, 48,* 147–160.

Dowell, G., Hart, S., & Yeung, B. (2000). Do corporate environmental standards create or destroy market value? *Management Science, 8,* 1059–1074.

Duerksen, C., & Leonard, H. J. (1980). Environmental regulation and the location of industry: An international perspective. *Columbia Journal of World Business* (Summer), 54–68.

Gereffi, G., Garcia-Johnson, R., & Sasser, E. (2001). The NGO – industrial complex. *Foreign Policy* (July–August), 56–65.

Guler, I., Guillen, M. F., & MacPherson, J. M. (2002). Global competition, institutions, and the diffusion of organizational practices: The international spread of ISO 9000 quality certificates. *Administrative Science Quarterly, 47*(2), 207–232.

Hart, S. L. (1995). A natural-resource-based view of the firm. *Academy of Management Review, 20,* 986–1014.

Hartman, R. S., Huq, M., & Wheeler, D. (1997). *Why paper mills clean up: Determinants of pollution abatement in four Asian countries.* Policy Research Working Paper, No. 1710, Washington, DC: World Bank.

Hettige, H., Huq, M., Pargal, S., & Wheeler, D. (1996). Determinants of pollution abatement in developing countries: Evidence from south and southeast Asia. *World Development, 24*(12), 1891–1904.

ISO World (1999). ISOWorld, The number of ISO14001/EMAS registration of the world, http://www.ecology.or.jp/isoworld/english/analy14k.htm

Jaffe, A. B., Peterson, S. R., & Portney, P. R. (1995). Environmental regulation and competitiveness of U.S. manufacturing. *Journal of Economic Literature, 33*(1), 132–163.

King, A., & Lenox, M. (2001). Who adopts management standards early? An examination of ISO 14001 Certifications. Best Paper Proceedings of the Academy of Management Annual Conference.

Korten, D. C. (1995). *When corporations rule the world*. San Francisco: Berrett-Koehler Publishers.

Kraatz, M. S. (1998). Learning by Association? Interorganizational networks and adaptation to environmental change. *Academy of Management Journal, 41*(6), 621–643.

Leonard, H. J. (1988). *Pollution and struggle for a world product: Multinational corporations, environment, and the struggle for international comparative advantage*. Cambridge: Cambridge University Press.

Low, P., & Yeats, A. (1992). Do dirty industries migrate? In: P. Low (Ed.), *International Trade and the Environment*. Washington, DC: World Bank.

Lucas, R. E. B., Wheeler, D. R., & Hettige, H. (1992). Economic development, environmental regulation and the international migration of toxic pollution: 1960–1989. In: P. Low (Ed.), *International Trade and the Environment* (pp. 89–103). Washington, DC: World Bank.

Lundan, S. M. (2001). Environmental standards and multinational competitiveness: A policy proposal. In: K. Fatemi (Ed.), *International Public Policy and the Regionalism at the Turn of the Century* (pp. 30–44). Oxford, England: Pergamon.

Montabon, F., Melnyk, S. A., Stroufe, R., & Calantone, R. (2000). ISO 14000: Assessing its perceived impact on corporate performance. *Journal of Supply Chain Management, 36*(2), 4–16.

Mowery, D. C., Oxley, J. E., & Silverman, B. S. (1996). Strategic alliances and interfirm knowledge transfer. *Strategic Management Journal, 17*, 77–91.

NEPA (National Environmental Protection Agency) (1997). 1996 Report on the State of the Environment. Beijing: NEPA (Chinese language edition).

Nunnally, J. C. (1978). *Psychometric theory* (2nd ed.). New York: McGraw-Hill.

Oliver, C. (1997). Sustainable competitive advantage: Combining institutional and resource-based views. *Strategic Management Journal, 18*(9), 697–713.

Penrose, E. T. (1959). *The theory of growth of the firm*. London: Blackwell.

Porter, M., & van der Linde, C. (1995). Green and competitive: Ending the stalemate. *Harvard Business Review, 73*(5), 120–151.

Qu, G. (1991). *Environmental management in China*. Beijing: UNEP and China Environmental Science Press.

Rugman, A., & Verbeke, A. (1998a). Corporate strategy and international environmental policy. *Journal of International Business Studies, 29*(4), 819–833.

Rugman, A., & Verbeke, A. (1998b). Corporate strategies and environmental regulations: An organizing framework. *Strategic Management Journal, 19*(4), 363–376.

Rumelt, R. P. (1991). How much does industry matter? *Strategic Management Journal, 12*, 167–185.

Salancik, G. R., & Pfeffer, J. (1977). An examination of need-satisfaction models of job attitudes. *Administrative Science Quarterly, 22*, 427–456.

Spar, D. L., & Yoffie, D. B. (2000). A race to the bottom or governance from the top? In: A. Prakash & J. A. Hart (Eds), *Coping with Globalization*. London and New York: Routledge.

Szulanski, G. (1996). Exploring stickiness: Impediments to the transfer of best practice within the firm. *Strategic Management Journal, 17*(Winter special issue), 27–43.

Teece, D. (1986). Profiting from innovation: Implications for integrity, collaboration, licensing, and public policy. *Research Policy, 15*, 295–305.

Terlaak, A., & King, A. (2001). *Contrasting institutional theory and signaling theory to explain the adoption process of and industry standard*. Working Paper.

Tobey, J. (1990). The impact of domestic environmental policies on the pattern of world trade: An empirical test. *Kyklos, 43*(2), 191–209.

Walter, I. (1982). Environmentally induced industrial relocation to developing countries. In: S. J. Rubin & T. R. Graham (Eds), *Environment and Trade*. Totowa, NJ: Allanheld, Osmun Publishers.

Wang, H. (2000). *Pollution charge, community pressure, and abatement cost: An analysis of Chinese industry*. Policy Research Working Paper, No. 2337, Washington, DC: World Bank.

Wang, H., & Chen, M. (1999). *How the Chinese system of charges and subsidies effects pollution control efforts by China's top industrial polluters*. Policy Research Working Paper, No. 2198, Washington, DC: World Bank.

Wang, H., & Wheeler, D. (1996). *Pricing industrial pollution in China: An econometric analysis of the levy system*. Policy Research Working Paper, No. 1644. Washington, DC: World Bank.

Wernerfelt, B. (1984). A resource based view of the firm. *Strategic Management Journal, 5*, 171–180.

Wolf, B. M., & Taylor, G. S. (1991). Employee and supplier learning in the Canadian automobile industry: Implications for competitiveness. In: D. McFetridge (Ed.), *Foreign Investment, Technology and Economic Growth*. Calgary: University of Calgary Press.

World Resources Institute (1998). 1998–1999 World Resources: Environmental Change and Human Health. A Report by World Resources Institute, UNEP, UNDP, and The World Bank. Oxford, UK: Oxford University Press.

APPENDIX

Measures

	Cronbach α
Dependent variables	
Likelihood of *ISO 14000* adoption — How likely is your company to start implementing *ISO 14000* in the next year? (1) Not at all likely; (2) Very unlikely; (3) Unlikely; (4) Neither likely nor unlikely; (5) Likely; (6) Very likely; (7) Already started; (8) Already certified.	
Independent variables	
Innovative capabilities — Relative to the major competitors in your industry, how important are the following strategy dimensions for your company? (a) Being the first in the industry to try new methods and technologies. (b) Using the latest technology in production. (c) Capital investment in new equipment and machinery.	0.85

APPENDIX   (*Continued*)

	Cronbach α
	(d) Being a leader in product innovation. (e) Being a leader in process innovation. (1) Not at all important; (2) Much less important; (3) Slightly less important; (4) About the same importance; (5) Slightly more important; (6) Much more important; (7) Most important.	
Level of employee education	What proportion of your company's employees has as highest level of general education? (a) Finished high school/secondary school. (b) Finished primary (elementary) school (*reverse coded*). (c) Did not finish primary school (*reverse coded*). (0) None; (1) Between 1 and 10%; (2) Between 11 and 25%; (3) Between 26 and 50%; (4) Between 51 and 75%; (5) More than 75%	0.59
Dispersed environmental management	(a) Environmental performance of operations is an important criterion for evaluating managers (*yes* = 1/*no* = 0) (b) How does your company assign responsibility for environmental issues to workers?	0.98

APPENDIX   (*Continued*)

	Cronbach α
	(1) All of the responsibility for environmental issues lies with specialized personnel; (2) Most of the responsibility for environmental issues lies with specialized personnel; (3) Some workers have responsibility for environmental issues; (4) Most workers have some responsibility for environmental issues; (5) Almost all workers in the company have important responsibilities for environmental issues.	
ISO 9000 certification	Dummy Variable: "1" if the company has received *ISO 9000* certification, "0" otherwise.	
MNE ownership	What proportion of your company is foreign owned? (0) None; (1) 1–25%; (2) 26–50%; (3) 51–75%; (4) More than 75%.	
Customer pressures for *ISO 14000* adoption	Has at least one of your customers indicated that they will *in the future* require their suppliers to become *ISO 14000* certified?	
Firm size	Number of employees (1) Less than 10; (2) 11–50; (3) 51–100; (4) 101–500; (5) 501–1000; (6) 1001–5000; (7) More than 5000.	
Industry controls	Dummy variables for three industries: *Electronics, Toys, Apparel*	

MULTINATIONALS, NGOs AND REGULATION: GREENPEACE AND THE GLOBAL PHASE-OUT OF CHLORINE BLEACHING

Sarianna M. Lundan

ABSTRACT

Empirical evidence from the past decade confirms that multinationals increasingly see the environment as a strategic issue, whether in terms of limiting damage to the bottom line from adverse publicity, or actually gaining in the marketplace by pioneering more environmentally conscious solutions. During the same period, NGOs have become a visible part of the political process, in influencing the environmental strategies of multinationals through direct action, as well as by forming broader coalitions aimed at influencing the agenda at multilateral institutions such as the WTO and the OECD regarding environmental concerns and the behavior of multinationals. This chapter explores the importance of different environmental drivers on the behavior of firms in the pulp and paper industry, with particular focus on the role of Greenpeace in changing industry practices. We discuss the extent to which the paper industry might be a special case in this respect, and conclude by assessing the implications for public policy.

Multinationals, Environment and Global Competition
Research in Global Strategic Management, Volume 9, 147–170
ISSN: 1064-4857/doi:10.1016/S1064-4857(03)09007-7

INTRODUCTION

The purpose of this chapter is to employ detailed evidence from the pulp and paper industry to illustrate a dynamic that is re-shaping national environmental policy in light of the growing role of multinational enterprises (MNEs) and non-governmental organizations (NGOs) in the policy process. We begin by briefly reviewing the theoretical argument linking multinationals and pollution havens, which suggested that trade and investment liberalization would result in increased specialization and relocation of pollution-intensive production to the developing countries. Next we illustrate how the development of multinational environmental strategy has changed both the way in which MNEs respond to regulation, as well as the way in which they respond to market pressures. We then move onto a detailed case study of environmental issues in pulp and paper industry, where MNEs and NGOs have played an important role in the standard-setting process. The chapter concludes with a discussion of the desirability and effectiveness of a model of public policy, where MNEs and NGOs are the de facto agents of change, and set the standards for the global economy.

FOREIGN INVESTMENT AND THE ENVIRONMENT

The "pollution haven" hypothesis predicted that increased capital mobility in the global economy combined with a tightening of environmental regulations would lead to the relocation of pollution-intensive industry to pollution havens in less developed countries (LDCs), unless regulatory harmonization was undertaken to remove this incentive. As this argument considered environmental regulations to operate solely on the cost dimension, a tightening of regulations in the home country of a multinational enterprise would precipitate a search for less costly production locales, with the implicit assumption that such locales would mostly be found in the developing countries. Since the 1970s, however, both empirical evidence and theoretical developments have refuted the underlying tenets of this hypothesis, namely that regulations only operate on the cost dimension, that such cost differentials would be sufficient to induce cross-border relocation, and that the most likely destination for such direct investment would be in the LDCs.

Three kinds of macro-level evidence would need to be present to confirm the pollution haven hypothesis. To begin with, one would expect to see a rise in outward investment in pollution-intensive industries from developed countries. Secondly, one should see an increase in pollution-intensive inward investment into developing (pollution haven) countries. Thirdly, one should see an increase in pollution-intensive exports from these pollution haven locations. Aggregate evidence on the patterns of trade and investment in pollution-intensive industries does not support this view, and we will proceed to discuss the likely reasons for this somewhat unexpected result. (For a concise review of the evidence see, e.g. Dean (1992) and OECD (1999).)

To begin with, the negative effect of environmental regulations on total costs has been refuted by Porter and van der Linde (1995) and other scholars based on empirical evidence from pollution-intensive industries on the grounds that "strict product regulations can also prod companies into innovating to produce less polluting or more resource-efficient products that will be highly valued internationally" (Porter, 1991). Furthermore, even if the primary effect of environmental regulations was felt in total costs (at least in the short run), Gladwin and Welles (1976) argued already more than two decades ago that there are other reputational and infrastructure considerations which would tend to weigh more heavily in the decision to relocate abroad than the simple cost differential. (Excluding natural resource-seeking investment, which is less sensitive to the infrastructure conditions of the recipient country.) It appears, that the costs of environmental compliance as a percentage of total cost (typically 1–2%, and only 5% at their highest) have not historically been high enough to significantly influence the decision to engage in foreign direct investment (FDI) and/or the international location decision (Walter, 1982).

As for the location issue, the developing nations most likely to attract foreign direct investment would be the higher GDP per capita, newly industrializing countries (NICs), whose development strategies have differed from the traditional path of European and American industrialization. In the process of FDI-assisted and export-led growth, many NICs have been able to set environmental standards equivalent to the home countries of the investing MNEs. In a study of the oil industry in Colombia and Peru, Moser (2001) found that Columbia's longer history of environmental management allowed local regulators to more effectively counterbalance the lobbying by multinationals than was the case in Peru, although in both countries multinationals have made a contribution towards sustainable development. Preliminary results from a recent World Bank report indicate that there has been an inverse relationship between foreign direct investment and air pollution in China, Brazil and Mexico (Wheeler, 2001), although it is acknowledged that the burden of pollution as measured by various indicators of environmental quality is often higher for low and particularly middle-income countries, and much lower for high-income countries. Ferrantino (1997) cites evidence, that levels of sulfur dioxide and particulates in the air, as well as water quality, urban sanitation and dissolved oxygen levels in rivers, improve with increases in per capita income, although they have been (temporarily) worse for middle-income countries. Nevertheless, it should also be noted, that instances of inadequate enforcement abound, such as in the case of Indonesia, where state-of-the-art pulp mills operate under a government that has come under severe criticism for failing to curb illegal logging.

Although the predicted large-scale migration of polluting industry never took place, there have been calls for uniform environmental standards to avoid a "race to the bottom" employing a variant of the pollution haven argument. While the pollution haven hypothesis saw the MNE as ready and able to transfer production abroad in response to cost differentials, the competitiveness argument stresses the relative short-term immobility of productive resources, and the (static) gains accruing to indigenous producers in pollution haven locations, who, if they sell their product in the global market, subject other MNEs to unfair price competition. In other words, the competitiveness argument is that either strategic or efficiency considerations prevent the MNEs from relocating abroad to capture the cost savings, or alternatively that considerable harm can be done to the competitiveness of domestic industry before such relocation takes place.

However, there is a danger of exaggeration of the competitiveness-eroding effects of divergent environmental regulations on the part of industry, particularly when the divergent regulations are deemed to result in "unfair" competition or "environmental dumping" from abroad. (The implicit assumption here is that the relevant reference point can be found in the domestic industry, and that any harmonization would involve the upgrading of competitors' standards, and not the other way around.) Given compliance with a minimum standard of performance, such as that posed by child-labor laws, it is not generally considered "unfair" for one nation to have a better educated or more skilled work force than another one. Analogously, whether a country is seen to benefit from the presence or absence of tough environmental standards, such differences are a part of the competitive landscape, and as such, form the basis for trade rather than a competitive obstacle, at least until proven otherwise. The point here is that the mere existence of differences is not proof of unfairness, while also recognizing that environmental regulations can be and have been used by powerful domestic firms to restrict competition (cf. Rugman, Kirton & Soloway, 1997) on U.S. restrictions on various Canadian products.

The theoretical possibility of a country attracting foreign investment on the grounds of lax regulation does exist, but such instances would in all likelihood involve either government corruption or mismanagement at the very least. A case in point is the group of ten new accession countries to the European Union. Out of these ten, the Czech Republic, Poland and Hungary face the highest cost of compliance with EU environmental directives. The negotiated timetables for compliance with the EU acquis, which range from the year 2004 to 2015, depending on the directive, should reassure foreign investors that the practices in these countries will converge to a European standard. However, in order for these countries to attract clean investment, the credibility of the negotiated timetables must not be in question. An unscrupulous government, or a government faced with increasing unemployment and low growth, might be desperate to attract investment and to overlook enforcement of the agreed timetables. This would be very unfortunate, as far from being a magnet for foreign investment, it would create a "market for lemons," and would only attract the lowest quality firms, if it attracted any investment at all (this case is explored more fully in Lundan, 2003). But what has led the multinationals to be so choosy about location?

MULTINATIONAL ENVIRONMENTAL STRATEGY

The environmental consequences of MNE activity essentially depend on whether multinationals will opt for global or local standards, and whose standards will form the relevant benchmark. The process of standard-setting *within* the multinational can either be a race to the top, also called "trading up" by Vogel (1995), or it can be a race to the bottom, depending on the extent to which the multinational is exposed to tough standards either through regulation or by consumers. What is notable about MNEs in this context is the extent to which they are influenced not only by the conditions in their home base (the original Porter case), but also by the conditions in important markets globally. Rugman and Verbeke (1998) provide a general framework for assessing the strategic implications of global vs. local standards for MNEs, and Lundan (in this volume) extends this framework to incorporate NGO activity.

The evolution of thinking about the environment as a strategic issue can usefully be split into three periods, and the timeline adopted here is broadly similar to Hoffman's (1999) carefully researched history of environmental issues in the chemical industry in the United States. The first phase gained momentum from the first UN conference on the environment held in 1972 in Stockholm, which was accompanied by the publication of some alarmist reports concerning population growth and the depletion of key natural resources (e.g. Paul Ehrlich in "The Population Bomb" and the Club of Rome in "Limits to Growth"). From a business perspective, the first phase was characterized by large-scale investment in pollution control with the objective of meeting new tougher emissions requirements, such as those imposed by the clean air (1970) and clean water (1977) acts in the United States.

The second phase in environmental thinking began sometime in the mid-1980s on the heels of corporate restructuring and the introduction of Total Quality Management (TQM) into the business vocabulary. While there is little disagreement over the movement from reactive to proactive environmental thinking, the timeline is dependent on geographical location, so that for instance Berry and Rondinelli (1998) identify the same process in the U.S. as lagging the European timeline by 5–10 years. The second phase was characterized by the emergence of a new win-win rhetoric concerning the effects of environmental standards on the competitiveness of firms. The most notable proponent associated with this line of thinking has been Michael Porter (1991), who has argued, consistent with his home country influenced diamond model of national competitiveness, that firms resident in countries with tough regulations do not suffer, but in fact benefit from the discipline imposed by strict regulations. The long-term pay-off from such investments was subsequently labeled as "innovation offsets" by Porter and van der Linde (1995). To capture such benefits firms will have to think of regulation as providing a long-term benefit at a short-term cost, and to move from a static conception of regulation as a cost to treating it as a strategic (resource) challenge. (See also Nehrt (1998) on the old vs. new thinking on environmental regulation.)

Alongside this argument of beneficial regulation, there is a technological as-pect to the win-win argument, which states that if firms move away from a reac-tive response to regulation, and adopt a proactive stance towards environmental challenges, the possibility of capturing first-mover benefits from environmental investments will emerge. The essential change in thinking is one that moves firms away from end-of-pipe solutions (i.e. addressing pollution problems once they have occurred) to process redesign, whereby all unwanted by-products and waste are eliminated. This process is analogous to that advocated in TQM, and has led many firms to institute a system of TQM for environmental management (some-times labeled TQEM) where pollution is seen as evidence of inefficient use of resources. The aim of such a process redesign is to create a closed facility, where any byproducts are captured and re-used.

Not surprisingly, the third phase in the evolution of environmental strategy is something of a critical review of the win-win rhetoric. On one hand, the notion that there is an economic rationale for environmental performance that exceeds compliance levels is well established, as is the idea that differentiating a product with environmental qualities can offer a competitive advantage for some firms (Reinhardt, 1998, 1999b). However, as environmental considerations in business strategy have moved from "heresy to dogma" (Hoffman, 1997), it is also becoming clear that not all firms are able to benefit from tackling environmental considerations in a proactive manner, and recently there have also been calls to "bring the environment down to earth" (Reinhardt, 1999a).

An important part of the present reassessment are a number of recent studies looking at the financial implications of strategic environmental management, and the results will be briefly reviewed here. In a study of 80 MNEs, Levy (1995) found no evidence of a relationship between environmental performance and subsequent financial performance, whereas Russo and Fouts (1997) found a positive relationship between environmental performance and profitability for a sample of 243 U.S. multinationals. Sharma and Vredenburg (1998) didn't directly assess the link between environmental performance and profitability, but looked instead at identifying environmentally related corporate capabilities that could be competitively valuable for the firm. Both Russo and Fouts (1997) and Sharma and Vredenburg (1998) relied on the resource-based theory of strategy, the basic tenet of which is that assets that are inimitable and difficult to acquire in the marketplace can generate value for their owners. In the environmental context, such assets can include a technological advantage in cleaner technology, as well as intangibles such as a corporate culture predisposed to accepting environmental responsibility, or a capability for generating a long-term vision of competitiveness and sustainability.

Continuing on the resource-based track, Klassen and Whybark (1999) looked at a sample of plants from the U.S. furniture industry and associated each plant's portfolio of investments in environmental technologies to its performance, both in terms of environmental performance as well as manufacturing performance. The results provide support for the win-win scenario whereby process improvements in manufacturing that were instigated for pollution prevention also improved manufacturing performance. However, in a study on 88 U.S. chemical companies, Christmann (2000) looked at the role of complementary assets in allowing firms to obtain a cost advantage from the implementation of best practices of environmental management, namely the focus on pollution prevention rather than control, innovation of proprietary pollution prevention technologies and first-mover advantages. Her results indicate that such benefits are not universal, and require the presence of process innovation to form a link between environmental best practices and cost advantage.

If firms are not rewarded directly for their environmental investments in ways that improve the bottom line, it is possible that they are nonetheless rewarded by the market because of expectations of reduced liability, improved image, or expectation of long-term cost savings. Using event methodology, Klassen and McLaughlin (1996) studied the stock market reaction to positive shocks such as environmental performance awards, and negative shocks such as environmental crises, and their results indicated that particularly first-time announcements of a firm instigated a significant increase in the stock price, while environmental crises had a predicted dampening effect on the firm's stock price. However, in another study employing event study methodology, Gilley et al. (2000) looked at the effects of the announcement of environmental initiatives and found no effect on stock price.

The problems of accurately measuring financial performance in diversified multinationals are considerable (see, e.g. Dunning & Lundan, 2001), and the limitations of event studies in dealing with long-term phenomena are evident. Additionally, there are a wide range of measures of environmental performance employed, including self-reported assessments of environmental proactivity, third party rankings of firms by green investment funds, and public evidence of toxic releases (e.g. the Toxics Release Inventory in the U.S.), or environmental fines levied against the firm. While this diversity is in itself not a problem, as each measure captures an important component of corporate environmental performance, it does make it difficult to group the results together. There are also significant deficiencies in environmental accounting within firms, and unfortunately, the more firms pursue advanced integrated pollution prevention solutions, the less tractable these investments become.

Whether firms manage to realize the win-win scenario or not, it is unquestionable that the thinking about environmental issues has changed, and that environmental strategy, whether aimed at first-mover advantages, or simply the lowest long-term cost of compliance, is a reality in global industries. The lowest long-term cost of compliance is most probably achieved in a "race to the top," i.e. the upgrading of standards within the firm, but the intensity with which a company will move up is dependent on the pressures put on it by regulators and the market. We will continue by presenting a case on the evolution of environmental standards in the pulp and paper industry, followed by a discussion of the role of NGOs as representatives of consumers in the marketplace.

CASE: THE GLOBAL PHASE-OUT OF CHLORINE BLEACHING

Data Collection

This case draws on research that was conducted at three different stages, with the first two stages covered originally in Lundan (1996). In the first stage, secondary data were collected at the industry level on patterns of trade and investment, as well as on the environmental issues specific to the pulp and paper industry. This was followed by primary data collection using a combination of semi-structured interviews and a mail-in questionnaire (not used in this chapter). The (current) third stage was again based on secondary sources, with an aim towards documenting the ongoing changes in the industry subsequent to the interviews.

The four most pollution-intensive industries, identified as chemicals, paper, petroleum refining and mineral processing (Leonard, 1988, p. 88), are highly capital intensive, implying that investment in process redesign is likely to be lumpy, and can only be undertaken as part of an overall investment plan. Furthermore, most of the product in these industries is sold in intermediate markets, where branding and advertising are less important, but where large buyers exercise a great deal of influence. While in this broad sense all four industries are alike, the paper industry was chosen because of the high visibility of the Greenpeace campaign against chlorine, and because the geographical concentration of the industry made it possible to target all of the major international firms in the industry. For information on the evolution of environmental issues and new technologies in the industry, every issue of *Pulp and Paper International* (PPI) was consulted from the year 1970 to 1995. Additional articles were sought from *Pulp and Paper* (U.S.), *Pulp and Paper Canada*, *Paper Technology* (U.K.) and *Svensk Papperstidning/Nordisk Cellulosa* (Sweden). For the targeted firms, the materials consulted included company environmental reports and annual reports, as well as papers written by company officials on environmental issues. For updating the information on industry developments from 1995 to 2001, online databases were used to identify relevant articles in *Pulp and Paper International*, *Pulp and Paper* (U.S.), *Pulp and Paper Canada*, and *Paperi ja Puu* (Finland).

The in-person interviews were conducted during 1995 and 1996. In all cases, the respondent sought was the highest ranking staff member with direct responsibility of environmental management at the corporate level. In Finland and Sweden the person's title was commonly Director of Environmental Affairs, or Vice President of Environmental Affairs. In Canada and the United States all but one of the interviewees had the title of Vice President, Group Vice President, Senior Vice President or President. Typically, the interviews ranged from one to three hours, averaging an hour and a half in length, except for two telephone interviews conducted in the United States, which lasted for half an hour.

Since the impact of internationalization on the transfer of environmental standards was central to this research, the selection of countries was based on the degree to which they contributed to world trade and production of pulp and paper. A secondary consideration was to include countries that have played a major role in the international arena since the early 1970s, which is when the first large environmental investments were made in the industry. These two criteria eliminate some major producing nations, such as Japan, China and the former Soviet Union, along with many smaller European and Asian producers, who are either too small or relative newcomers, and do not thus contribute significantly to world trade in pulp and paper. For the final group of countries, namely the United States, Canada, Sweden and Finland, the data on world exports of pulp and paper indicate that while the global share attributable to this group has declined with the growth in production in East Asia, their share of world market pulp production was still 71% in 1991, down from 80% in 1971. Also, despite their declining share in the overall paper and board category, world production of newsprint was still dominated (76% in 1991) by these four countries.

The selection of firms was limited to those that had annual sales above of $365 million in 1989 in pulp and paper, as identified in PPI (1989). For all the firms included in the sample, Worldscope/Disclosure company profiles and the Economist Intelligence Unit's *World Pulp and Paper: Profiles of 150 leading manufacturers* were also consulted in the selection process. Considerable care was exercised in trying to ensure that all of the companies included in the sample were broadly comparable in terms of their global activities in pulp, paper and paperboard production. Since using a selection criterion based on sales (size) brings in a large number of American firms, a further selection was made among the American firms to achieve approximately equal numbers of firms from all four countries. The second selection was made based on the degree of internationalization as expressed by the ratio of foreign sales to total sales in the Worldscope database. In the end, four to six of the most important, and most directly comparable, firms were chosen from each country for the interviews. The list of companies targeted for interview (21 firms, of which 18 were interviewed) is provided in Table 1.

Table 1.   Firms Targeted for Interviews.

Ahlström	Finland
Enso-Gutzeit	Finland
Kymmene	Finland
Metsä-Botnia	Finland
Metsä-Serla	Finland
United Paper Mills (Yhtyneet)	Finland
AssiDomän	Sweden
MoDo	Sweden
SCA	Sweden
Abitibi-Price	Canada
Canfor	Canada
Domtar	Canada
MacMillan Bloedel	Canada
Noranda	Canada
Repap	Canada
Tembec (Temboard)	Canada
Champion International	United States
International Paper	United States
Stone Container	United States
Westvaco	United States
Weyerhaeuser	United States

Market Structure and Regulatory Context

In Finland and Sweden, there has been a concerted move towards higher value-added production, which is indicated by the increasing share of printing and writing papers of total production. Both markets are export-driven with exports accounting for over four fifths of total production of paper and board. The primary export markets for Finnish and Swedish firms have continued to be within the EU, with Germany as the single largest market. The Canadian market continues to be dominated by newsprint production, while the United States is concentrated on printing and writing papers and paperboard, and linerboard in particular. The destination for Canadian newsprint is predominantly the United States, while the Unites States has large export markets both in Asia and Europe. While Kraft (chemical) pulp is the most common pulp entering the world market, mechanical pulp (used for newsprint) has a large share of Canadian production.

While Finland and Sweden internationalized their pulp and paper production mostly thorough direct investment within the EU in the 1980s, inward investment into Scandinavia remained almost non-existent. In Finland, 1997 was a watershed year, when capacity increases abroad (as a result of acquisitions) for the first time exceed capacity increases in Finland. In addition to pulp and paper, Finland and Sweden are still host to some of the leading machine manufacturers in pulping and papermaking, namely Ahlstrom Machinery (a part of the Austrian-Finnish Andritz-Ahlstrom) and Metso (a combination of the Finnish Valmet and Rauma), which now also includes the Swedish Sunds Defibrator. The United States and Canada engage in significant two-way investment, along with increasing investment directed towards Central and South America. Mergers and acquisitions in the late 1990s reduced the number of large firms in each producer market, while at the same time further increasing the scale of production, so that by 2001 there were 54 firms making more than one million tons of paper and board annually. Furthermore, the Top 20 firms accounted for 60% of world sales from pulp, paper and converting, and nearly half of this was due to the firms in our sample.[1]

Due to the tremendous amount of consolidation, the small size of their home market, and the central role the forest industry plays in the economic structure of both countries, there are virtually no firms in the Swedish or Finnish industries that could be classified as lagging. The remaining players are an essential part of the forest cluster in both countries, which includes not just the firms themselves, but technical universities, government research centers, and trade associations, which until relatively recently also functioned as cooperative sales organizations for the industry. In spite of the prominence of the forest sector in economic life, the number of individuals in leading positions is small, the key individuals know one another, and information is generally widely disseminated within the cluster.

Owing to the economic importance of the sector, and a corporatist model of collective bargaining, state-business relations have not traditionally been as adversarial in Finland or Sweden as in the United States. The relationship between regulators and industry has been relatively uncomplicated, and early on, industry representatives have been consulted regarding the feasibility and timetables for proposed new regulations. This system had allowed the Scandinavian firms to incorporate new investment into their investment cycle better than their North American counterparts, and it may be the reason why the Swedish regulators already in the 1980s, and Finnish regulators a bit later on, were successful in promoting in-process rather than end-of-pipe solutions. Already then, a part of the solution originated within the industry, and the one-tier regulatory structure combined with small numbers made it possible for a trust-based relationship to develop between the firms and their regulators.

The regulatory context in Canada and the United States has been markedly different from the Scandinavian example. In Canada, environmental protection is the outcome of a two-tier system of regulation, where provincial governments and the federal government have their own areas of responsibility. In practice some of the most contentious issues in the industry, like chlorinated organics (AOX) releases have been regulated at the provincial level, with some provinces lobbying for more stringent regulations, while others would prefer a federal standard. In the United States, federal regulations have been generally more influential on the industry than state regulation, and although the process of developing the new cluster rules for the pulp and paper industry involved extensive industry participation, the size and diversity of the U.S. market do not allow for the same kind of two-way flow of information as is possible in the Scandinavian context.

In the United States, and to a somewhat lesser extent in Canada, the industry seems to consist of two very different kinds of participants. At one end are a handful of global forest firms, whose strategic outlook is very similar to the Scandinavian producers, and who, prior to the mergers undertaken in the last ten years, have dominated the global market by their sheer size. The rest of the industry consists of hundreds of smaller firms, which tend to lag the global industry leaders in terms of technology, and consequently environmental performance. For example, a report on the International Non-Chlorine Bleaching Conference held in 1996 in Orlando, Florida stated that companies like Weyerhaeuser, which had worked closely with the Paper Task Force,[2] Champion (later acquired by UPM-Kymmene of Finland) and Union Camp (later acquired by International Paper) in many ways shared the same environmental philosophy as the Scandinavian producers, while most of the North American firms not sharing the same vision of the industry were conspicuously absent from the conference.

Greenpeace and Chlorine Bleaching

The first major appearance of the issue of the harmful effects of organochlorides to human and animal health occurred in 1987 when, aware that information on its earlier findings had been leaked to Greenpeace, the U.S. Environmental Protection Agency (EPA) announced that dioxins had been found in pulp mill effluent, as well as in fish caught downstream from pulp mills, and in various paper products, including coffee filters and disposable diapers. The news of these findings was relayed around the world, but it came as no surprise in Sweden, where grassroots citizen groups had already been campaigning since the 1970s on the issue, and where government funded research on the effects of chlorine in pulping had been conducted since the early 1980s.[3] The research results from this project were reported as early as 1985, and limits were proposed for chlorinated organic discharges in the form of adsorbable organic halides (AOX) in Sweden. Early on, the Swedish regulators were focused on promoting process solutions rather than improvements in secondary treatment, as was initially done in Finland.

The issue of organochlorides was picked up by Greenpeace, who actively disseminated the Swedish research results to North America (Harrison, 2002). The Greenpaece campaign against chlorine reached its climax in Germany in 1991, with the publication of a mock version of the popular magazine Der Spiegel entitled Das Plagiaat, printed on totally chlorine free paper to demonstrate that this was a commercially viable product. The Finnish and Swedish producers reacted to the concerns surrounding chlorine by offering two alternatives: the elementally chlorine free (ECF) pulping process, where chlorine gas is replaced by a small amount of chlorine dioxide, and the totally chlorine free (TCF) process. Some firms, like the Swedish Södra, positioned themselves heavily in favor of TCF, and were able to derive a premium on TCF pulp for a few years. Most other firms opted for the ECF process with a possibility to produce TCF as well, citing research results that showed no significant differences in the mill effluent from the two processes.

Meanwhile, Canadian researchers, who had worked in close contact with the scientists in Sweden, launched their own program to study the environmental impact of bleached pulp mill effluent in 1990, and new federal rules for the pulp and paper industry were issued in 1992 (Harrison, 2002). These included limits on dioxins, but not on AOX. In the coming years, their research revealed that it was likely that the organic residue from the wood, rather than the chlorine itself, accounted for the majority of the environmental impact. This became apparent, as more evidence emerged that the same environmental effects were observed downstream from mills that had not used any chlorine in the bleaching process.

By the mid-1990s there was a broad consensus among scientists that attention should shift from chlorine towards technologies that would help to "close the loop."[4] However, in spite of these findings, AOX continues to be used as a regulatory parameter in Sweden, Finland, Canada (on the provincial level), and the United States. (Harrison (2002) provides an extremely interesting account of the competing standard setting process on the issue of chlorine by regulatory authorities in Sweden, Canada and the United States.)

In the United States, the process of revamping the emission standards for the pulp and paper industry began in 1993, but it took until 1998 before the new "cluster rules" actually came into effect. The "cluster rules" were the first of their kind to combine simultaneous regulation of air and water pollution to discourage the transfer of pollution from one medium to another.[5] The standard finally adopted in the United States required ECF as the best available technology, but the AOX limits were carefully chosen to leave open the possibility that mills might not have to install extended cooking and oxygen delignification in the process, as was the practice in Scandinavia, since this would necessitate further capital investment, which would adversely affect some mills. This outcome was a result of prolonged negotiations with industry and NGOs prior to the release of the cluster rules, and it has come to some criticism on the part of the environmentalists, who claimed that ECF bleaching in an average American mill might consequently have very different environmental outcomes than an ECF mill in Scandinavia.

By the mid-1990s, the use of elemental chlorine (Cl_2) had disappeared from Sweden and Finland, and its use has been drastically reduced in the United States and Canada, as well as in other modern ECF installations around the world. Indeed, ECF pulp accounted for 62% of world production of bleached Kraft pulp in the year 1999.[6] While Sweden is still the largest producer of TCF, all of the large Scandinavian companies produce either grade as required, and the environmental focus of the industry has moved towards "closing the loop" both in pulping and bleaching, as well as issues of energy efficiency and forestry practices. In the United States and Canada, chlorine remains an issue, and Greenpeace, which has stuck to its view on the dangers of chlorine, argues that the cluster rules should instead have focused on the TCF process, and hence a total elimination of chlorine.[7] A similar line was taken by the Sierra Legal Defence Fund of Canada, who filed a complaint at the Commission for Environmental Cooperation in 2002 accusing the Canadian government of a lack of sufficient enforcement of the existing regulations of the pulp and paper industry, and argued that totally chlorine free production should have been adopted as the industry goal.[8]

Triggers of Environmental Change

Why did the Greenpeace campaign have such an impact on the pulp and paper industry, and what would have happened in its absence? It is apparent from the interviews, that the Greenpeace campaign did not directly cause the ECF or TCF technologies to come about. In fact, the technology had existed since the 1970s, but the removal of chlorine implied fundamental changes in the production process, and due to the size of the required investment, the new process was waiting for the right time to be introduced. There were many technological and economic reasons why firms would have wanted to move to a chlorine-free process, since it was more efficient, consuming for example one tenth of the fresh water compared to older processes, and it opened up the possibility to "close the loop." In effect, it was the window of opportunity for capital investment that was created by the Greenpeace campaign in Germany. Since Germany was the largest export market for both Finnish and Swedish firms, and all of the leading firms were affected by the changing market conditions, the risks of a large unilateral investment were removed.

In a highly capital-intensive industry like pulp and paper, capital investment decisions are among the most profound strategic decisions made by the firm, since the operational repercussions are felt for the next 20 or 30 years. In many ways, this does not seem to be an industry where first movers in environmental investment could reap great benefits, and there was little enthusiasm among the interviewees for the possibility that a firm could have gained first mover benefits by moving into ECF or TCF. In this industry, the capital investment is very lumpy, the investment cycle is slow, and the technology is relatively stable, despite the improvements made in the past few decades. The firms are conservative in their outlook on investment, and tend to move in unison. Indeed, as far as investment timing is concerned, the paper industry has a record of exacerbating the natural cyclicality of the industry by investing in capacity additions when pulp prices are rising, only to find that the additional capacity comes online as the prices have already begun to decline, resulting in chronic bubbles of oversupply on the market. Under such conditions, the leading firms will all adopt the new technology, while the lagging firms generally lack the means to make the necessary investment. Indeed, it is quite possible that the somewhat better financial performance of the early adopters of ECF in the sample of Nehrt (1996), which included many of the same firms as this study, reflected the overall performance of the global industry leaders in comparison to the lagging (American) firms, many more of which were included in his sample.

Overall, the interviewees emphasized the difficulties they faced in communicating about their environmental performance to different stakeholders, mostly because their claims were either not understood or believed. Consequently the industry executives did not believe in the market's ability to reward good deeds, but they did, however, believe in the power of the market to punish the firm if it was seen as lagging behind acceptable norms in the industry. This is understandable in terms of the information asymmetry between the firm and the consumers (or NGOs) in the marketplace. In order to reward a first-mover firm, you would need to be able to assess the unknown value of the firm's innovative efforts as compared to other firms, whereas to shun a firm, you only need to demonstrate that it is not meeting an established standard. This dynamic again pushes firms towards becoming more similar in their environmental strategies, particularly with issues involving large capital investment.

But to what extent are the changes brought about in the paper industry a special case, and why should the actions of an NGO such as Greenpeace have such impact? We have argued, that in capital-intensive industries, the dynamics of capital investment explain a lot of the change. Effective action by NGOs reduces the risk of investment, because the investment is no longer a unilateral commitment by one firm, but shared by all the major players in the industry. Since the most polluting industries are also the most capital intensive, we believe that such investment represents major steps in the move towards cleaner production. However, the growing influence of NGOs is not limited to direct action directed at multinationals, but also extends to policy making at the local, national and international levels. In the final part of this chapter, we explore the implications of the changing dynamic between multinationals, regulators, and the NGOs.

NGOs, MULTINATIONALS AND REGULATION

The unrest that took place at the intended opening of a new round of trade negotiations under the auspices of the WTO in Seattle in December 1999 was the first concrete manifestation of the new status acquired by NGOs (as well as MNEs) in the global economy. Those events were the next step in a process that has included the 1992 United Nations conference on the environment in Rio de Janeiro, the Kyoto agreement on curbing greenhouse gases, and most importantly the derailment of the talks for the multilateral agreement on investment (MAI) under the auspices of the Organization for Economic Co-operation and Development (OECD). In all four cases, the concerns of the large and increasing number of NGOs, framed in terms of eroding national sovereignty, as well as the interests of the MNEs, framed mostly in terms of effects on competitiveness, were to be at the forefront of the discussions. Indeed, in the 10-year follow-up meeting to Rio held in Johannesburg in 2002, large MNEs were prominent as critical "partners" in the process of sustainable development.

Since the Rio de Janeiro conference and the talks leading to the Kyoto agreement on the curbing of greenhouse gases, hundreds of NGOs have become an integral part of the international regulation of the environment (see, e.g. Levy & Egan, 1998 on the climate change negotiations). Although it is not their aim, by focusing on the actions of multinationals and by launching campaigns against practices that are damaging to the environment, the NGOs have helped to legitimate the role of multinationals in addressing environmental problems. Based on their study of the organizations involved in the preservation of global biodiversity, Westley and Vredenburg (1997) argue that the underorganization of interest groups without well-established formal structures of authority may in fact result in more effective problem solution when the problems are highly interrelated and complex, and require collaborative decision-making processes. On the other hand, the loosely defined relationships within NGO networks can also result in a lack of political responsibility which might undo some of the positive representational role that NGOs play in the global economy (Jordan & Tuijl, 2000). This danger is exacerbated if the political space within which NGOs operate is unusually large, and coalitions of NGOs are effective in pressurizing governments or firms to change their policies. Most NGOs operate with a considerable scarcity of resources, and consequently may choose to focus on issues that have the most visible impact, based on information that is not always reliable. In some instances, NGOs can also become co-opted by multinationals, who have become quite skilled in speaking the language of the environmentalists in their marketing communications and environmental reporting (see, e.g. King & Baerwald, 1998 on how to say the right things).

Given that there is little agreement even among firms on the details of what good environmental performance consists of, it is not surprising that environmental NGOs have been particularly effective in "naming and shaming" firms which are seen as laggards in the industry rather than rewarding well-performing firms. Furthermore, while consumers frequently express a great deal of concern for the environment in opinion polls, there have been few instances in which they have voted with their money, and actually paid a premium for "green" products (see, e.g. Lampe & Gazda, 1995), and instead most consumers seem willing to delegate the duty of oversight to the NGOs. However, even when faced with consumers who are more effective in employing a stick than offering carrots, the pursuit of proprietary gains from environmental investment remains viable for firms, because environmental concerns have become integrated into the overall strategic management of multinationals. But since consumers are unwilling to accept a price premium, they do not directly bear the costs of environmental investments, and instead industry can be pushed (by NGOs) towards alternatives that can become prohibitively expensive and contribute only marginally to overall environmental quality.

Many NGOs have formed a part of the antiglobalization backlash aimed particularly at the (symbolic) institutions that have been set up for the international control and regulation of multinationals. While the reasons for the demise of the MAI in 1998 were numerous, and included developing countries unhappy about their exclusion from the negotiations, along with French (and Canadian) concerns over the preservation of certain cultural exemptions, there was also a significant unease on behalf of many NGOs that the MAI was giving multinationals the power to effectively regulate labor and environmental standards. While this concern does not seem entirely warranted in light of the evidence (Brewer & Young, 2000; Graham, 2000), the proposed right of multinationals to sue governments for denying national treatment plays directly into the NGOs concerns that multinationals are taking precedence over national governments in the global economy. The exclusive and opaque process of decision making particularly in connection with the OECD and the WTO is fundamentally incompatible with what Kobrin (1998) has called the "electronically networked global civil society," in other words, the hundreds or thousands of NGOs mobilizing public opinion, particularly over the internet.

There is no denying that NGOs play an important role in open democracies, and their participation in processes where decisions are made that affect the living conditions of people around the world should be encouraged. However, it is possible that for every case of beneficial interaction such as the introduction of chlorine free pulping, there will be another one such as the Brent Spar, where a great deal of resources were used to combat a problem that independent analyses indicated wasn't there.[9] The paper industry case illustrated how multinational firms, and particularly those in capital intensive industries, are faced with many irreversabilities once they embark on a particular approach to address environmental concerns. There is a danger that if the market increasingly guides public policy, and the marketplace is dominated by NGOs, a vacuum is created where neither the regulators, nor the firms, nor the NGOs, are able to set a long-term vision of environmental strategy.

At the present time, there is little evidence to warrant such a negative scenario, but an analogy to the evolution of class action lawsuits in the United States presents a cautionary example. The barrage of class action litigation, where a case is brought with a few plaintiffs representing the collective claims of thousands, has resulted in a situation where firms are effectively blackmailed into settlements, the cost of which is treated as a form of insurance against adverse publicity.[10] Not only are multinationals liable to be sued for things directly connected to the product they produce, but they have also been called to account for past wartime atrocities, such as the use of slave labor by German industrial firms, or by Japanese firms during its occupation of China, with the latter case being brought in California against Japanese multinationals.[11] While class action lawsuits make it possible for individually powerless claimants to seek redress from powerful corporate entities, if such lawsuits emerge particularly frequently in areas vacated by government regulation, they amount to the substitution of a system of regulation by a system of civil litigation. A substitution of regulation for markets in the environmental arena is not desirable if it results in an unpredictable and costly process whereby multinationals try to adjust their actions primarily to the demands of the NGOs. Environmental progress is only achieved when it is possible for firms to engage in large-scale re-designs of the production system, which requires a lengthy planning-horizon to be present.

Following the general acceptance of the idea that environmental protection and profit are not necessarily in conflict in the long run, new forms of regulation have gained ground, which rely on the economic incentive of firms to pursue improved technological solutions to environmental problems. They require cooperation and flexibility, and represent a definitive move away from command-and-control approaches. Negotiated rule-making and flexible regulation require continuous consultation with industry in order to allow individual firms to adjust their investment horizons in the most economic manner. The role of the regulator is to set targets, and the means to achieve the targets are selected by the firms. In practice, flexible regulatory measures can include reduced monitoring for firms with certified environmental management systems, such as EMAS or ISO 14001,[12] and they can also involve negotiated timetables and individual compliance agreements for firms that pursue innovative pollution control strategies. At least in the case of the electric utilities, regulations that allow firms to develop new technologies according to their own schedule have resulted in a competitive advantage for the firms (Majumdar & Marcus, 2001).

Another new means of regulation that has received increasing interest in recent years is voluntary codes of conduct, drawn up by the firms themselves, often in collaboration with NGOs (see, e.g. Kolk, Tulder & Welters, 1999 on the overall use of codes by multinationals and Kolk (2001) for a study of codes of conduct in the sporting goods industry). One of the earliest codes initiated by firms was the chemical industry's Responsible Care program, although two recent studies (Howard, Nash & Ehrenfeld, 2000; King & Lenox, 2000) found that members of Responsible Care included poor performers, and members did not improve their environmental performance faster than non-members.

If multinationals are the de facto guardians of environmental standards in the world economy, and their performance is responsive to consumer demand, the market system can be a cost-effective means of upgrading standards, developing new technology, and in the process producing a cleaner environment. Increased industry self-regulation, and the substitution of bureaucracy by markets can therefore become the future of environmental regulation, but a few very significant caveats are also introduced. The effective oversight of a policy of enlightened self-regulation requires a constant two-way communication between the regulators, who set the targets, and the multinationals that develop the technological solutions. However, a market-led system is not really led by a market, composed of large numbers of individuals making decisions on the environmental attributes of products. Rather, the market consists of NGOs that allow individuals to reduce the significant information costs associated with being a "green" consumer. Evidence has been presented in this chapter which has demonstrated the mechanism of "trading up" and the emergence of improved standards in response to the interaction between MNEs and NGOs. However, it is also possible to replace bad regulation with bad markets if excessive short-termism is introduced to the policy process. NGOs are responsible for raising issues, not necessarily finding solutions to them, and if MNEs do not continue to develop long-term policy jointly with national regulators, it is possible for environmental strategy to turn into another nuisance tax firms pay to avoid bad publicity.

CONCLUSIONS

This chapter has presented evidence indicating that MNEs have learned to operate in the new era of negotiated regulation and target setting (rather than command and control), and are increasingly taking their signals from the market rather than regulation. The marketplace is in turn increasingly influenced by NGOs, and the growing tendency of the technological solutions to environmental problems to reside within the MNE coincides with an overall trend towards trade and investment liberalization, and a recognition of the role of the MNE as a political entity. NGO involvement in standard-setting has both positive and negative consequences. In a global economy where multinationals are very influential and national regulators are keen on maintaining a good working relationship with large firms, NGOs can pose awkward questions on behalf of affected citizens. On the other hand, most NGOs operate with very limited resources, and by their very nature are likely to focus on issues that are easily recognizable and likely to generate publicity.

While multinationals may have grown increasingly comfortable with their role as negotiating partners with national regulators, it is not clear whether they are ready or willing to assume a new role in the global economy, where performance objectives are often being set by a group of NGOs instead of, or in addition to, national regulators. If multinationals respond to NGO initiatives in a reactive manner, this would make it impossible for them to concentrate on a long-term strategy of sustainability, in the same way that command-and-control regulation resulted in end-of-pipe solutions, and turned the firms' focus on short-term costs. In practice, this would mean that firms would increasingly agree on standards or codes that involve relatively trivial but highly visible aspects of their activities. It might also mean that multinationals will increasingly learn to shape their environmental visions in a defensive manner with an eye to minimizing future liability.

The rising influence of NGOs also coincides with the general antiglobalist concerns that essential aspects of the national economy have been handed over to the multinationals. MNEs used to be able to take refuge in demonstrating compliance with national regulation in order to avoid looking bad in the eyes of the NGOs. To the extent that MNEs are now increasingly a part of setting national and international standards, that refuge has lost much of its effectiveness, and if MNEs were to start reconsidering their role as virtual state actors, this would require unprecedented openness and transparency regarding their long-term vision for sustainability, and willingness to take on the NGOs to defend such policies. This would mean a rather radical departure for many multinationals, content over the years on being led by market forces and being responsive to the marketplace, but not necessarily to society as a whole.

The case of the pulp and paper industry discussed in this chapter could well be considered a model of the desired outcome from such an MNE-NGO interaction, where the industry is prodded towards more efficient and cleaner solutions. Nonetheless, the same dynamic of market-led regulation, and NGOs representing the market, can also produce inefficient and haphazard results, and under such a scenario there is a distinct possibility that multinationals would move towards risk limitation or damage control as their predominant environmental strategy. A model of public policy where the future direction is set by NGOs in collaboration with multinationals requires a strong presence by national regulators as a counter balance.

NOTES

1. Rhiannon James, Caroline Jewitt, Laura Galasso and Genevieve Fortemps, Consolidation changes the shape of the Top 150, *Pulp and Paper International*, September 2001, 31–41.

2. The Paper Task Force was a joint effort by Duke University, the Environmental Defence Fund, Johnson & Johnson, McDonald's, Prudential and Time.

3. I am indebted to Charles Berkow, former Head of Friends of the Earth in Europe for emphasizing this aspect.

4. Pulp and paper Canada Special Report, No. 10, 1997, Mill closure has taken over the ECF vs. TCF debate.

5. EPA fact sheet, November 1997, EPA's Final pulp, paper and paperboard "Cluster Rule."

6. Jurgen D. Kramer, Pulping/Bleaching Technology View Shows North America Lagging, *Pulp & Paper*, April 2000, 51–59.

7. Greenpeace Technical Report 7/96, Toward zero-effluent pulp and paper production: The pivotal role of totally chlorine free bleaching.

8. Sierra Legal Defence Fund Report, November 2000, Pulping the law: How pulp mills are ruining Canadian water with impunity.

9. The Brent Spar was an oil storage buoy Shell wanted to dispose of by sinking it in the sea. Greenpeace intervened, and got Shell to tow the facility to Norway, where it was due to be dismantled on land. There is no consensus on what the best solution would have been from an environmental point of view, but the cost of the disposal was significantly increased.

10. Patti Waldmeir, "Legal eagles rule the roost," *Financial Times*, December 11th–12th, 1999.

11. Ex-slaves sue Japanese: Chinese seek redress in California court, *International Herald Tribune*, October 3rd, 2000.

12. Although it should be noted that EMAS and ISO 14000 certify processes and movement towards stated objectives, and do not guarantee an absolute level of performance.

REFERENCES

Berry, M. A., & Rondinelli, D. A. (1998). Proactive corporate environmental management: A new industrial revolution. *Academy of Management Executive, 12*(2), 38–50.

Brewer, T. L., & Young, S. (2000). *The multilateral investment system and multinational enterprises.* Oxford: Oxford University Press.

Christmann, P. (2000). Effect of "best practices" of environmental management on cost advantage: The role of complementary assets. *Academy of Management Journal, 43*(4), 663–680.

Dean, J. M. (1992). Trade and the environment: A survey of the literature. In: P. Low (Ed.), *International Trade and the Environment – World Bank Discussion Papers.* Washington, DC: World Bank.

Dunning, J. H., & Lundan, S. M. (2001). The geographical sources of competitiveness and multinational financial performance. *Global Economy Quarterly, 2*(3), 165–188.

Ferrantino, M. J. (1997). International trade, environmental quality and public policy. *World Economy,* 43–72.

Gilley, K. M., Worrell, D. L., Davidson, W. N., & El-Jelly, A. (2000). Corporate environmental initiatives and anticipated firm performance: The differential effects of process-driven versus product-driven greening initiatives. *Journal of Management, 26*(6), 1199–1216.

Gladwin, T. N., & Welles, J. G. (1976). Environmental policy and multinational corporate strategy. In: I. Walter (Ed.), *Studies in International Environmental Economics.* New York: Wiley.

Graham, E. M. (2000). *Fighting the wrong enemy: Antiglobal activists and multinational enterprises.* Washington, DC: Institute for International Economics.

Harrison, K. (2002). Ideas and environmental standard-setting: A comparative study of regulation of the pulp and paper industry. *Governance: An International Journal of Policy, Administration and Institutions, 15*(1), 65–96.

Hoffman, A. J. (1997). *From heresy to dogma: An institutional history of corporate environmentalism.* San Francisco: New Lexington Press.

Hoffman, A. J. (1999). Institutional evolution and change: Environmentalism and the U.S. chemical industry. *Academy of Management Journal, 42*(4), 351–371.

Howard, J., Nash, J., & Ehrenfeld, J. (2000). Standard or smokescreen? Implementation of a voluntary environmental code. *California Management Review, 42*(2), 63–82.

Jordan, L., & Tuijl, P. V. (2000). Political responsibility in transnational NGO advocacy. *World Development, 28*(12), 2051–2065.

King, A., & Baerwald, S. (1998). Using the court of public opinion to encourage better business decisions. In: K. Sexton, A. A. Marcus, K. W. Easter & T. D. Burkhardt (Eds), *Better Environmental Decisions: Strategies for Governments, Business and Communities.* Washington, DC: Island Press.

King, A., & Lenox, M. (2000). Industry self-regulation without sanctions: The chemical industry's responsible care program. *Academy of Management Journal, 43*(4), 698–717.

Klassen, R. D., & McLaughlin, C. P. (1996). The impact of environmental management on firm performance. *Management Science, 42*(8), 1199–1214.

Klassen, R. D., & Whybark, D. C. (1999). The impact of environmental technologies on manufacturing performance. *Academy of Management Journal, 42*(6), 599–615.

Kobrin, S. J. (1998). The MAI and the clash of globalizations. *Foreign Policy, 118*(Fall), 97–109.

Kolk, A. (2001). Multinationality and corporate ethics: Codes of conduct in the sporting goods industry. *Journal of International Business Studies, 32*(2), 267–284.

Kolk, A., Tulder, R. V., & Welters, C. (1999). International codes of conduct and corporate social responsibility: Can transnational corporations regulate themselves? *Transnational Corporations, 8*(1), 143–180.

Lampe, M., & Gazda, G. M. (1995). Green marketing in Europe and the United States: An evolving business and society interface. *International Business Review, 4*(3), 295–312.

Leonard, H. J. (1988). *Pollution and the struggle for the world product: Multinational corporations, environment, and international comparative advantage.* Cambridge: Cambridge University Press.

Levy, D. L. (1995). The environmental practices and performance of transnational corporations. *Transnational Corporations, 4*(1), 44–67.

Levy, D. L., & Egan, D. (1998). Capital contests: National and transnational channels of corporate influence on the climate change negotiations. *Politics and Society, 26*(3), 337–361.

Lundan, S. M. (1996). *Internationalization and environmental standards in the pulp and paper industry.* Unpublished Ph.D. dissertation, Rutgers University, NJ, USA.

Lundan, S. M. (2003). The role of environmental issues in the competition for inward investment within Europe. In: P. Ghauri & L. Oxelheim (Eds), *European Union and the Race for Foreign Direct Investment in Europe.* Oxford: Pergamon.

Majumdar, S. K., & Marcus, A. A. (2001). Rules versus discretion: The productivity consequences of flexible regulation. *Academy of Management Journal, 44*(1), 170–179.

Moser, T. (2001). MNCs and sustainable business practice: The case of the Colombian and Peruvian petroleum industries. *World Development, 29*(2), 291–309.

Nehrt, C. (1996). Timing and intensity effects of environmental investments. *Strategic Management Journal, 17*, 535–547.

Nehrt, C. (1998). Maintainability of first mover advantages when environmental regulations differ between countries. *Academy of Management Review, 23*(1), 77–97.

OECD (1999). *Foreign direct investment and the environment.* Paris: OECD.

Porter, M. E. (1991). America's green strategy. *Scientific American* (April), 168.

Porter, M. E., & van der Linde, C. (1995). Toward a new conception of the environment-competitiveness relationship. *Journal of Economic Perspectives, 9*(4), 97–118.

Reinhardt, F. L. (1998). Environmental product differentiation: Implications for corporate strategy. *California Management Review, 40*(4), 43–73.

Reinhardt, F. L. (1999a). Bringing the environment down to earth. *Harvard Business Review* (July–August), 149–157.

Reinhardt, F. L. (1999b). Market failure and the environmental policies of firms: Economic rationales for "beyond compliance" behavior. *Journal of Industrial Ecology, 3*(1), 9–21.

Rugman, A. M., Kirton, J., & Soloway, J. (1997). NAFTA, environmental regulations, and Canadian competitiveness. *Journal of World Trade, 31*(4), 129–144.

Rugman, A. M., & Verbeke, A. (1998). Corporate strategies and environmental regulations: An organizing framework. *Strategic Management Journal, 19*, 363–375.

Russo, M. V., & Fouts, P. A. (1997). A resource-based perspective on corporate environmental performance and profitability. *Academy of Management Journal, 40*(3), 534–559.

Sharma, S., & Vredenburg, H. (1998). Proactive corporate environmental strategy and the development of competitively valuable organizational capabilities. *Strategic Management Journal, 19*, 729–753.

Vogel, D. (1995). *Trading up: Consumer and environmental regulation in a global economy.* Cambridge, MA: Harvard University Press.

Walter, I. (1982). Environmentally induced industrial relocation to developing countries. In: S. J. Rubin & T. R. Graham (Eds), *Environment and Trade: The Relationship of International Trade and Environmental Policy.* Totowa, NJ: Allanheld, Osmun & Co.

Westley, F., & Vredenburg, H. (1997). Interorganizational collaboration and the preservation of global biodiversity. *Organization Science, 8*(4), 381–403.

Wheeler, D. (2001). *Racing to the bottom? Foreign investment and air pollution in developing countries.* Unpublished manuscript, Washington, DC.

MULTINATIONALS AND GLOBAL CLIMATE CHANGE: ISSUES FOR THE AUTOMOTIVE AND OIL INDUSTRIES

Ans Kolk and David Levy

ABSTRACT

This chapter analyzes the strategic responses by U.S. and European multinational enterprises (MNEs) in the oil and automobile industries to the global climate change issue. We examine and attempt to explain the differences across regions, across industries, and the changes over time. Traditional economic drivers of strategy do not provide a satisfactory account for these differences, and the chapter focuses instead on the conflicting institutional pressures on MNEs and the implications for their climate strategy. The home-country institutional context and individual corporate histories can create divergent pressures on strategy for MNEs based in different countries. At the same time, the location of MNEs in global industries and their participation in "global issues arenas" such as climate change generate institutional forces for strategic convergence. It appears that local context influenced initial corporate reactions, but that convergent pressures predominate as the issue matures.

Multinationals, Environment and Global Competition
Research in Global Strategic Management, Volume 9, 171–193
Copyright © 2004 Elsevier Ltd.
All rights of reproduction in any form reserved
ISSN: 1064-4857/doi:10.1016/S1064-4857(03)09008-9

INTRODUCTION

Climate change is an international environmental issue that presents a profound strategic challenge to firms. Measures to control the emissions of greenhouse gases (GHGs), for example, threaten firms that produce fossil fuels as well as firms that depend on these fuels, such as airlines and chemical companies. Other sectors, such as automobile and aircraft manufacturing, are indirectly dependent on fossil fuels. Considerable uncertainties exist concerning the extent and pace of climate change, the likely regulatory response, and the potential impact on markets and technologies. Given the import and scope of the issue, and the risks and uncertainties associated with it, it is perhaps not surprising that companies vary considerably in their perspectives and strategies regarding climate change. Indeed, it is a testament to the significance of the issue that many large firms in the auto and oil industries have assembled senior level climate strategy teams to formulate a coherent response in the face of this complex web of uncertainties.

The climate issue poses a number of strategic dilemmas. Companies can attempt to postpone regulation by debating the science of climate change and the economic cost of greenhouse gas controls, or they can attempt to invest in new low-emission technologies. This "debate or innovate" decision is not a strict dichotomy, of course, as companies may engage in a hedging strategy, or attempt to postpone regulation until they are better prepared. A related question is whether a firm should attempt to invest early and gain first mover advantages, or wait until the technological turmoil and regulatory uncertainty has subsided. R&D resources can be directed toward incremental improvements to existing technologies or radically different ones. Companies also need to decide whether to commit substantial resources to a single technology, or adopt a portfolio strategy, alone or with partners. The decisions are difficult because, while the evidence of climate change is growing, investments in R&D for low-GHG products and processes still appear highly risky. The technologies associated with low-emission vehicles and renewable energy require radically new capabilities that threaten to undermine the competencies and strategic assets of existing companies, and open the industries to new entrants (Anderson & Tushman, 1990; Tushman & Anderson, 1986). Although the long-term nature of the climate issue affords companies a window of time to adapt strategies and invest in new technologies, it is unclear to what extent companies can successfully "reinvent themselves," given the specificity and inertia of corporate competencies (Hannan & Freeman, 1984). Moreover, the unpredictable path of technological evolution makes the task of choosing among competing technologies a treacherous business (Arthur, 1989). Finally, although energy and automotive industries are concentrated, no single company possesses the market power to establish new standards and ensure success for new products.

The different responses to the threat of climate change by European and North American multinational enterprises (MNEs), particularly in the oil and automobile sectors, point to a wide gulf between a more proactive perspective in Europe and a more conservative approach on the part of many American businesses. These differences were especially pronounced during the 1990s. American companies expended considerable energies in aggressively challenging climate science, pointing to the potentially high economic costs of greenhouse gas controls and lobbying against the Kyoto protocol. Technological strategies have tended to focus on long-term, more radical approaches, such as fuel cell vehicles. In Europe, by contrast, companies have been much quicker to proclaim their acceptance of the need for precautionary action and have acquiesced to, if not actively supported, policies leading to mandatory emission controls. The European firms have invested more modest resources in political efforts to shape the emerging climate change regime and to experiment in emission trading schemes. European companies have also engaged in a range of substantial investments in low-emission technologies, including more short-term approaches such as diesel cars and wind energy, as well as solar and fuel cells (Levy & Kolk, 2002; Levy & Rothenberg, 2002).

Over time, however, the positions of European and U.S.-based MNEs have moved towards convergence, although the timing and pace of these shifts has varied. Such convergence should, perhaps, not be surprising, given that the companies involved are large multinationals engaged in each other's markets, are actively involved in a process of globalization of production and management structures, and are frequently active in the same industry associations. As former U.S. Labor Secretary, Robert Reich, has argued, the question of national ownership and identity in international business is increasingly moot as companies pursue their economic objectives internationally (Reich, 1991). This convergence is also driven by a wave of international mergers, joint ventures, as well as the growth of international institutional structures for business coordination such as the International Chamber of Commerce and the Trans-Atlantic Business Dialogue.

For multinational enterprises, the formulation of a climate strategy has been especially complex because they are confronted with very different, often conflicting pressures, originating from the variety of contexts in which they operate. Rosenzweig and Singh (1991, p. 340) write that: "On one hand, a multinational enterprise is a single organization that operates in a global environment, with a need to coordinate its far-flung operations. On the other hand, an MNE is comprised of a set of organizations that operate in distinct national environments." Bartlett and Ghoshal (1989) point to the benefits of economies of scale and global sourcing that derive from a unified strategy coordinated across an MNE's global operations. At the same time, they recognize the considerable value of a multidomestic strategy, adapting to each country's local culture, market conditions, regulatory environment, and technical standards.

This chapter examines the responses of MNEs to the climate change issue in the oil and automobile industries, and attempts to explain some of the major differences as well as the dynamics involved in the trend toward convergence. We argue that home country effects and individual firm-level characteristics present MNEs with different social, economic, and political pressures that can lead to divergent strategies. At the same time, these firms compete in industries with strong global dimensions and participate in the same debates concerning climate change, providing some convergent influences on strategy. The chapter draws from a study of eight MNEs, four in the oil and four in the automobile industry; two of the companies in each industry were based in the U.S., and two in Europe. The study encompassed most of the major companies in these regions: in oil, Exxon, Texaco, BP, and Shell, and in autos, GM, Ford, Volkswagen, and Daimler-Chrysler. Data were collected from a series of interviews in the U.S. and Europe with more than fifty senior personnel in corporate management, industry associations, government agencies, and environmental non-governmental organizations (NGOs). For detailed accounts of these studies, see Kolk and Levy (2001), Levy and Kolk (2002) and Levy and Rothenberg (2002).

THEORETICAL BACKGROUND

When economic interests are clearly defined, companies generally view environmental concerns in a similar way and are likely to adopt similar response strategies, wherever their headquarters might be located. For example, the threat to coal, the most carbon-intensive of all fossil fuels, from GHG controls is clear and immediate, and the reaction around the world has been uniformly hostile. Nuclear, gas, and renewable energy industries, on the other hand, see opportunities in emission controls and have been broadly supportive of the international negotiations. Trans-Atlantic differences in corporate responses to the climate issue have been most noticeable in the auto and oil sectors.

These differences are not easily explicable in terms of the traditional determinants of strategy, such as the possession of particular assets and capabilities. While significant regional differences exist in the auto industry, it is particularly hard to find rational economic explanations for trans-Atlantic differences among oil companies. The external competitive environment and internal resources and capabilities are similar for the companies. The more obvious economic and technological characteristics of the companies, such as the carbon intensity of their production and reserves, are comparable (Rowlands, 2000). Perhaps more than any other industry, oil companies approach strategy in an internationally coordinated manner, while utilizing global sourcing, integration, and rationalization to achieve economies of scale and low costs (Ernst & Steinhubl, 1999; Yergin, 1991).

Here, we make the case that institutional factors are particularly important in explaining strategic differences in responses to climate change. Oliver (1991) has argued that institutional influences are stronger under conditions of uncertainty, because managerial discretion is higher when the economic consequences of actions are unclear. For MNEs facing the climate issue, great uncertainty surrounds the future of climate science, emission regulation, and markets for alternative technologies. The future of the Kyoto Protocol remains unclear, nor is there any degree of certainty concerning the future level of carbon taxes or credits. As a result, there is no straightforward method for calculating optimal strategies a priori. Investments in alternative technologies might yield first mover advantages in vast new markets or could prove to be a waste of money.

Institutional environments are associated with particular organizational fields, which comprise "those organizations that, in the aggregate, constitute a recognized area of institutional life: key suppliers, resources and product customers, regulatory agencies, and other organizations that produce similar services or products" (DiMaggio & Powell, 1991, p. 143). In situations where managers have significant discretion, corporate strategy can be influenced by the location of firms in organizational fields with strong cognitive, normative, and regulatory pressures for conformity (Scott & Meyer, 1994). These institutional environments shape corporate perceptions and interpretations of technological and market potential, regulatory constraints, and firm-specific capabilities (Sharma, 2000). These cognitive and normative frames of reference in turn affect the strategy formation process. Murtha, Lenway and Bagozzi (1998, p. 97), for example, argue that "key aspects of international strategic capabilities derive from managers' cognitive processes" and Prahalad and Doz (1987) suggest that strategic change in MNEs begins with a reorientation of the mind-sets of senior managers. The institutional drivers of strategy are important because, as Hoffman and Ventresca (1999, p. 1369) put it, "the debate over environmental issues such as climate change is determined by which actors are engaged, what kinds of problems are debated, how those problems are defined, and what kinds of solutions are considered appropriate."

Multinational corporations are subject to conflicting strategic pressures arising from the institutional environments of their home country, the host countries, and the global industry (Gooderham, Nordhaug & Ringdal, 1999; Kostova, 1999; Westney, 1993). The distinct regulatory and cultural contexts of countries suggests that the home country environment is a coherent organizational field that exerts a powerful influence on MNE strategy formulation, creating divergent pressures on companies headquartered in different countries (Kostova & Roth,

2002; Rosenzweig & Singh, 1991). Sethi and Elango (1999) note that cultural values and norms are an important element of the country of origin effect. These institutional influences are likely to preserve the legacy of the country of origin, even in highly internationalized companies, because most MNEs still concentrate their senior management responsible for strategy in the country of origin.

The country of origin effect is not the only source of strategic heterogeneity. Each company's unique history and culture affects its response to institutional pressures. For example, companies that experienced a history of losses associated with alternative energy sources are likely to institutionalize a negative view toward the future prospects of such technologies. While some companies still believe that environmental regulations are a burdensome imposition, others are embracing the notion that proactive environmental management practices can offer "win-win" strategic opportunities (Porter & van der Linde, 1995a, b; Reinhardt, 2000). Within the MNE itself, strategies and practices developed in the home country are not necessarily transmitted evenly to all subsidiaries, particularly when home and host countries possess different institutional profiles (Kostova, 1999).

While country of origin and individual company differences create divergent pressures on strategy, MNEs competing in global industries participate in a common industry-level field, creating some tendencies toward convergence for companies in the same industry. The progressive delinking of MNEs from their home countries and the growing importance of the global industry as the dominant organizational field in industries such as autos and oil constitutes an important force for strategic convergence. The trend toward cross-border mergers and acquisitions, such as BP-Amoco and Daimler-Chrysler, reinforces this orientation. The oil industry is even more global in scope than the auto industry, given the undifferentiated nature of the product and the international scope of oil extraction, refining, and retail operations. Given the keen awareness of interdependence in a global oligopoly, companies are likely to copy each others' moves to prevent rivals gaining undue advantage (Chen & MacMillan, 1992; Chen & Miller, 1994; Knickerbocker, 1973). Industry interdependence also takes a collaborative form, within industry associations and in alliances and joint ventures. Executives read the same trade journals and the same industry studies.

The emergence of climate change as a "global issues arena" constitutes a second convergent influence. While the literature on business-government relations has focused on the home-host country axis, little scholarly attention has been paid to the implications for MNEs of the multilateral negotiations and binding international treaties associated with issues such as climate change, ozone depletion, and biodiversity. The network of actors involved in a global issues arena interact frequently and develop their own organizational frameworks, thus constituting sub-fields with isomorphic pressures. The senior managers responsible for climate-related strategy in the companies studied know each other well and meet regularly at international negotiations, conferences and other events. They interact within issue-specific sub-groups of groups such as the International Chamber of Commerce, which are developing institutional structures around the climate issue. These managers are therefore likely to develop common perspectives, so that they come to view climate science and the threats and opportunities arising from regulation and new technologies in similar ways.

A key question here is whether MNEs need to pursue globally coordinated responses to climate change or are able to differentiate their responses according to local economic and regulatory conditions. Corporate political strategies generally need to respond to local political and cultural contexts to a greater extent than product market strategies. Baron (1997, p. 146) argues that "Non-market strategies . . . tend to be less global and more multi-domestic, that is, tailored to the specific issues, institutions, and interests in a country." Similarly, Hansen and Mitchell (2001) found that foreign subsidiaries of MNEs adapt their political strategies to meet host country conditions, though foreign firms tended to try to avoid high-profile activities. However, this emphasis on local responsiveness may not hold for industries and issues that are more global in scope (DeSombre, 2000; Lin, 2001). The evolution of the Kyoto Protocol to control GHGs is clearly an on-going global process entailing multi-lateral negotiations and an international scientific assessment team, the Intergovernmental Panel on Climate Change (IPCC). It would make little sense for one arm of an MNE to be opposing the protocol while another is supporting it. Not only would this entail a waste of resources, but it could also lead to charges of hypocrisy. This became evident for Shell in the mid-1990s, when Shell Europe moved toward acceptance of the need for internationally agreed greenhouse gas emission controls while Shell U.S. was still a member of the Global Climate Coalition (GCC), the industry association which lobbied aggressively against any such measures. This inconsistency complicated the company's efforts to pursue a particular political strategy, and became a severe liability when it was publicized by environmental NGOs, leading Shell U.S. to leave the GCC in 1998.

In the following two sections, we analyze in more detail home-country contexts and individual, firm-specific characteristics, which help to explain some of the strategic differences between firms in the same industry. Subsequently, we examine industry-specific and issue-level factors, in order to characterize the common environment in which firms from different countries are located. These various influences are summarized in Table 1, below. Finally, we consider trends over time and some of the salient differences between the automobile and oil industries.

Table 1.   Important Explanatory Factors for Corporate Positions on
Climate Change.

Factors	Components
Home-country factors	Societal concerns about environment/climate change
	Societal views on corporate responsibilities
	Regulatory culture (litigious or consensus-oriented)
	Ability of companies to influence regulation
	National environmental policies
	National industrial promotion strategies
Firm-specific factors	Economic situation and market positioning
	History of involvement with (technological) alternatives
	Degree of (de)centralisation
	Degree of internationalization of top management
	Availability and type of internal climate expertise
	Nature of strategic planning process
	Corporate culture
Industry-specific factors	Nature and extent of threat posed by climate change
	Availability and cost of alternatives
	Degree of globalization of supply chain
	Political power of the industry
	Technological and competitive situation
Issue-specific factors	Impact of issue on various sectors, countries
	Institutional infrastructure for addressing issue
	Degree to which issue and regulation are global
	Complexity and uncertainty associated with issue

HOME-COUNTRY FACTORS

Three aspects of the home country could influence MNEs' strategies: the home country's economic and physical resources, national economic and industrial policies, and thirdly, cultural values and institutional norms regarding environmental regulation and business lobbying. Porter's perspective on national competitiveness suggests that the economic and regulatory environment of the home country play an important role in shaping corporate capabilities and hence strategies (Porter, 1990; Porter & van der Linde, 1995a, b). Illustrating this logic, several oil industry interviewees mentioned that U.S.-based companies have developed sophisticated technologies for enhancing oil extraction, because many U.S. fields are quite depleted. Although this could result in a more optimistic view of the adequacy of global oil supplies, companies expressed only minor differences on this point. All expected oil production to peak around 2020–2030, though Shell's estimate was toward the earlier end of the range. Moreover, the companies concurred that regulation and new technologies rather than inadequate supply would drive the market for alternative energy. Overall, home country economic and resource conditions are unlikely to affect competencies very much in this industry because the oil companies can tap their subsidiaries and independent specialist companies for technologies and resources.

Inconsistent industrial policy in the U.S. toward renewable energy appears to be a more important factor. Large subsidies initiated under the Carter administration were abruptly cut under Reagan. One Exxon manager stated that: "we are not looking to get into any business supported by government subsidies. We lost more than $500 million on renewables, and learnt a lot of lessons." European companies lacked this history of large losses. Moreover, where policy in the U.S. generally favored oil exploration through various subsidies, European policies of high fuel taxation and support for rail rather than road transportation signaled a less secure future for oil.

In the auto industry, which is more regional in scope, home country conditions are likely to influence corporate strategy more significantly. The regulatory context differed substantially between the U.S. and Europe. The primary concern in the U.S. for many years has been local air quality. U.S. industry was already subject to CAFE standards under the Clean Air Act, and the California Air Review Board (CARB) was mandating zero emission vehicles in the longer-term. Strict controls on SO_x, NO_x, and hydrocarbons have led to precise electronic control of combustion and catalytic converter technology. The focus on local air quality induced U.S.-based companies to lose considerable sums on more radical technologies. GM, for example, had invested more than $1 billion in its electric vehicle, of which less than 1,000 had been sold (Lippert, 1997; Shnayerson, 1996). Although a few GM managers thought that the company had gained valuable expertise in electric drive chains, company managers generally interpreted the experience as a commercial mistake. Ford had invested an estimated $500 million in sodium-sulfur batteries, only to abandon the project because of safety concerns. American companies were also relatively unsuccessful in their efforts to downsize vehicles in the response to the oil shocks of the 1970s and 1980s, and GM managers felt that they had rushed too quickly to downsize their vehicles in response to earlier oil price shocks. With this shared historical experience, American companies did not appreciate the advantages of being a first mover in emerging low-emission automotive technologies.

Initially, U.S.-based companies understood climate change as a continuation of this pressure to improve local air quality, thus not requiring a major strategic change in direction. As a Ford VP responsible for government affairs put it, "There was already huge pressure for reduction of smog precursors. So climate did not require a step function change in strategy; it was more of an organic evolution." Over a period of time, companies came to appreciate that many technological approaches involved trade-offs. Electric vehicles charged by coal-generated electricity can be worse than conventional vehicles in terms of GHG emissions. Similarly, the introduction of catalytic converters in the early 1980s caused a noticeable decrease in fuel efficiency. It was not easy for American companies to shift their technology strategies toward carbon reduction, however, because the regulatory system was still ratcheting up controls on non-GHG emissions while paying no attention to CO_2.

In Europe, by contrast, pre-existing environmental concerns about automobiles were more aligned with the strategic challenge of climate change. Instead of a focus on local air quality, concerns about resource depletion and congestion had led to high fuel prices and investments in public transportation that reduced fuel consumption and vehicle use overall. European innovation efforts were therefore already more directed toward lighter weight, smaller vehicles with high fuel efficiency, and companies were more aware of potential challenges to the private automobile in the broader transportation system. This has not only given European companies greater expertise in small, fuel-efficient vehicles, but also created more confidence that they can adjust to a carbon-constrained world.

It is important to note that these differences between U.S.-based and European MNEs appear to be more related to perceptions than to possession of firm-specific competencies. There is no reason to think that European oil companies have more expertise in renewables than U.S. firms, quite the opposite. It is the history of U.S. losses that colors managerial perceptions of the future. In the auto industry, all the world's major companies have made significant efforts toward fuel efficiency since the first oil price shock in late 1973. If anything, European companies might find it relatively harder to squeeze additional weight and efficiency out of their product range, and appear to be basing their low-emission strategies on the widespread adoption of diesel, at least in the short-term. Indeed, it is the U.S. companies that are investing in advanced light-weight materials and high-efficiency conventional engines. American auto companies tend to view the future potential market for low-emission vehicles through the lens of their earlier failures with electric vehicles.

A third aspect of the home country environment is the context of cultural values and institutional norms regarding business-government interactions. The conventional wisdom is that "Europeans demonstrate their considerable concern about environmental issues in their behavior as voters, consumers, corporate managers, and policy makers . . . (while) people in the United States are more individualistic, more concerned about their lifestyles than about the environment, and more ideologically averse to regulation" (Levy & Newell, 2000). A survey by

Kempton and Craig (1993) supported this view, finding that Europeans expressed more concrete concerns about environmental impacts on future generations and viewed their responsibility for sustainability as part of their national identity and heritage. At the same time, sensitivity to societal concerns regarding environmental issues as expressed in annual corporate reports is also stronger in Europe than in the U.S. (Kolk, van de Wateringen & Walhain, 2001).

In our study, interviewees from European oil companies expressed explicit concern for their legitimacy and image. A BP manager stated that "as a company trying to act with corporate social responsibility, is it sensible to turn a blind eye to this issue? Our response was no." Similarly a Shell executive discussed the ramifications of negative publicity "Here there is a real concern for legitimacy and what the community thinks. There is a fight for the hearts and minds of the public; this is a long-term force affecting our business." Following the Brent Spar incident, consumer boycotts were organized in European countries and Shell's market share dropped noticeably in Germany. One of Shell's long term planning scenarios, termed People Power, discussed the risk of significant public pressure. Exxon, by contrast, saw little value in improving its image. As one manager put it, "If we appear more green, it might get us a better seat at the policy table, but the real question is whether it would improve our access to resources and markets."

In the political arena, the American system of business-government relations is often characterized as adversarial, with a tradition of contentious policy battles being waged on the basis of detailed technical studies (Jasanoff, 1990). Several U.S. managers acknowledged that adopting an adversarial stance concerning climate change did not cost them much credibility with regulators; one GM manager said, "The Hill works by compromise, so you need to go to the extreme. It ends up completely polarized." An Exxon manager stated "they cannot ignore us anyway; we are the big elephant at the table." This aggressive approach was typified in the activities of The Global Climate Coalition (GCC), an industry association formed in 1989 to represent major fossil fuel users and producers, which has strongly challenged the scientific basis for action, questioned the legitimacy of the Intergovernmental Panel on Climate Change (IPCC), and highlighted potential economic costs (Leggett, 2000; Newell, 2000).

By contrast, key stakeholders in Europe tend to engage in more collaborative bargaining, resulting in a more corporatist and consensual system (Jasanoff, 1991; Kruck, Borchers & Weingart, 1999; Vogel, 1978). European managers viewed GHG regulation as inevitable and thought that an adversarial approach would only hurt their credibility and political access. As a result, challenging the scientific basis for regulation was seen as futile. An official with the German environmental ministry said: "If the companies here argued the way they do in the

States, it would create an image disaster. And they wouldn't argue the science to me or I would kill them." Similarly, a representative with the VDA, the German auto industry association, commented that: "if the auto industry were to support a specific study, the people would think that scientists were bought by the industry and they would not believe them." These differences created some interesting tensions between the European operations and U.S. headquarters of one auto company. A European manager reported that:

> my boss in Detroit said we should argue about the science and the economics. It was an education process to get them on board. We had to explain that it's not constructive to challenge the science in Europe, and if we want to influence the debate we cannot move back. Here, the IPCC reports are accepted without question by policy makers. We would be thrown out of the room if we challenged them.

Over a period of time, and perhaps as a result of these interactions among MNE units, the Americans began to soften their position. Ford's VP of Economics and Strategy, Michael Kaericher, acknowledged that "appearing negative hurts. We lost the first round of battles. We are now trying to be more positive with the science, while still pointing to the high cost of precipitate action before scientific uncertainties are resolved. Our actions will be less strident in the future."

The home country influence would also diminish as top management teams became more international. By 1995, Exxon, Mobil and Texaco still had no board members from outside North America, but annual reports indicate that an increasing number of senior executives have spent significant portions of their careers outside the home country. Top management in Detroit was becoming increasingly cosmopolitan in outlook in the mid-1990s and was therefore perhaps more sensitive to the market and regulatory environments in Europe and elsewhere. Ford implemented its Ford 2000 project, which pushed toward the rationalization and integration of production and management worldwide, and GM began to move in a similar direction. Ford Europe, for example, became responsible for the Fiesta-size class of small cars worldwide, as well as for the development of advanced diesel technology. According to one Ford Europe manager,

> What has changed is the global focus. In the old days, senior management in the U.S. spent some of their careers in Europe. Alex Trotman had a European pedigree. But now we have global managers in top management, people who grew up in other cultures. Ford understands the importance of Europe now, and this really puts pressure internally on the U.S. focus.

FIRM-SPECIFIC FACTORS

MNEs are likely to respond differently to the climate change issue because of the specificities of their own histories, cultures, and structures. In the oil industry, for example, Exxon has been the most aggressive and successful in implementing a lean model of cost reduction and efficiency, leading to the highest returns in the industry on capital employed. The company's status as the most profitable of the oil majors created little stimulus to reconsider its successful strategic focus on supplying oil for transportation and gas for power markets. Instead of investing in renewables, on which it had lost large sums in the 1980s, Exxon has focused its efforts on fuel cell research and carbon sequestration, technologies which complement oil-related technologies. For Texaco, by contrast, one impetus to re-evaluate strategy was the financial crisis caused when oil prices fell below $15 a barrel at the end of the 1990s. Texaco managers also expressed the belief that their gasification technologies could generate hydrogen for fuel cells.

BP, Shell and Texaco expressed the belief that early investments in renewables would generate significant first-mover advantages, but that new competencies would take time to build. For Shell, this approach was a continuation of the company's institutional history of organic, internal growth. Interviewees at Exxon, by contrast, had a very clear perception of their company's strategic strengths. One commented: "we have learnt from the experiment with diversification that businesses such as office products, with rapid product cycles and very different technologies, require competencies that Exxon lacks." If the more dire predictions about climate change came to pass, Exxon managers expressed confidence that an acquisition strategy would enable the company to obtain the required technologies and capabilities in an environment of much lower risk.

Firm-level differences in organizational structures and processes also appeared to play a role. MNEs such as Exxon and Ford tightly controlled their strategic planning from the center, leaving little room for local discretion or dissent. Perspectives from these companies' European operations did not easily permeate into the deliberations of top management. By comparison, GM was more decentralized, enabling its research labs to develop an electric vehicle and a product division to commence limited production even in the face of opposition from corporate headquarters (Shnayerson, 1996). Similarly, a traditionally decentralized multinational like Shell, having grown from two separate national bases, was less prone to insular thinking and more open to international perspectives. The company's renowned scenario planning process emphasized a longer time horizon than at Exxon and deliberately set out to incorporate diverse perspectives and challenge conventional thinking.

Sometimes, individuals can make a difference. Texaco's CEO Peter Bijur, appointed in 1996, had extensive experience in Canada and Europe, and he formed a new team of senior vice-presidents, all with substantial international experience. Texaco managers explicitly associated the change in the company's position on climate with the appointment of Bijur and his openness to European perspectives.

Exxon's Brian Flannery, who played a key role in developing the company's climate strategy, was a well-known climate skeptic with significant internal credibility, who had published articles in scientific journals and was engaged in the international scientific review process. Ruth Reck, a scientist working in GM's research laboratories, began tracking the issue in the mid-1970s, long before it came onto the radar screen of other companies, and became a powerful internal advocate. In an effort to inform and motivate the company, she organized a large GM conference on the subject in 1985, which was attended by more than 700 company personnel. Product managers were asked to speak about the relevance of their existing emission reduction strategies for greenhouse gas emissions.

INDUSTRY CHARACTERISTICS

To the extent that industries are more global in scope, we might expect MNEs from different countries to be facing similar competitive conditions. In terms of institutional theory, the relevant field exerting pressures for conformity is more global than national or regional. Oil is the archetypal global industry. It is a commodity with a uniform international price and the major companies tend to adopt global rather than multidomestic strategies, at least in their extraction, production and refining operations (Grant & Cibin, 1996; Yergin, 1991). If alternative energy sources, such as wind or solar, become available at competitive costs, they will affect global demand for fossil fuels. Shell and BP will likely be seeking global opportunities for their large investments in renewable energy sources. All of the oil companies studied are large, integrated multinationals with comparable strategic capabilities, and they possess production and distribution operations throughout North America, Europe, and the Middle East. As a result, they are subject to similar sets of regulatory pressures. Their technological capabilities are also comparable, according to interviewees, and they all access the services of independent specialized exploration and drilling companies. The ratio of oil to gas reserves, and the proportion of operations in developing countries not covered by the Kyoto Protocol are quite comparable among the companies (Rowlands, 2000). As a result of this global oligopolistic structure, the companies have tended to move through phases of diversification, restructuring, and consolidation in a synchronized fashion (Ernst & Steinhubl, 1999; Grant & Cibin, 1996). Despite the fact that oil companies are among the oldest MNEs, it is only during the 1990s that they have abandoned geographic structures and moved toward globally integrated business units, increasingly based in subsidiary locations. Accompanying this structural shift, senior management has become more internationalized, further reducing the institutional dominance of the home country.

The auto industry is somewhat more regional in nature, both in terms of supply chain integration and the degree of product differentiation (Eden & Molot, 1993; Shaffer, 1992). These regional differences can explain, in part, the more accommodating stance of European companies. Under intense pressure from the EU authorities, in 1998 the European Automobile Industry Association (ACEA) accepted a voluntary agreement to reduce CO_2 emissions to 140 g/km by 2008 (about 38 mpg), with a 120 g/km target for 2012. The agreement included Ford and GM's European subsidiaries, but not Japanese manufacturers (Bradsher, 1998). European companies have addressed these regulatory pressures by introducing very small, light-weight cars such as Daimler-Chrysler's SMART car, and investing substantial amounts in a range of technologies from diesel to fuel cells. Daimler has aggressively pursued fuel cell technology, investing $320 million in Ballard in April 1997, and has announced plans for a limited commercial launch by 2004. The short-term commitments would be met through large investments in advanced diesel technology.

By comparison, U.S.-based auto companies were planning a car of the future that would not require any change in transportation patterns, road infrastructure, or social conceptions of cars; rather, all the burden of emissions reduction would be placed on advanced automotive technologies. This was the conception underlying a collaborative venture called the Partnership for a New Generation of Vehicles (PNGV), launched in 1993 with substantial government funding and the participation of the three U.S. manufacturers. This project focused on longer-term and more radical approaches to emission reduction, without sacrificing car size, comfort, or other features. Such efforts were necessarily expensive, generating pessimism about the likely markets for such cars and political resistance to emission controls in the short-term. Meanwhile, companies were free to sell large and highly profitable SUVs and trucks in the U.S. market, where fuel remains cheap and particulate emissions from diesels are more tightly regulated. At the same time, U.S. auto companies have successfully fought off efforts to raise CAFE (corporate average fuel economy) standards above the current 27.5 mpg.

Despite these regional differences, a trend toward convergence can also be observed in the auto industry. By January 1998, GM Chairman Jack Smith was acknowledging that climate change was a cause for concern, and GM entered a project organized by the World Resources Institute called Safe Climate, Sound Business. At the end of 1999, Ford resigned from the Global Climate Coalition. The technology strategies of U.S. companies increasingly began to converge with those of European firms. In December 1997, Ford invested $420 million in the joint venture between Daimler-Chrysler and the Canadian fuel cell company Ballard. GM formed an alliance with Toyota to invest in a range of technologies. This level of investment would not be undertaken for one region only. To satisfy needs for shorter-term technologies, Ford and GM turned to outside suppliers for diesel expertise (Simison & Quintanilla, 1998).

One reason for this convergence lies in the nature of the threat posed by climate change to the auto industry. In some ways, the threat to the American auto industry is more immediate and severe than to oil. No practical substitutes for oil exist in the transportation sector for the next 10–15 years, but a sharp increase in price in the short-term could shift demand for cars substantially to smaller, more efficient cars in which American companies lack market strength and lose money. American managers did not want to be caught unprepared again in a high oil price environment and acknowledged that if the more pessimistic scientific forecasts were borne out, implications for the industry could be drastic. A Ford VP was concerned about relying on information filtered through the corporate institutional lens: "The trick from a management standpoint is how to get information through the layers of the organization and be able to make a judgment. We want to know what's really going on, not just what we want to hear." Top management began to arrange briefings directly with outside scientists, including some who were known as climate advocates.

At the same time, low emission technologies constitute less of a fundamental threat to the auto industry than to oil. Low-emission automotive technologies represent a radical change at the component level, but are more incremental at the architectural level – a car would still comprise a chassis, power train, accessories and so on. The core competencies of automobile companies in applying lean production techniques to large-scale assembly and in managing complex supply chain relationships would not be fundamentally threatened. In contrast, renewable energy sources such as photovoltaics and wind present a profound long-term threat to oil company capabilities in prospecting, extracting, refining, and distributing petroleum products. Oil companies are experts at geology, chemistry, large-scale continuous process operations, and managing vertically integrated supply chains. Photovoltaics and wind rely on electronics and turbine-based technologies respectively, and are appropriate for more distributed and disaggregated supply chain configurations.

The global oligopoly in the oil industry promoted frequent interactions among senior executives and a shared perspective on the energy sector. For example, all the oil companies had initially perceived climate change as a serious threat to their core business, but over time the companies became less pessimistic. None of the oil company managers interviewed expected renewables to pose major threats to oil before mid-century due to cost and infrastructure limitations. Emission controls were not expected to be severe due to flexibility in the Kyoto implementation mechanisms, and the common view was that the outlook for core oil and gas businesses remained strong in the medium term; demand for gas for power generation was booming even without carbon controls, while oil would remain the primary fuel for transportation. Any improvements in fuel efficiency would be more than offset by growth in air transportation, car sales and miles traveled, particularly in developing countries, while radical technologies such as fuel cells still faced many cost and technical barriers.

The oligopolistic nature of these industries also sensitized companies to each other's actions and stimulated emulation. Companies are sometimes willing to invest to match competitors' moves even when expected returns are highly uncertain or negative rather than risk ceding strategic advantage (Chen & MacMillan, 1992; Chen & Miller, 1994; Knickerbocker, 1973). The 1989 Exxon Valdez oil spill, for example, stimulated concern among competitors and constituted a "catalyst for change throughout BP" (Reinhardt, 2000). Similarly, BP learnt from Shell's misfortune with the Brent Spar incident in 1995 that legitimacy and reputation can be more important than technical analysis. In turn, the 1997 speech by BP's Browne caused other companies to reconsider their positions. One Texaco executive stated that "Texaco has always been stronger in engineering than public relations, but we're trying to change. We saw how much mileage BP got from Browne's speech." Texaco also began inventorying greenhouse gas emissions in 1998. An interviewee commented that: "we looked at how BP and Shell were inventorying their emissions and evaluating the business impact of greenhouse gases. Texaco took the best pieces of their protocols." Exxon closely monitored these developments, and one interviewee noted that: "if emissions trading becomes real, it would only take a few months for us to come up with a system."

A similar dynamic was observed in the auto industry. Toyota's commercial launch into the U.S. market in 2000 of the Prius, a hybrid electric-gasoline engine car, took the industry somewhat by surprise and caused other companies to accelerate their plans. Honda leapfrogged Toyota and launched its hybrid Insight in the U.S. market in December 1999. Although most American executives were dismissive of the prospects for the car, they were nervous that they might misread the market or fall behind a competitor. A Ford V.P. remarked that:

> of course we are concerned about what competitors are doing. We have to build a product that satisfies consumers and any insights into consumer demands are a scarce and valuable commodity. Look at what happened with the mini-van, which was a Ford idea that Chrysler made happen.

Daimler's investment in April 1997 in the Canadian fuel cell company Ballard had a similar effect, with Ford joining the venture in December 1997. After Daimler announced a target date of 2004 for introducing a commercial fuel cell vehicle, Ford, GM, BMW, and Honda followed with similar pronouncements. This "follow-the-leader" behavior has been observed before in the international business literature (Knickerbocker, 1973). It has been suggested that fuel cell vehicles, by many accounts, are not the most promising low-emission technology, due to their cost, technological difficulties with fuel reformers to produce hydrogen, and relatively small advantage in GHG emissions. Nevertheless, in institutional terms, these moves confer some legitimacy on the technology and create pressures on others.

ISSUE-LEVEL FACTORS: CONVERGENCE ACROSS COUNTRIES AND INDUSTRIES

Multinational corporations are increasingly engaged with global issues such as climate change, ozone depletion, and labor standards in developing countries, with concomitant sets of institutions for negotiating, monitoring and enforcing agreements. Not only are MNEs likely to develop a global rather than a multidomestic response to such issues, but these global issues are likely to exert institutional pressures for convergence on MNEs from different countries and industries. In the case of climate change, participation in industry associations and a multitude of negotiation sessions, scientific meetings, and conferences have provided arenas within which expectations concerning science, policy, markets, and technologies tended to converge. Key managers responsible for climate strategy in each of the companies studied were on first name terms and had met each other frequently during the many years over which the issue emerged from scientific curiosity to the foremost environmental and policy concern facing the international community.

In addition to negotiations and conferences, the dense institutional infrastructure established by industry has tended to encourage convergent views and attitudes. The Global Climate Coalition represented multiple sectors and included some European companies. The International Chamber of Commerce has an active climate change working group. American automobile manufacturers were members of ACEA, the European industry association, while European companies were members of the Alliance of Automobile Manufacturers, the new industry association formed in January 1999 to represent the interests of manufacturers with U.S. production, whatever their home country. In the oil industry, European companies have participated in the American Petroleum Institute while American companies attend European industry meetings. The London-based International Petroleum Industry Environmental Conservation Association (IPIECA), in which all the major oil companies participate, has four active working groups, including one on climate change. IPIECA has served as a particularly important venue for companies to discuss their views, and staff gave an example of how a series of meetings helped to reconcile differences. A July 1998 workshop on Kyoto implementation mechanisms produced a stalemate, with U.S. companies concerned that any mention of possible mechanisms could imply agreement to a binding treaty. By 2000, IPIECA was able to produce a document representing a common approach to mechanisms.

More broadly, these intense interactions promote the diffusion of new conceptual frames for considering the business-environment relationship. American companies have moved toward accepting the need for some precautionary action in the absence of definitive scientific evidence, though without endorsing Kyoto. While European companies were quicker to embrace the concept of ecomodernism (Hajer, 1995), suggesting the compatibility of environmental and business goals, this thinking has increasingly permeated industry-wide discussions. One example of this process was a series of open discussions in Washington, DC in 1998 and 1999 on business and climate change organized by the Business Council for Sustainable Energy. Michael Marvin, director of the organization, observed that "companies don't come expecting to change their positions, but they move by a process of osmosis. At our meetings they talk about positive, reasonable solutions. It makes a big impact when Enron, ARCO, and Shell come out ahead on the issue."

CONCLUSION

This chapter has analyzed the factors driving the strategies of multinationals in the oil and automobile industries based in the U.S. and Europe regarding climate change. Industry characteristics and the nature of the technological threat accounted for some of the cross-industry differences, but conventional drivers of strategy could not adequately explain the marked differences observed between U.S. and European based MNEs' responses. We have argued that, given the conditions of considerable uncertainty relating to the issue and its business impact, the institutional environment plays an important role in influencing corporate strategies. MNEs facing global issues such as climate change are immersed in multiple institutional contexts, subjecting them to competing pressures. The disparate reactions of U.S. and European companies in the early phase of the climate issue were found to be related to corporate histories and experiences with alternative technologies, norms concerning the conduct of business-government relations, and cognitive assumptions regarding the future of fossil fuels and substitute technologies. Divergent pressures initially tended to predominate, as home country context and individual corporate experiences influenced initial corporate reactions to this emerging environmental issue. When a new issue such as climate change first emerges, uncertainty is very high regarding the scientific issues, technological alternatives, and potential regulatory responses. In the absence of significant inter-firm communication and coordination, firms are likely to respond based on their existing institutionalized repertoires of understanding that are firm-specific and related to their home country's national cultural and regulatory contexts.

It is notable, however, that convergent pressures tended to increase as the issue matured. Over a period of time, a more sophisticated understanding of the science emerged and mechanisms for regulating emissions, monitoring, and enforcement became institutionalized. In the case of climate change, this maturity was signaled by the release in 2001 of the Third Assessment Report of the Intergovernmental Panel on Climate Change, the voluminous official output of collaborative efforts by more than two thousand scientists to inform the international negotiating body concerning climate science, likely impacts, and approaches to mitigation. The report, drafts of which were available during 2000, significantly strengthened the scientific consensus concerning the anthropogenic causes of climate change and its likely severity. A number of corporate scientists were also drafted to participate in writing and reviewing the report. Detailed mechanisms for emission trading and for funding technology transfer to less developed countries were devised at the fifth Conference of the Parties (COP-5) in Bonn in 1999 and at COP-6 in the Hague in 2000. By this stage, corporate representatives from a core group of oil, coal, automobile, and chemical companies had been meeting several times a year at negotiation sessions, conferences, and industry associations. As the companies became more aware of their competitors' responses and more enmeshed in issue-specific international regulatory and scientific institutions, they began to coordinate their responses to the issue within national and cross-national industry associations and issue-specific working groups. These intense interactions strengthened the industry and issue-level organizational fields within which strategic convergence might be expected. As a result of frequent interactions in these institutional environments, the companies have developed similar outlooks on markets and technologies.

It is noteworthy that those companies with prior experience in renewable technologies were most reticent in investing in renewables in response to climate change. Strategic responses were thus driven less by accumulated technological competencies and more by the institutionalized memory of losses associated with prior investments. In general, managerial perceptions of markets, technologies, and regulatory prospects appeared more important as strategic drivers than any objective assessment of these factors. Indeed, it was the uncertainty surrounding these issues which afforded management considerable discretion and increased the influence of institutional factors. A significant managerial implication of this study is, therefore, that institutional frames provide strategic guidelines derived from historical and home country experiences, which are not necessarily relevant to future global market conditions. The failure of renewable energy markets to maintain growth in the 1980s does not doom their prospects for the twenty-first century. MNEs need to develop strategy based on a broad set of inputs gained from interactions with subsidiaries, industry associations, and NGOs.

REFERENCES

Anderson, P., & Tushman, M. L. (1990). Technological discontinuities and dominant designs: A cyclical model of technological change. *Administrative Science Quarterly, 35*, 604–633.

Arthur, W. B. (1989). Competing technologies, increasing returns, and lock-in by historical events. *The Economic Journal, 99*(394), 116–131.

Baron, D. P. (1997). Integrated strategy, trade policy, and global competition. *California Management Review, 39*(2), 145–169.

Bartlett, C., & Ghoshal, S. (1989). *Managing across borders: The transnational solution.* Boston: Harvard Business School Press.

Bradsher, K. (1998). European auto division calling for improved fuel economy. *New York Times*, April 26th, 24.

Chen, M.-J., & MacMillan, I. C. (1992). Non-response and delayed response to competitive moves: The roles of competitor dependence and action irreversibility. *Academy of Management Journal, 35*, 539–570.

Chen, M.-J., & Miller, D. (1994). Competitive attack, retaliation and performance: An expectancy-valence framework. *Strategic Management Journal, 15*, 85–102.

DeSombre, E. R. (2000). *Domestic sources of international environmental policy: Industry, environmentalists, and U.S. power.* Cambridge, MA: MIT Press.

DiMaggio, P., & Powell, W. (Eds) (1991). *The new institutionalism in organizational analysis.* Chicago: University of Chicago Press.

Eden, L., & Molot, M. A. (1993). Continentalizing the north American auto industry. In: R. Grinspun & M. A. Cameron (Eds), *The Political Economy of North American Free Trade* (pp. 297–313). New York: St. Martin's Press.

Ernst, D., & Steinhubl, A. M. J. (1999). Petroleum: After the megamergers. *The McKinsey Quarterly* (2), 49–57.

Gooderham, P. N., Nordhaug, O., & Ringdal, K. (1999). Institutional and rational determinants of organizational practices: Human resource management in European firms. *Administrative Science Quarterly, 44*(2), 507–531.

Grant, R. M., & Cibin, R. (1996). Strategy, structure, and market turbulence: The international oil majors, 1970–1991. *Scandinavian Journal of Management, 12*(2), 165–188.

Hajer, M. A. (1995). *The politics of environmental discourse: Ecological modernization and the policy process.* Oxford: Clarendon Press.

Hannan, M., & Freeman, J. (1984). Structural inertia and organizational change. *American Sociological Review, 82*, 929–964.

Hansen, W. L., & Mitchell, N. J. (2001). Globalization or national capitalism: Large firms, national strategies, and political activities. *Business and Politics, 3*(1), 5–19.

Hoffman, A. J., & Ventresca, M. J. (1999). The institutional framing of policy debates: Economics versus the environment. *American Behavioral Scientist, 42*(8), 1368–1392.

Jasanoff, S. (1990). *The fifth branch*. Cambridge, MA: Harvard University Press.

Jasanoff, S. (1991). Cross-national differences in policy implementation. *Evaluation Review, 15*(1), 103–119.

Kempton, W., & Craig, P. P. (1993). European perspectives on global climate change. *Environment, 35*(3), 17–45.

Knickerbocker, F. T. (1973). *Oligopolistic reaction and multinational enterprise*. DBA Thesis, Harvard Business School, Division of Research.

Kolk, A., & Levy, D. (2001). Winds of change: Corporate strategy, climate change and oil multinationals. *European Management Journal, 19*(5), 501–509.

Kolk, A., Van de Wateringen, S. L., & Walhain, S. (2001). Environmental reporting by the Fortune Global 250: Exploring the influence of nationality and sector. *Business Strategy and the Environment, 10*(1), 15–29.

Kostova, T. (1999). Transnational transfer of strategic organizational practices: A contextual perspective. *Academy of Management Review, 24*(2), 308–324.

Kostova, T., & Roth, K. (2002). Adoption of an organizational practice by the subsidiaries of the MNC: Institutional and relational effects. *Academy of Management Journal, 45*(1), 215–233.

Kruck, C., Borchers, J., & Weingart, P. (1999). Climate research and climate politics in Germany: Assets and hazards of consensus-based risk management. In: C. Miller & P. Edwards (Eds), *Changing the Atmosphere: Science and the Politics of Global Warming*. Cambridge, MA: MIT Press.

Leggett, J. (2000). *The carbon war: Dispatches from the end of the oil century*. London: Penguin books.

Levy, D. L., & Kolk, A. (2002). Strategic responses to global climate change: Conflicting pressures on multinationals in the oil industry. *Business and Politics, 4*(3), 275–300.

Levy, D. L., & Newell, P. (2000). Oceans apart? Business responses to the environment in Europe and North America. *Environment, 42*(9), 8–20.

Levy, D. L., & Rothenberg, S. (2002). Heterogeneity and change in environmental strategy: Technological and political responses to climate change in the automobile industry. In: A. Hoffman & M. Ventresca (Eds), *Organizations, Policy and the Natural Environment: Institutional and Strategic Perspectives*. Stanford: Stanford University Press.

Lin, K. C. (2001). Finding the right chemistry: The U.S. chemical industry in Asia. *Business and Politics, 3*(2), 185–203.

Lippert, J. (1997). New R & D policy powers GM engine quest. *Automotive News*, April 14th, 20.

Murtha, T. P., Lenway, S., & Bagozzi, R. P. (1998). Global mind-sets and cognitive shifts in a complex multinational corporation. *Strategic Management Journal, 19*(2), 97–114.

Newell, P. (2000). *Climate for change: Non-state actors and the global politics of the greenhouse*. Cambridge: Cambridge University Press.

Oliver, C. (1991). Strategic responses to institutional processes. *Academy of Management Review, 16*, 145–179.

Porter, M. E. (1990). *The competitive advantage of nations*. New York: Free Press.

Porter, M. E., & van der Linde, C. (1995a). Green and competitive. *Harvard Business Review*, 120–134.

Porter, M. E., & van der Linde, C. (1995b). Toward a new conception of the environment-competitiveness relationship. *Journal of Economic Perspectives, 9*(4), 97–118.

Prahalad, C. K., & Doz, Y. L. (1987). *The multinational mission: Balancing local demands and global vision*. New York: Free Press.

Reich, R. (1991). *The work of nations: Preparing ourselves for 21st-century capitalism*. New York: Knopf.

Reinhardt, F. (2000). Global climate change and BP Amoco. *Harvard Business School Case Study*.

Reinhardt, F. L. (2000). *Down to earth: Applying business principles to environmental management.* Boston: Harvard Business School Press.

Rosenzweig, P. M., & Singh, J. V. (1991). Organizational environments and the multinational enterprise. *Academy of Management Review, 16,* 340–361.

Rowlands, I. H. (2000). Beauty and the beast? BP's and Exxon's positions on global climate change. *Environment and Planning, 18,* 339–354.

Scott, W. R., & Meyer, J. W. (Eds) (1994). *Institutional environments and organizations.* Thousand Oaks, CA: Sage.

Sethi, S. P., & Elango, B. (1999). The influence of "country of origin" on multinational corporation global strategy: A conceptual framework. *Journal of International Management, 5,* 285–298.

Shaffer, B. (1992). Regulation, competition, and strategy: The case of automobile fuel economy standards 1974–1991. In: J. Post (Ed.), *Research in Corporate Social Performance and Policy* (Vol. 13, pp. 191–218). Greenwich, CT: JAI.

Sharma, S. (2000). Managerial interpretations and organizational context as predictors of corporate choice of environmental strategy. *Academy of Management Journal, 43*(4), 681–702.

Shnayerson, M. (1996). *The car that could.* New York: Random House.

Simison, R., & Quintanilla, C. (1998). Navistar is Ford's choice to supply diesel engines. *Wall Street Journal,* March 6th.

Tushman, M. L., & Anderson, P. (1986). Technological discontinuities and organizational environments. *Administrative Science Quarterly, 31,* 439–465.

Vogel, D. (1978). Why businessmen distrust their state: The political consciousness of American corporate executives. *British Journal of Political Science, 8,* 45–78.

Westney, E. (1993). Institutionalization theory and the multinational corporation. In: S. Ghoshal & E. Westney (Eds), *Organization Theory and the Multinational Corporation.* New York: St. Martin's Press.

Yergin, D. (1991). *The prize: The epic quest for oil, money, and power.* New York: Touchstone.

MULTINATIONALS, THE ENVIRONMENT AND THE WTO: ISSUES IN THE ENVIRONMENTAL GOODS AND SERVICES SECTOR AND IN CLIMATE CHANGE MITIGATION

Thomas L. Brewer

ABSTRACT

Two linked topics concerning environmental issues at the WTO and their implications for MNEs are considered – namely, international business in the environmental goods and services sector, and the relationship of the WTO to the emerging climate change regime, particularly the Kyoto Protocol. Liberalization of barriers to international trade and investment in environmental goods and services could expand market access and otherwise change competitive conditions for multinational firms. The relationship of the WTO to the Kyoto Protocol is on the broader agenda of environmental and economic diplomacy. Decisions concerning these two sets of issues during the next few years will affect multinational firms' competitive positions, strategies and operations in many industries. For instance, the liberalization of barriers to trade and FDI in the environmental goods and services industry creates new international market opportunities for firms that want to expand abroad; it also creates new competitive threats in home markets. The chapter

Multinationals, Environment and Global Competition
Research in Global Strategic Management, Volume 9, 195–217
© 2004 Published by Elsevier Ltd.
ISSN: 1064-4857/doi:10.1016/S1064-4857(03)09009-0

was in press when the WTO Cancun ministerial meeting collapsed in mid-September 2003.

INTRODUCTION

This chapter examines the environmental agenda at the World Trade Organization (WTO) and its implications for multinational firms. Two sets of environmental topics receive special attention because of their intrinsic importance and because they reveal the diverse ways the WTO affects multinational enterprises' (MNEs') strategies and operations. The issues are: (a) trade and investment in the environmental goods and services sector; and (b) the relationship of the WTO to the emerging climate change regime, particularly the Kyoto Protocol. The former issue is on the negotiating agenda at the WTO, and liberalization of barriers to international trade and investment in that sector could expand market access and otherwise change competitive conditions for multinational firms. The latter issue is on the broader agenda of environmental and economic diplomacy; although the United States has prevented it from being officially included on the Doha round agenda, there are nevertheless many potential overlaps between specific provisions in WTO agreements and the Kyoto Protocol. Whether and how the issues in those overlapping areas are addressed, and perhaps resolved, will have important implications for MNEs in many sectors.

The two sets of issues, furthermore, are linked.[1] For the extent of access to foreign technology and providers of environmental goods and services can affect a firm's response to climate change issues. For instance, technology to monitor and/or reduce greenhouse gas emissions in its production processes or reduce such emissions from the use of its products may find such technology unavailable or more expensive because of barriers to international trade and investment.

The analysis in the chapter explicitly includes foreign direct investment (FDI), which is of course central to the strategic choices and operations of MNEs. In addition, the chapter addresses issues concerning services and intellectual property, as well as goods, because they are all covered by WTO agreements. As a result, MNEs' competitive positions, strategic modes of entry into markets and their strategic and operational choices about how to serve markets and where to produce goods and services – all of these are potentially affected by WTO agreements (Brewer & Young, 2001a, b; Condon, 2002).

The chapter is divided into the following main sections:

(1) Overview of Environmental Issues at the WTO.
(2) Trade and FDI in the Environmental Goods and Services Sector.

(3) Climate Change Issues: The WTO, the Kyoto Protocol and Multinational Firms.
(4) Competitive, Strategic and Operational Implications for MNEs.

OVERVIEW OF ENVIRONMENTAL ISSUES AT THE WTO

The Preamble to the Marrakech Agreement establishing the World Trade Organization (WTO) notes that "The parties to this agreement (recognize) that their relations in the field of trade and economic endeavour should be conducted with a view to raising standards of living . . . while allowing for the optimal use of the world's resources in accordance with the objective of sustainable development, seeking both to protect and preserve the environment and to enhance the means for doing so in a manner consistent with their respective needs and concerns at different levels of economic development, . . ." (GATT, 1994).

In the *Doha Communiqué*, which officially inaugurated the current negotiating round, the members of the WTO observe that "the aims of upholding and safeguarding an open and non-discriminatory multilateral trading system, and acting for the protection of the environment and the promotion of sustainable development can and must be mutually supportive" (WTO, 2001a).

Beyond these formal statements about a concern with environmental objectives, there are numerous WTO agreements that have explicit provisions concerning environmental issues or that otherwise affect environmental policies directly – and they affect MNEs' strategic and operational choices as well. Contrary to common impressions, WTO rules provide many opportunities for environmental considerations to prevail over trade and investment liberalization. The rules themselves as written, therefore, are not necessarily or inherently environment-unfriendly. Their practical effect, however, depends on the interpretation of those rules and their application in particular circumstances.

Of course, these are often matters at issue in dispute cases that are brought to the WTO. For some people, these cases have created the impression that there is an inherent conflict between the WTO liberalization agenda and an environmental protection agenda, and furthermore that in those conflicts the WTO will consistently resolve the conflict in favour of trade-investment liberalization and against environmental protection. In fact, neither of these is necessarily true. As to the former assumption, there are in fact opportunities for simultaneously promoting trade-investment liberalization and environmental protection. As to the latter assumption, there may well be dispute cases in the future in which the WTO allows environment-based exceptions to trade-investment liberalization. Selected dispute cases are discussed in more detail below in relationship to specific WTO agreements and rules.[2]

ERTMS, ERIMS, TREMS, AND IREMS

Several new acronyms can be crafted to encapsulate the overlaps of the WTO and Multilateral Environmental Agreements (MEAs). There are national policies and associated multilateral rules concerning trade and/or investment that are related to environmental policies. These are the focus of the present paper, and they can be identified and illustrated as follows:

ERTMs: Environment Related Trade Measures – e.g. provisions in the GATT concerning trade in goods providing for exceptions to national treatment on environmental grounds.

ERIMs: Environment Related Investment Measures – e.g. provisions in the GATS for liberalization of FDI measures in the environmental services sector.There are also provisions concerning trade and investment in environmental agreements, and they include provisions such as those in the Kyoto Protocol.

TREMs: Trade Related Environment Measures – e.g. Kyoto Protocol provision for establishing an international emissions trading regime.

IREMs: Investment Related Environment Measures – e.g. Kyoto Protocol provisions concerning the establishment of a Clean Development Mechanism (CDM) to promote FDI in emission-reducing projects in developing countries.

Additional examples of overlapping of issues and regimes – and hence issues for MNEs, as well as governments – are evident in the numerous provisions of the GATT agreement on goods as well as other WTO agreements.

Trade in Goods: Environmental Exceptions to National Treatment

GATT 1994 Article XX, "General Exceptions," provides for exceptions to the principle of national treatment, i.e. the principle of non-discrimination against foreign products or foreign firms. The conditions for allowable exceptions that are particularly pertinent to environmental issues are contained in the preamble and in sections (b) and (g): "Subject to the requirement that such measures are not applied in a manner which would constitute a means of arbitrary or unjustifiable discrimination between countries where the same conditions prevail, or a disguised restriction on international trade, nothing in this Agreement shall be construed to prevent the adoption or enforcement by any contracting party of measures: ... (b) necessary to protect human, animal or plant life or health; ... (g) relating to the conservation of exhaustible natural resources if such measures are made effective in conjunction with restrictions on domestic production or consumption; ..." (GATT, 1994, p. 518).

The result of these provisions is a complex set of "tests" that a national environmental policy may have to pass in order to be considered an allowable exception to the provisions concerning national treatment embedded in the GATT agreement. The distinction between products and production processes has been particularly contentious in dispute cases (Charnovitz, 2002), but there are many other issues as well. The decision tree in Fig. 1 is one way to depict the issues schematically; these are issues that may emerge to determine the consistency of a particular national environmental measure with the GATT principle of national treatment.

Other, more narrowly-focused, agreements at the WTO include provisions about environmental matters: The Agreement on Technical Barriers to Trade takes explicitly into account the use by governments of measures to protect the environment as well as human, animal and plant life and health. The Agreement on Sanitary and Phytosanitary Measures has extensive provisions about the harmonization of standards and the adoption of international standards, including environmental standards. The Agreement on Subsidies and Countervailing Measures treats as a non-actionable subsidy government assistance to industry covering up to 20% of the cost of adapting existing facilities to new environmental legislation. (Non-actionable subsidies are those that cannot be challenged as a basis for undertaking countervailing duties.)

Trade and FDI in Services Industries

The General Agreement on Trade in Services (GATS) also contains environment-related provisions. The GATS Preamble and Article XIV(b) are nearly identical to the provisions of GATT Article XX, though the GATS does not have an equivalent provision to GATT Article XX paragraph (g) concerning "exhaustible natural resources." With respect to the GATS and its coverage of environment-related matters, the 1999 Report of the Committee on Trade and the Environment (WTO, 1999) notes that discussions have not led to the identification of any measures that Members feel may be applied for environmental purposes to services trade which are not already adequately covered by GATS provisions. This could be interpreted

1. Is the target a product or a process?
product
process
other issues
2. Is the process domestic or foreign?
domestic
foreign
ok
3. Does the measure discriminate against like products ?
no
yes
ok
4. Is the measure necessary to protect the environment?
no
yes
not ok
5. Does the measure constitute arbitrary or unjustifiable discrimination or a disguised restriction on trade?
yes
no
not ok
6. Is the measure less trade restrictive than available alternatives?
yes
no
ok

Fig. 1. Decision Tree for Exceptions to GATT Article XX (a, g).

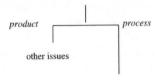

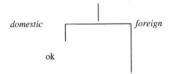

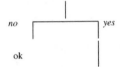

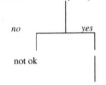

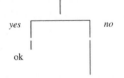

7. Are the affected lives or resources in the country imposing the barrier?

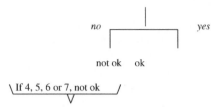

8.   Does the measure qualify for a GATT Article IX waiver?

no   *yes*

not ok   ok

Fig. 1.   (Continued)

to imply a potentially wide-ranging application of environment-related exemptions from national treatment. As with the analogous provisions in the GATT, however, the meaning of this provision will depend on the resolution of specific dispute cases and broader political developments concerning trade-environment relationships.

Agricultural Subsidies for Environmental Purposes

The Agreement on Agriculture exempts subsidies in the form of direct payments under environmental programs from governments' commitments to reduce domestic support for agricultural production. (The exception, however, is subject to several conditions.)

Intellectual Property and Technology Transfer

The Trade Related Intellectual Property Rights (TRIPs) agreement also has important environment-related consequences. For instance, the establishment of uniform standards of intellectual property rights and the requirements for greater transparency in the enforcement of such standards can facilitate international transfers of advanced environmentally-benign technologies. However, there are no *explicit* environmental provisions in the TRIPs agreement.

Dispute Cases[3]

There have been many formal dispute cases during the history of the GATT and WTO that raised serious and complex questions about the relationship between GATT/WTO rules and environmental issues. There were several such cases during the GATT (the first in 1982 and the last in 1994), and there have been several in the WTO since it entered into force on 1 January 1995. There had been a total of 276 disputes as of the end of 2002 (WTO, 2003); of these, only a few had concerned environmental issues, though they had attracted much attention.

It is beyond the scope of this chapter to examine the details of the issues, arguments, facts and outcomes of these cases. However, it can be noted that the cases involve questions such as the following: When are imported and domestic products "like products" or "directly competitive or substitutable" products? Can producer characteristics and/or production process methods – and their consequences for the environment – be taken into consideration in determining whether otherwise similar goods can be treated differently in order to protect the environment? How can it be determined whether a particular measure has the "aim and effect" of discriminating against imported products? What qualifies a national measure as "necessary" to protect the health or life of humans or other animals? Answers to these questions within the context of the dispute settlement process have varied across cases and between the Panel reports and Appellate reports on the same case.

Summaries of key WTO dispute cases are presented in Box 1.

Box 1: Key Dispute Cases Involving Environmental Issues

U.S. – Tuna/Dolphin and U.S. – Shrimp/Turtle Cases
The *Tuna/Dolphin* case, in which Mexico prevailed in its complaint that a U.S. prohibition on imported tuna was a violation of national treatment, the environmental objective of the U.S. policy was to discourage fishing methods for tuna that also routinely killed dolphins. In the *Shrimp/Turtle* case, the sea life involved were obviously different, and the complaining countries were also different (India, Malaysia, Pakistan, Thailand). But the underlying issues were similar: the U.S. was accused of violating its national treatment obligations not to discriminate against foreign produced-goods. At issue was U.S. law that prohibited importation of shrimp that were harvested using methods that also routinely trapped sea turtles. The U.S. lost both cases; in both instances, the WTO panel found that the U.S. measures did not qualify as exceptions to its obligation to provide non-discriminatory treatment to imports.

U.S. – Reformulated Gasoline Cases

Two of the early WTO dispute cases were environmental cases – the *Gasoline* cases, in which Venezuela and Brazil challenged a U.S. regulation that imposed different production process certification requirements on imported gasoline, as compared with domestically produced gasoline. The ostensible environmental purpose of the regulations was to insure that certain pollution standards were being met. But the regulations were also clearly protectionist in effect – and perhaps in intent as well. The two complaints by Venezuela and Brazil were considered together as a single "matter" in the dispute settlement process. The U.S. lost on the grounds that its regulations were discriminatory against imports and thus a violation of national treatment. In particular, U.S. regulations allowed U.S. producers to document their historical baseline gasoline quality in ways that they did not allow foreign producers. It was generally perceived as discriminatory in intent as well as in effect.

EU – Beef Hormones

Other WTO cases have been focused on food safety issues, but they are often considered environmental cases as well. These are the *Beef hormones* cases brought by the United States and by Canada against the EU. In both cases, which were considered together as a single "matter," the WTO panel ruled against the EU, and in both cases an appellate body upheld the panel report. This dispute was of course part of a much larger EU-U.S. conflict over EU agricultural policies, including subsidies and restrictive import regimes (as in the *Bananas* case). In the context of this chapter, however, the beef hormones dispute is of special interest in relationship to other environmental dispute cases. The panel found the EU had not followed appropriate risk assessment procedures.

Trade and FDI in the Environmental Goods and Services Sector

As noted in the introduction to the chapter, one way to understand in greater detail the nature of WTO agreements and procedures – and their implications for MNEs' strategies and operations – is to focus on particular sectors and industries. Because this chapter is in a volume devoted to environmental issues, an obvious sector of interest is the environmental goods and services sector, and it is considered in this section of the chapter.

The worldwide environmental goods and services sector entails more than U.S.$400 billion per year in sales (OECD, 1999b). A major segment is in water treatment services and equipment and water utilities, which together represent

Table 1. Size of the Environmental Goods and Services Sector.

	U.S. Dollars (Billions)
Equipment	215
Water equipment and chemicals	109
Air pollution control	39
Instruments and information	30
Waste management	5
Process/prevention technology	32
Services	229
Solid waste management	102
Hazardous waste management	17
Consulting and engineering	27
Remediation and industrial	15
Analytical services	3
Water treatment	65
Resources	116
Water utilities	73
Resource recovery	38
Environmental energy	5

Source: OECD (1999a, p. 7, Table 2). Data, which are for 1996, have been rounded to the nearest billion dollars.

approximately U.S.$200 billion; waste management services and equipment represent U.S.$150 billion. Although about 90% of the world market is now in the industrialized countries of North America, Western Europe and Japan, the market has been increasing more rapidly in the rest of the world in recent years. Further details are presented in Table 1.

Barriers to Trade and FDI

MNEs strategies and operations as they serve these markets are constrained by tariffs and other barriers to international trade and investment. Such barriers are addressed in three different WTO agreements – the GATT, the Government Procurement agreement, and the GATS.

Bound tariff rates on environmental goods in the tariff schedules listed in the GATT average less than 3% in the EU, U.S., Japan and Canada, but they average more than 20% in major developing country markets. Current levels and commitments, as noted in Table 2, are subject to reductions in the future, depending on the outcome of the Doha round negotiations.

In addition, there are diverse non-tariff barriers – which are not so readily summarized or quantified. These include, in particular, restrictions on international investment (FDI) as well as trade in services, and also restrictions on government

Table 2. Tariff Levels on Environmental Goods.

Country Group	Average Bound Rates[a]		
	Pollution Management Goods	Other	Overall
Canada, U.S., EU, Japan	2.3	3.0	2.5
Korea, Mexico, Turkey	24.7	29.5	25.2
Emerging economies[b]	29.4	31.0	28.7

Source: OECD (1999a, p. 10, Table 5).
[a] Bound rates at end of implementation of WTO Uruguay Round commitments.
[b] Argentina, Brazil, Chile, Malaysia, India, Indonesia, Thailand.

procurement. Thus, the GATS and the Government Procurement agreement are both also relevant to MNEs' strategies and operations.

Restrictions on government procurement are especially important (OECD, 1999b) because the government procurement market is a significant proportion of the total market in environmental goods and services. Indeed, much of the market is dominated by sales to government agencies at all levels – local and regional as well as national. However, most countries have not signed the WTO Government Procurement agreement – which is technically a "plurilateral" agreement and therefore not part of the WTO "single undertaking" according to which all members must accept all of the core WTO agreements as a single package.

As for the services sector, including FDI in environmental services industries, aside from the EU, U.S., Japan and Canada, fewer than twenty countries have listed the environmental services sector in their "specific commitments" to liberalize market access and national treatment in the GATS. The differences in their commitments across firms' "modes of supply" are varied and complex, and therefore so are their consequences for MNEs' choices and competitive positions.

Firms' Modes of Supply

In order to assess the implications for firms' strategic choices, it is essential to understand countries' specific commitments in the GATS in relation to four different modes of supply that firms use to provide services internationally. The following modes are explicitly included in the GATS:

(1) "Cross-border trade," i.e. traditional export-import transactions in which service providers as exporters and service consumers as importers are in two different countries – for instance, a bank in one country making a loan to a firm in another country.

(2) "Consumption abroad," i.e. transactions in which the consumers are in the countries of the exporters – for instance, a foreign tourist's consumption of meals or use of lodging facilities.
(3) "Commercial presence," i.e. sales of foreign affiliates created through foreign direct investment – for instance, a loan to a local resident by the local affiliate of a foreign-owned bank.
(4) "Movement of natural persons," i.e. transactions in which the service provider is a temporary resident of a foreign country – for instance, an employee of a foreign-owned consulting firm transfers from the firm's headquarters to a local affiliate for six months to work on a consulting project with a local client.

For each of these modes, there are potential exceptions to a government's otherwise binding commitments to provide market access and national treatment to foreign firms. As a practical matter, since environmental services cannot generally be provided by cross-border trade or by consumption abroad (modes 1 and 2), the issues about the governments' commitments are mostly about commercial presence and the movement of natural persons (modes 3 and 4).

There is no WTO agreement specifically and exclusively on *investment* in environmental *goods* manufacturing, because there is no single comprehensive multilateral agreement on FDI at the WTO. Only the GATS in services and the TRIMs in manufacturing – which only pertains to a narrow range of trade-related restrictions on investments – include FDI provisions. The coverage of the combinations of trade and FDI in goods and services is therefore incomplete, as summarized in Fig. 2.

The nature and significance of signatories' specific commitments under the GATS can be illustrated by China's commitments, which were undertaken as part of its accession process (WTO, 2001b); they are summarized in Box 2. China has

	Goods	Services
Trade	GATT	GATS (modes 1 & 2)
Investment	Not covered (except TRIMs)	GATS (modes 3 & 4)

Fig. 2.   WTO Coverage of Trade and Investment in Environmental Goods and Services.

excluded some sub-sectors from its commitments – in particular, environmental quality monitoring and pollution source inspection. However, it commits itself to providing market access and national treatment in seven other sub-sectors: sewage services, solid waste disposal services, cleaning services of exhaust gases, noise abatement services, nature and landscape protection services, sanitation services, and other environmental protection services. Yet, for all of these sub-sectors, "foreign service suppliers engaged in environmental services are permitted to provide services only in the form of joint ventures, with foreign majority ownership permitted." That is, wholly-owned subsidiaries through FDI are not permitted, but foreign majority ownership is permitted in a joint venture with a local partner. MNEs must therefore find local joint venture partners if they want to undertake FDI projects in environmental services.

Box 2: Summary of China's Schedule of Specific Commitments Concerning Environmental Services in the General Agreement on Trade in Services (GATS)

Services Sub-Sectors Covered
Sewage, Solid Waste Disposal, Cleaning Services of Exhaust Fumes, Noise Abatement, Nature and Landscape Protection, Other Environmental Protection, Sanitation.

Sub-Sectors Explicitly Excluded
Environmental Quality Monitoring, Pollution Source Inspection.

Limitations on Market Access or National Treatment by Mode of Supply

Mode of Supply	Market Access Limitations	National Treatment Limitations
1. Cross-border	Not bound	None
2. Consumption abroad	None	None
3. Commercial Presence [FDI]	Joint Ventures required	None
4. Presence of Natural Persons	Same as other sectors[a]	Same as other sectors[a]

Source: Adapted from WTO (2001b, p. 29).
[a] So-called "horizontal" commitments apply. These are commitments that pertain to all services sectors unless otherwise indicated. In the case of China, these commitments are as follows: "managers, executives and specialists defined as senior employees of a corporation of a WTO member that has established a representative office, branch or subsidiary . . . temporarily moving as intra-corporate transferees, shall be permitted entry for an initial stay of three years."

As for the presence of natural persons, so-called "horizontal commitments," which pertain to *all* sectors in the GATS, including environmental services, are applicable. Because there are politically sensitive immigration and labor market issues associated with the movement of natural persons as service providers, most countries have formulated quite limited and precise liberalization commitments for this mode of supply. Essentially, they do not bind themselves except to allow in transferred employees of MNEs for specified periods of time. Thus, the commitments in this respect must be interpreted in conjunction with the commitments for FDI in mode 3. In the case of China, for instance, "managers, executives and specialists defined as senior employees of a corporation of a WTO member that has established a representative office, branch or subsidiary ... temporarily moving as intra-corporate transferees, shall be permitted entry for an initial stay of three years."

Such commitments by China are illustrative more generally of the types of policies concerning FDI and trade in services that governments have made in the WTO, and they are thus indicative of the relevance of WTO agreements and dispute cases to multinational firms' strategic and operational choices and ultimately to their competitive position. Because of the potential win-win outcomes of further liberalization agreements in the environmental goods and services sector, reductions of barriers during the WTO Doha round of negotiations is likely.

CLIMATE CHANGE ISSUES: THE WTO, THE KYOTO PROTOCOL AND MULTINATIONAL FIRMS

The nexus of the trade-investment regime centered in the WTO and the climate regime centered in the Kyoto Protocol of the Framework Convention on Climate Change poses issues of importance to the strategic and operational choices of multinational firms in a broad range of industries.[4] Although trade and FDI issues involved in the emerging multilateral regime for climate change mitigation are not likely to be addressed in the current round of negotiations at the WTO, such issues are being considered in other forums by individuals in firms, non-governmental organizations (NGOs) and think tanks, as well as governments (Brewer, 2002).

In any case, the trade and FDI policies that are being developed at the national, regional and multilateral levels to mitigate climate change have important implications for multinational firms' strategic and operational decisions and for their competitive positions. For instance, a basic question concerns the business transactions covered by the "flexibility mechanisms" of the Kyoto Protocol. In particular, what is the nature in international business transaction terms of the credit units that firms and countries will gain for contributing to the reduction of emissions of greenhouse gases or to the enhancement of carbon sequestration goods or services or something else? These items in the Protocol's flexibility mechanisms have been variously described as being one or more of the following:

- carbon and thus commodities,
- services such as "decarbonization,"
- permits that convey property rights,
- financial instruments, and
- investment goods.

Discussions in the WTO's Committee on Trade and the Environment (CTE) have suggested that emissions' credits are neither services because they are not activities, nor goods because they are not tangible materials. Thus, they would presumably not be subject to WTO. Yet, one might suppose that brokerage, consulting and insurance services associated with emissions trading could be considered commercial services within the normal meaning of the term and thus potentially covered by the GATS. In that case, governments' policies concerning such services would be subject to the limits of the individual WTO members' schedules of specific commitments under the GATS. Briefly, countries' GATS commitments pertain to granting market access and/or national treatment for each of four different types of "modes of supply" of services; the four modes are cross-border trade by export of the supplier of the service, consumption by a foreigner in the country of the provider, commercial presence through foreign direct investment, and movement of natural persons such as employees of multinational firms. There are, therefore, two different, though closely related issues, about the coverage of such emissions trading services by GATS: (a) whether and how particular types of services are included by definition in the categories of types of services covered by GATS, and consequently whether they are covered by MFN and other general obligations under the GATS; and (b) what kinds of specific liberalization commitments and/or exceptions to such commitments individual countries have made for each of the types of services. In any case, the GATS seems more likely than the GATT to be applicable to at least some aspects of international emissions trading.

However, if emissions' credits are defined as services to which the General Agreement on Trade in Services (GATS) applies, then there is a question about whether the most favored nation (MFN) principle of non-discrimination would be violated. Limiting the trading of emissions permits to Kyoto Protocol parties could violate GATS Article 1. Further, if emissions trading privileges are linked to compliance with other Kyoto Protocol provisions, this could also violate the MFN principle.

Other issues emerging from provisions in the Kyoto Protocol concerning Clean Development Mechanisms (CDM) and Joint Investment (JI) projects represent foreign direct investment projects, which involve trade in goods as well as provide services. Because of ambiguities about some distinctions (e.g. the difference between goods and services) in WTO agreements, there is not yet a consensus on these basic issues of coverage. The WTO Agreement on Subsidies and Countervailing Measures (SCMs), as it entered into force at the beginning of 1995, included a provision in Article 8 that subsidies to industry covering up to 20% of the cost of adapting existing facilities to new environmental requirements would not be actionable. However, the provision was limited to five years and thus expired at the end of 1999. Whether it will be re-instituted in the future is unclear. Non-actionable subsidies are those that cannot be challenged as a basis for undertaking countervailing duties. In Part IV, Article 8; 8.1, the agreement said:

> The following subsidies shall be considered as non-actionable: . . . 8.2(c) assistance to promote adaptation of existing facilities to new environmental requirements imposed by law and/or regulations which result in greater constraints and financial burden on firms, provided that the assistance:

(i)   is a one-time non-recurring measure;
(ii) is limited to 20% of the cost of adaptation;
(iii) does not cover the cost or replacing and operating the assisted investment, which must be fully borne by firms; and
(iv) is directly linked to and proportionate to a firm's planned reduction of nuisances and pollution, and does not cover any manufacturing cost savings which may be achieved; and is available to all firms which can adopt the new equipment and/or production processes.

These provisions prompt the question of whether CDM and JI projects would qualify as environmental exceptions if those or similar provisions are adopted in the future.

These are but a few of the questions about the future of the international regulatory regime in greenhouse gas emissions that multinational firms are now facing. Yet, they are indicative of the nature, scope and significance of such questions. In one forum or another, such issues about the relationship of the WTO trade-investment regime and the Kyoto Protocol climate regime are likely to be addressed with increasing intensity, and the outcome will be increasingly significant for MNEs.[5]

COMPETITIVE, STRATEGIC AND OPERATIONAL IMPLICATIONS FOR MNES[6]

WTO agreements and their implementation in more than 140 countries pose a variety of issues for multinational firms' competitive positions, strategies and operations. Indeed, whether or not executives are fully aware of the nature or the extent of the agreements, their firms are affected in many ways. For instance, governments' commitments to liberalize barriers to international transactions in goods and services are quite specific to individual sectors, sub-sectors and products; as a result there are variations among substitutable products in the extent to which they face protectionist government policies. A firm's competitive position and its strategic choices about what to sell and where to sell it can be affected, therefore, by the relative severity of the barriers faced by its products and their substitutes. Further, the barriers are variable across countries since each country is able to negotiate its own barriers. Thus, firms' strategic choices about what to produce where are affected by cross-national differences in the nature and severity of the barriers. Finally, strategic and operational decisions about where to locate various stages of international production processes also depend on the nature and extent of the barriers to trade and investment.

These and other issues for firms are evident in the two sets of environmental issues that have been considered above – WTO agreements concerning international business in the environmental goods and services sector, and the relationship of WTO agreements to the emergence of a new multilateral regime concerning greenhouse gas emissions and other aspects of climate change issues. The implications of these two sets of issues for multinational firms are quite different, however.

Environmental Goods and Services

The liberalization of barriers to trade and FDI in the environmental goods and services industry creates new international market opportunities for firms that want to expand abroad; it also creates new competitive threats in home markets. Firms' stakes in the liberalization of the barriers are tangible, evident and immediate. Further, since liberalization offers win-win opportunities for international business and environmental protection, it has natural political constituencies among environmental NGOs as well as multinational firms that are in strong competitive positions. Thus, MNEs and NGOs are natural political allies on these items during WTO negotiating rounds.

The following illustrative issues for multinational firms in the environmental goods and services industry suggest the relevance of the WTO negotiating agenda:

- Will the current round of WTO negotiations open new markets that are less protected than previously?
- Which firms will face increased competition in their home markets and foreign markets because of the greater access that their rivals have via trade and/or FDI?

- Will further liberalization of barriers to FDI be transparent enough so that there will be less regulatory uncertainty associated with FDI projects?
- Will local government barriers undermine the principle of national treatment and thus make FDI projects vulnerable to discrimination at the local level, where many environmental goods and services are purchased?
- Will the list of signatories to the "plurilateral" government procurement agreement, which now includes only a small proportion of WTO members as signatories, expand significantly to include many developing countries and economies in transition, where there is much potential for market growth?

Climate Change Mitigation

The nature and implications of the business and political issues for firms are different on climate change issues. In the first place, there is resistance even to consider the international trade and investment aspects of the climate regime in the WTO, partly because the U.S. has kept them off the WTO agenda since it decided not to participate in the Kyoto Protocol. Yet, as we have seen above, there are significant issues concerning the international trade and investment implications of key provisions in the Kyoto Protocol, especially the "flexibility mechanisms" that provide for international emissions trading and FDI projects to gain credits for emissions reductions.

Multinational firms have already been involved in many such emission credit trades and projects. Whether the rules established by the Kyoto Protocol for these types of international business transactions will be challenged or constrained or even negated by WTO processes in the future obviously remains to be seen. But, in any case, these and other climate change issues and the rules concerning international trade and investment are clearly of interest to multinational firms in many industries – in the services and agriculture sectors as well as manufacturing.

The following issues about multinational firms' strategies, operations and competitive positions are thus on the agendas of MNEs as a result of past and prospective developments concerning climate change and its mitigation:

- Will there be new rules and/or dispute cases in the WTO concerning emissions trading and/or FDI projects for emission mitigation or for carbon sink preservation or enhancement? What business opportunities or constraints will these developments create for multinational firms?
- Will multinational firms with headquarters in the U.S., which is not participating in the Kyoto Protocol, and subsidiaries in countries that are participating in the Protocol adopt similar production processes in the U.S. to reduce emissions as they do so in their foreign subsidiaries?

- Will national governments or the EU impose special border taxes on imported goods to offset the competitive advantages enjoyed by firms that produce in countries that are not participating in the Kyoto Protocol emissions limits?
- Will U.S.-based firms encounter consumer boycotts outside the U.S. because the U.S. is not participating in the Protocol?
- Will multinationals such as BP and Shell, which are headquartered outside the U.S., enjoy competitive advantages in the U.S. market over their U.S.-based rivals because they have adopted forward-looking internal emissions trading schemes and adopted "green" advertising campaigns in the U.S.?
- Will firms from home countries that have mandatory emissions reduction programs experience learning-curve advantages as compared with firms from other countries?
- Will multinational firms with subsidiaries in countries with relatively advanced emissions trading regimes transfer relevant technologies to affiliates in other countries?
- Will mandatory governmental regimes concerning climate change be limited to the EU, or will other countries such as Japan that are home to many multinationals also develop mandatory programs?

Thus, climate change has placed new issues on the agendas of firms as well as governments and multilateral organization – alongside the traditional issues of trade in goods and the more recent issues of FDI and intellectual property. As climate change and other environmental issues become more salient in the future, multinational firms will find that their strategic and operational choices, as well as their competitive positions, will be increasingly shaped by the WTO and other multilateral agreements.

NOTES

1. I am indebted to Sarianna Lundan for pointing out this linkage.
2. The literature on the WTO – including environmental issues – is of course voluminous. The following are useful starting points: On trade, see Hoekman and Kostecki (1995) and Jackson (1997); on FDI, see Brewer and Young (1998, 2000, 2001b) and Graham (1996). Also see the collection of studies in Brewer (1999). For developments since the creation of the WTO in 1995, including the ministerial meeting at Seattle and the background to the Doha round negotiations, see Krueger (1998), Schott (2000) and Rugman and Boyd (2001). On environmental issues, see especially Brack (1998), Charnovitz (1998, 2002) and Esty (1994, 2000, 2001), Heinrich Boll Foundation and Woodrow Wilson Center for Scholars (2001) and Shaw and Schwartz (2002). On the environmental practices of MNEs, see Bora (2002), Gentry (1997), Jun and Brewer (1997) and OECD (1999b). Graham (2000) is a well-known analysis of a broad range of current issues concerning MNEs, including

environmental issues. Also see Picciotto and Mayne (1999). Focused discussions of the business strategy implications of the WTO and trade and investment policies more generally are available in Brewer and Young (2001a), Condon (2002) and Rugman and Verbeke (1990).

3. For detailed legal analyses of the cases and their implications for environmental policy, see especially Charnovitz (1998, 2002) and Esty (1994). More generally, on the WTO dispute settlement process, see *International Lawyer* (1998), Petersmann (1997) and Shoyer (1998). On FDI dispute resolution, which is not in the WTO, see Brewer (1995).

4. Discussions of the trade and investment implications of the FCCC and Kyoto Protocol are available in Brack, Windram and Grubb (2000), Brewer (2002), Forsyth (1999), Grubb, Brack and Vroijk (1999), Muller (2002), Sampson (1999, forthcoming), Springer (2000), Werksman (1999), Werksman, Baumert and Dubash (2001), Werksman and Santoro (1999), Wiser (1999), Petsonk (1999) and Zhang (1998).

5. These and related issues are discussed more extensively in Brewer (2002).

6. In addition to other chapters in this volume, there are of course substantial bodies of literature on each of these and other related topics concerning FDI and MNEs' strategies concerning environmental issues; see for instance Gentry (1997), Jun and Brewer (1997), OECD (1999a) and Rugman and Verbeke (1998).

ACKNOWLEDGMENTS

Portions of this chapter appeared as Policy Briefs and/or Policy Papers for conferences at the Centre for European Policy Studies (CEPS) in Brussels and at Georgetown University in Washington, DC, during 2001–2002; I am indebted to Christian Egenhofer, Thomas Legge and many other participants in those conferences for their comments. Other portions of the material were originally prepared for the AIB-UK Conference at Strathclyde University, Glasgow, in 2000, and I am indebted to Stephen Young for his observations. Finally, some of the material was presented in a lecture at the Copenhagen Business School in 1999, and I am indebted to members of the audience for their reactions.

REFERENCES

Bora, B. (2002). FDI and the environment. In: B. Bora (Ed.), *Foreign Direct Investment: Research Issues* (pp. 211–229). London and New York: Routledge.

Brack, D. (1998). International trade and environment. In: B. Hocking & S. McGuire (Eds), *Trade Politics*. London and New York: Routledge.

Brack, D., Windram, C., & Grubb, M. (2000). *International trade and climate change policies*. London: RIIA and Earthscan.

Brewer, T. L. (1995). International investment dispute settlement procedures: The evolving regime for foreign direct investment. *Law and Policy in International Business*, 26(3), 633–672.

Brewer, T. L. (Ed.) (1999). *Trade and investment policy* (Vol. 2). Cheltenham, UK: Edward Elgar.

Brewer, T. (2002). The Kyoto Protocol and the WTO: Institutional Evolution and Adaptation. Policy Paper, Brussels: Centre for European Policy Studies. Available at http://www.ceps.be

Brewer, T. L., & Young, S. (1998). Investment issues at the world trade organization: The architecture of rules and the settlement of disputes. *Journal of International Economic Law, 1*, 457–470.

Brewer, T. L., & Young, S. (2000). *The multilateral investment system and multinational enterprises*. Oxford: Oxford University Press.

Brewer, T. L., & Young, S. (2001a). The multilateral regime for FDI: Institutions and their implications for business strategy. In: A. M. Rugman & T. L. Brewer (Eds), *Oxford Handbook of International Business* (pp. 282–313). Oxford, UK: Oxford University Press.

Brewer, T. L., & Young, S. (2001b). The USA in the WTO. In: A. M. Rugman & G. Boyd (Eds), *The World Trade Organization in the New Global Economy: Trade and Investment Issues in the Millennium Round* (pp. 128–54). Cheltenham, UK: Edward Elgar.

Charnovitz, S. (1998). Environment and health under WTO dispute settlement. *The International Lawyer, 32*, 901–921.

Charnovitz, S. (2002). The law of environmental 'PPMs' in the WTO: Debunking the myth of illegality. *The Yale Journal of International Law, 27*(1), 59–110.

Condon, B. J. (2002). *NAFTA, WTO and Global Business Strategy*. Westport, CT: Quorum.

Esty, D. (1994). *Greening the GATT: Trade, environment and the future*. Washington, DC: Institute for International Economics.

Esty, D. (2000). Environment and the trading system: Picking up the post-Seattle pieces. In: J. J. Schott (Ed.), *The WTO After Seattle* (pp. 243–52). Washington, DC: Institute for International Economics.

Esty, D. (2001). Bridging the trade-environment divide. *Journal of Economic Perspectives, 15*(3), 113–130.

Forsyth, T. (1999). *International investment and climate change*. London: RIIA and Earthscan.

General Agreement on Tariffs and Trade (GATT) (1994). *Guide to GATT law and practice* (6th ed.). Geneva: GATT.

Gentry, B. (1997). Making private investment work for the environment. In: *Finance for Sustainable Development: The Road Ahead* (pp. 342–402). New York: United Nations.

Graham, E. M. (1996). *Global corporations and national governments*. Washington, DC: Institute for International Economics.

Graham, E. M. (2000). *Fighting the wrong enemy*. Washington, DC: Institute for International Economics.

Grubb, M., Brack, D., & Vrolijk, C. (1999). *The Kyoto Protocol: A guide and assessment*. London: RIIA and Earthscan.

Heinrich Boll Foundation and Woodrow Wilson Center for Scholars (2001). *Trade and environment, the WTO, and MEAs*. Washington, DC.

Hoekman, B. M., & Kostecki, M. M. (1995). *The political economy of the world trading system*. Oxford: Oxford University Press.

International Lawyer (1998). Special issue, first three years of the WTO dispute settlement system (Fall).

Jackson, J. H. (1997). *The world trade system*. Cambridge, MA: MIT.

Jun, K. W., & Brewer, T. L. (1997). The role of foreign private capital flows in sustainable development. *Finance for Sustainable Development* (pp. 109–138). New York: United Nations.

Krueger, A. O. (Ed.) (1998). *The WTO as an international organization*. Chicago: University of Chicago Press.

Muller, B. (2002). The Kyoto mechanisms – linking technology to ratification. *Journal of World Trade Law, 36*(1), 57–66.

Organization for Economic Cooperation and Development (OECD) (1999a). *Foreign direct investment and the environment*. Paris: OECD.

Organization for Economic Cooperation and Development (OECD) (1999b). *Future of liberalisation of trade in environmental goods and services: Encouraging environmental protection as well as economic benefits*. Paris: OECD.

Petersmann, E.-U. (1997). *The GATT/WTO Dispute settlement system*. London: Kluwer Law International.

Petsonk, A. (1999). The Kyoto protocol and the WTO: Integrating greenhouse gas emissions allowance trading into the global market place. *Duke Environmental Law and Policy Forum, 10*(1), 185–220.

Picciotto, S., & Mayne, R. (Eds) (1999). *Regulating international business: Beyond liberalization*. London: Macmillan and New York: St. Martin's.

Rugman, A. M., & Boyd, G. (Eds) (2001). *The World Trade Organization in the new global economy: Trade and investment issues in the millennium round*. Cheltenham, UK: Edward Elgar.

Rugman, A. M., & Verbeke, A. (1990). *Global corporate strategy and trade policy*. London: Routledge.

Rugman, A. M., & Verbeke, A. (1998). Corporate strategies and environmental regulations: An organizing framework. *Strategic Management Journal, 14*, 363–375.

Sampson, G. (1999). WTO rules and climate change: The need for policy coherence. In: Chambers & W. Bradnee (Eds), *Global Climate Governance: A Report on the Inter-Linkages between the Kyoto Protocol and Other Multilateral Regimes*. Tokyo: United Nations University.

Sampson, G. P. (forthcoming). *WTO rules and climate change: The need for policy coherence*. Brussels: Centre for European Policy Studies.

Schott, J. J. (2000). *The WTO after Seattle*. Washington, DC: Institute for International Economics.

Shaw, S., & Schwartz, R. (2002). Trade and environment at the WTO – state of play. *Journal of World Trade, 36*(1), 129–154.

Shoyer, A. W. (1998). The first three years of WTO dispute settlement: Observations and suggestions. *Journal of International Economic Law, 1*, 277–302.

Springer, U. (2000). GATS and the Kyoto mechanisms: Open markets for climate change mitigation services? *Swiss Review of International Economic Relations, 55*, 65–84.

Werksman, J. (1999). Greenhouse gas emissions trading and the WTO. *Review of European Community and International Environmental Law, 8*(3), 251–264.

Werksman, J., Baumert, K. A., & Dubash, N. K. (2001). *Will International Investment Rules Obstruct Climate Protection Policies?* Climate Notes. Washington, DC: World Resources Institute.

Werksman, J., & Santoro, C. (1999). Investing in sustainable development: The potential interaction between the Kyoto protocol and the multilateral agreement on investment. In: Chambers & W. Bradnee (Eds), *Global Climate Governance: A Report on the Inter-Linkages between the Kyoto Protocol and Other Multilateral Regimes*. Tokyo: United Nations University.

Wiser, G. M. (1999). The clean development mechanism versus the world trade organizaion: Can free-market greenhouse gas emissions abatement survive free trade? *Georgetown International Environmental Law Review, 11*(3), 531–598.

World Trade Organization (WTO) (1999). *1999 Report of the committee on trade and the environment*. Geneva: WTO.

World Trade Organization (WTO) (2001a). *Doha WTO ministerial declaration*. Adopted on 14th November 2001, retrieved from http://www.wto.org on 5th January 2003.

World Trade Organization (WTO) (2001b). *Report of the working party on the accession of China.* Addendum, Schedule CLII – The People's Republic of China, Part II – Schedule of Specific Commitments on Services, retrieved from http://www.wto.org on 5 January 2003.

World Trade Organization (WTO) (2003). *Disputes, chronologically*, retrieved from http://www.wto.org on 5th January 2003.

Zhang, Z. X. (1998). Greenhouse gas emissions trading and the world trading system. *Journal of World Trade, 32*(5), 219–240.

SUBJECT INDEX